Lecture Notes of the Institute for Computer Sciences, Social Informatics and Telecommunications Engineering   290

More information about this series at http://www.springer.com/series/8197

Yuyu Yin · Ying Li · Honghao Gao ·
Jilin Zhang (Eds.)

Mobile Computing, Applications, and Services

10th EAI International Conference, MobiCASE 2019
Hangzhou, China, June 14–15, 2019
Proceedings

 Springer

Editors
Yuyu Yin
Hangzhou Dianzi University
Hangzhou, China

Honghao Gao
Shanghai University
Shanghai, China

Ying Li
Zhejiang University
Hangzhou, China

Jilin Zhang
Hangzhou Dianzi University
Hangzhou, China

ISSN 1867-8211   ISSN 1867-822X (electronic)
Lecture Notes of the Institute for Computer Sciences, Social Informatics
and Telecommunications Engineering
ISBN 978-3-030-28467-1   ISBN 978-3-030-28468-8 (eBook)
https://doi.org/10.1007/978-3-030-28468-8

This Springer imprint is published by the registered company Springer Nature Switzerland AG
The registered company address is: Gewerbestrasse 11, 6330 Cham, Switzerland

Preface

We are delighted to introduce the proceedings of the 10th European Alliance for Innovation (EAI) International Conference on Mobile Computing, Applications, and Services (MobiCASE). This conference brought together researchers, developers, and practitioners from around the world who are interested in mobile computing and leveraging or developing mobile services, mobile applications, and technologies that improve the mobile eco-system.

The technical program of MobiCASE 2019 consisted of 18 full papers that were selected from 48 paper submissions. The conference tracks were: Track 1—Mobile Application with Data Analysis; Track 2—Mobile Application with AI; Track 3—Edge Computing; and Track 4—Energy Optimization and Application. Aside from the high-quality technical paper presentations, the technical program also featured one keynote speech about image processing and deep learning, by Dr. Jun Yu from Hangzhou Dianzi University, China.

Coordination with the steering chair, Imrich Chlamtac, and Steering Committee members was essential for the success of the conference. We sincerely appreciate their constant support and guidance. It was also a great pleasure to work with such an excellent Organizing Committee team and we thank them for their hard work in organizing and supporting the conference. In particular, we thank the Technical Program Committee, led by our TPC co-chairs, Dr. Honghao Gao and Dr. Jilin Zhang, who completed the peer-review process of technical papers and compiled a high-quality technical program. We are also grateful to the conference manager, Karolina Marcinova, for her support and all the authors who submitted their papers to the MobiCASE 2019 conference and workshops.

We strongly believe that the MobiCASE conference provides a good forum for all researchers, developers, and practitioners to discuss all scientific and technological aspects that are relevant to mobile computing, applications, and services. We also expect that future MobiCASE conferences will be as successful and stimulating as indicated by the contributions presented in this volume.

July 2019

Yuyu Yin
Ying Li
Honghao Gao
Jilin Zhang

Organization

Steering Committee

Chair

Imrich Chlamtac   University of Trento, Italy

Members

Ulf Blanke	ETH Zurich, Switzerland
Martin Griss	Carnegie Mellon University, USA
Thomas Phan	Samsung R&D
Petros Zerfos	IBM Research

Organizing Committee

General Chairs

Yuyu Yin	Hangzhou Dianzi University, China
Ying Li	Zhejiang University, China

TPC Chairs

Honghao Gao	Shanghai University, China
Jilin Zhang	Hangzhou Dianzi University, China

Local Chair

Gangyong Jia   Hangzhou Dianzi University, China

Workshops Chair

Li Kuang   Central South University, China

Publicity and Social Media Chair

Congfeng Jiang   Hangzhou Dianzi University, China

Publications Chair

Youhuizi Li   Hangzhou Dianzi University, China

Web Chair

Yucong Duan   Hainan University, China

Technical Program Committee

Gerold Hoelzl	University of Passau, Germany
Xiaobing Sun	Yangzhou University, China
Honghao Gao	Shanghai University, China
Ella Peltonen	University of Oulu, Finland
Lianyong Qi	Qufu Normal University
Kanae Matsui	Tokyo Denki University, Japan
Yuyu Yin	Hangzhou Dianzi University, China
Brahim Benaissa	Kyushu Institute of Technology, Japan
Youhuizi Li	Hangzhou Dianzi University, China
Yihai Chen	Shanghai University, China
Christian Meurisch	TU Darmstadt, Germany
Wenmin Lin	Hangzhou Dianzi University, China
Stephan Reiff-Marganiec	University of Leicester, UK
Shoji Sano	Kanazawa Institute of Technology, Japan
Congfeng Jiang	Hangzhou Dianzi University, China
Xiaolong Xu	Nanjing University of Information Engineering, China
Xiaoxian Yang	Shanghai Polytechnic University, China
Yueshen Xu	Xidian University, China
Rui Li	Xidian University, China
Jinyu Kai	Zhongyuan University of Technology, China
Dongjing Wang	Hangzhou Dianzi University, China
Xuan Liu	Southeast University
Paula Lago	Los Andes University, Colombia
Shoji Sano	Kanazawa Institute of Technology, Japan
Li Kuang	Central South University

Contents

Edge Computing

Energy Optimization and Application

Mobile Application with Data Analysis

A Location and Intention Oriented Recommendation Method for Accuracy Enhancement over Big Data

Wajid Rafique[1,2], Lianyong Qi[3], Zhili Zhou[4], Xuan Zhao[1,2], Wenda Tang[1,2], and Wanchun Dou[1,2(✉)]

[1] State Key Laboratory for Novel Software Technology,
Nanjing University, Nanjing, People's Republic of China
rafiqwajid@smail.nju.edu.cn, douwc@nju.edu.cn
[2] The Department of Computer Science and Technology, Nanjing University,
Nanjing, People's Republic of China
[3] School of Information Science and Engineering, Qufu Normal University, Qufu,
People's Republic of China
[4] Nanjing University of Information Science and Technology,
Nanjing, People's Republic of China

Abstract. Big data recommendation systems provide recommendations based on user history and optimize this process using feedback information. Recent developments in location-based social networks reveal that spatial properties of users greatly affect their opinion. Traditional location-aware recommendation systems do not consider user intentions to produce personalized recommendations. This paper proposes LIOR, a Location and Intention Oriented Recommendation method that uses spatial properties of users and their intentions to produce personalized recommendations. LIOR hierarchically employs user location and rating information to generate location-aware predictions, it then integrates user intentions to produce highly accurate recommendations. Extensive experimental evaluation performed on a real-world location-aware Movielens dataset demonstrates that LIOR provides exceptional performance on producing recommendations, it is highly scalable, and efficiently reduces the sparsity problem.

Keywords: Intention-oriented recommendation ·
Location-based clustering · Spatial · Performance improvement

1 Introduction

Recommender systems assist users in finding items of interest from considerably large item space by utilizing community opinion (e.g., Amazon [1], Netflix [9]). Item-based collaborative filtering (CF) is a widely used recommendation technique which analyzes previous public opinions to ascertain underlying similarities between users and items and present top-k item recommendations to a

Y. Yin et al. (Eds.): MobiCASE 2019, LNICST 290, pp. 3–17, 2019.
https://doi.org/10.1007/978-3-030-28468-8_1

target user [14]. Public opinions are usually represented by $(user, item, rating)$ triple which determines how much a user likes or dislikes an item.

In the current context, numerous systems generate location-aware ratings for users or items. For example, current social networks (e.g., Facebook) allow individuals to provide ratings of their visited places (eg., restaurants, cinemas, and parks) and are capable of storing location-aware ratings. Similar users tend to have same preferences, hence, there exists a correlation among similar user preferences and their intentions (e.g., watching a movie, visiting a place) [25]. The location-based ratings and user intentions provoke an interesting phenomena of location and intention-oriented recommendations where the recommender system utilizes spatial properties of users and their intentions while producing recommendations. Current recommendation systems ascertain that ratings are expressed using the $(user, item, rating)$ triple and are not capable of considering location and intention context to produce personalized recommendations [5].

This research proposes LIOR a location and intention-oriented recommendation method to provide highly accurate recommendations. LIOR generates recommendations using two latent information resources including *location* and *intention* represented by a five-tuple $(user, ulocation, uintention, item, rating)$.

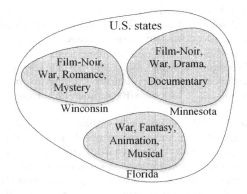

Fig. 1. U.S. states movie preferences in Movielens dataset [16].

The motivation for this research comes by the analysis of a real-world location-aware rating dataset, Movielens [8] and by ascertaining the significance of intentions in endorsing user opinion of doing some business activity (eg., watching a movie, buying a product). We observe two interesting characteristics: locality preferences and intention preferences that stimulate the need for location and intention-oriented recommendations. Locality preferences suggest that users from a specific location (e.g., neighbors) like items (e.g., food, movies, places) that are inherently distinct from people in other spatial regions [16,20,22]. Figure 1 suggest top-4 movie genres in three U.S. states, as all three lists are different, top movie preferences from the state of Florida are vastly disparate from the other states. The "Animation", "Fantasy", and "Musical" movie genres of Florida are not present in the preference list of other states. This fact implies that movie preferences are unique in different spatial regions. Intentions determine user's motivation of doing some activity (e.g., watching a movie, buying a product), hence, are a critical component for personalized recommendations. Intention preferences imply that user intentions are influenced by other users having similar taste. To predict user intention for an item, use the opinion of other similar users [25], in this regard, user-based similarity can ascertain current user intentions which can help to produce personalized recommendations in the future.

LIOR provides top-k personalized recommendations in the same way as most of the other traditional recommender systems. However, LIOR is novel because of its characteristic of producing location and intention-oriented recommendations by employing locality preferences and user intentions. LIOR produces initial predictions by exploiting a user clustering strategy based on user preference locality. This technique partitions users on the basis of their location into different regions and use the item-based collaborative filtering technique on segregated users to produce locality-aware recommendations. LIOR then computes user intentions by employing the user-based similarity technique for each target user. We get the final recommendations by aggregating user intention attribute values with the predictions generated by $(user, ulocation, item, rating)$ tuple.

We experimentally evaluate LIOR using real-world location-aware Movielens big dataset by comparing with state-of-the-art location-aware recommendations techniques MLTRS [20], LARS [16], and ULA-LDA [22]. The results demonstrate that LIOR outperforms all these techniques on the basis of Mean Absolute Precision (MAP) and $accuracy$ as well as efficiently reduces the sparsity problem. Hence, we propose a location and intention-oriented recommendation method that utilizes user location, intention, and rating information to enhance accuracy in big data service recommendation systems. This research provides the following contributions:

- We model the problem of location and intention-oriented recommendations and prove how intention and location-oriented hierarchical recommendations increase the service recommendation accuracy.
- This research proposes LIOR, a novel big data service recommendation method capable of producing effective recommendations by exploiting user locality preferences, user intentions, and rating information.
- Experimental evidence on a real-world Movielens dataset demonstrates that LIOR outperforms state-of-the-art location-based recommendation techniques as well as it is highly scalable for larger datasets.

Rest of this paper is organized as follows: Sect. 2 provides LIOR problem formulation while Sect. 3 discusses the detailed LIOR method. Section 4 elaborates the experimental evaluation whereas Sect. 5 explains the related work and comparison analysis. Section 6 provides a discussion on the results and finally, Sect. 7 concludes the paper and provides some future insights.

2   Problem Formulation for Location and Intention-Oriented Recommendation

In this section, we formalize the problem and provide preliminary knowledge about LIOR.

Definition 1: Intention Preferences. *The intention preferences denoted by* $T_{(ij)}$ *of a user* u_i *for an item/movie* i_j *is the desire of a user to watch a specific movie.*

In this research, we generate a user-item, intention matrix $T_{m \times n}$ where m is the set of movies and n is the set of users where each entry in T_{ij} contains intention values of the user u_i for the movie i_j in a range of $T_{ij} \in \{0, \ldots, 5\}$ based on a user intention of watching a movie. Higher values of T_{ij} range shows that a user is more inclined towards watching that specific movie. In this way, we extend traditional user-item, rating tuple to $(user, item, rating, uintention)$, where $uintention$ is a numerical value, showing the current user's intention.

Definition 2: Locality Preferences. *Locality preferences suggest that users in a spatial geographical location share the same movie preferences as the other users in the same locality that are different from the people living in other regions.*

Locality adds location dimension $(user, ulocation, item, rating)$ in the user-item, rating matrix where user preferences are unique with respect to their locations. The location dimension accompanies a set of hierarchies in terms of the city, state, region, and country which affect user's preferences.

Definition 3: Multi-dimensional Ratings. *It is a set of a user given ratings for items at different levels of the multidimensional cube (e.g., user location) that are a discrete set of ordered numbers used to indicate the intensity of a user likes or dislikes an item in a range of 0–5.*

In this research, we propose that ratings are affected by both location and intention dimensions which extends the traditional user-item rating matrix into a multidimensional cube. We exploit traditional user-item rating matrix to calculate the item similarities and predictions at a specific location.

Definition 4: Locality and Intention-Aware Tuple. *For a user u and item i, locality, and intention-aware tuple is an ordered set of values representing user, ulocation, uintention, item, and rating denoted by a 5-tuple* $(user, ulocation, uintention, item, rating)$.

The traditional user-item, rating tuple is represented by a 3-tuple $(user, item, rating)$, adding location and intention dimension converts it into a 5-tuple represented by $(user, ulocation, uintention, item, rating)$.

This section provides preliminary knowledge involved in the current study including intention and locality preferences, multidimensional ratings, and locality and intention-aware tuple. Next section elaborates the detailed recommendation generation procedure using LIOR.

3 Location and Intention-Oriented Recommendation Method

In this section, we describe how LIOR produces recommendations using location-based user ratings for items and user intentions denoted by the tuple $(user, ulocation, uintention, item, rating)$. We perform the recommendation process in three phases, in the first phase we, exploit locality preferences of the users to produce location-oriented predictions. For this purpose, LIOR employs user clustering strategy to partition $(user, ulocation, item, rating)$ tuple into different regions by utilizing user location attribute $(ulocation)$. Subsequently, we compute recommendations using item-based collaborative filtering on each partitioned cluster using Eqs. 1 and 2. In the second phase, user intentions are computed by employing the user-based collaborative filtering technique where similar users are first identified using Eq. 3, then intention values are computed by employing Eq. 4. In the third phase, we compute recommendations using location and intention preference-aware tuple $(user, ulocation, uintention, rating, item)$. LIOR leverages two main components, locality preferences and intention preferences of spatial users to enhance service recommendation accuracy as defined in the previous section. We explain LIOR components in the following subsections.

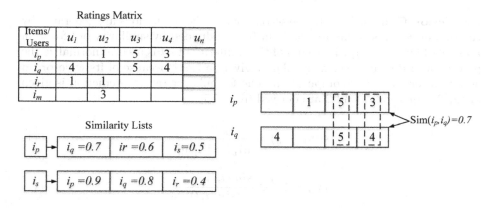

Fig. 2. Item-based similarity computation.

3.1 Item-Based Collaborative Filtering Computation

LIOR utilizes item-based collaborative filtering method to compute recommendations, we chose this technique because it is widely being used in multiple commercial systems [1]. The notion behind item-based collaborative filtering is that similar items will be rated in the same manner by the same users in the future.

Item-based collaborative filtering analyzes a set of n users and m items represented by $U = \{u_1, \ldots, u_n\}$ and $I = \{i_1, \ldots, i_m\}$ respectively. Users express ratings (usually numeric) about a set of items. The ratings are expressed as a matrix $(m \times n)$ where n and m represent dimensions of the matrix. The steps to compute item-based collaborative filtering involve similarity computation and prediction generation.

Similarity Computation. The recommendations are generated in two phases, the initial phase computes similarity $sim(i_p, i_q)$ for the item i_p and i_q which owns minimum one common rating given by the same user. Subsequently, a model is built that stores an ordered list $\mathcal{L}$ of items based on the similarity score of each item i as given in Eq. 1. The recommendations for a specific user u are generated by employing the formula of predicted ratings $(P_{u,i})$ using Eq. 2 for user u on every item i which is not previously rated by u. Prior to similarity computation, each similarity list $\mathcal{L}$ is reduced in a way that it only contains the items that are rated by the target user u.

Figure 2 demonstrates the steps to compute item-based similarity here, the similarity among item i_p and item i_q can be computed by first extracting users who have rated same items and then applying the similarity computation method on the co-rated items. Figure 2 shows the similarity value of 0.7 among i_p and i_q.

Prediction Generation. In the second phase, the predictions are generated by the sum of user u's rating for the item $(l \in \mathcal{L})$ divided by similarity of l for item i, denoted by $sim(i, l)$, where sum of the similarity of i, l is used to normalize the prediction. LIOR uses cosine similarity given in Eq. 1 because of its widespread adoption for similarity computation. The formula for rating prediction is given in Eq. 2. Equations 1 and 2 are derived from [15].

$$sim(i_p, i_q) = \frac{\overrightarrow{i_p} \cap \overrightarrow{i_q}}{||\overrightarrow{i_p}|| * ||\overrightarrow{i_p})||}.$$ (1)

$$P_{u,i} = \frac{\sum_{l \in \mathcal{L}} sim(i, l) * r_{u,l}}{\sum_{l \in \mathcal{L}} |sim(i, l)|}$$ (2)

Here, $P_{(u,i)}$ is the predicted rating which is the sum of a user u's rating on a similar item i and $r_{u,l}$ is the user u's rating for the item l. Moreover, the weighted sum is normalized by the sum of similarity scores to restrict the predictions within a predefined range. The predicted ratings are arranged according to the prediction score and top-k items are selected for the target user denoted by R_{itemCF}.

3.2   Intention Preferences Generation

LIOR utilizes the fact that similar users share the same item preferences to compute the intention values for the users [25]. To generate intention value for a target user u_i and a movie i_j, we first identify a set of nearest neighbors of u who have watched that specific movie i_j using the adjusted cosine similarity given in Eq. 3. The reason behind using adjusted cosine similarity is that the traditional cosine similarity measurement techniques treat missing values as 0 which produces a non-normalized similarity results. However, adjusted cosine similarity normalizes all the ratings prior to similarity computation. It provides a kind of Bayesian Regularization where the difference in rating scale of different users is normalized. For all the users in the dataset, centering value $\bar{r}$ is produced by computing every user's row mean and subtracting it from his/her rating values as given in Eq. 3. Subsequently, the intention values are generated by a weighted aggregate of the neighbors for the movie that the user have not watched previously using Eq. 4. This process has been performed for all the movies that a user have not watched to generate intention values. We derive Eqs. 3 and 4 from the [14,19] research and extend them for intention generation.

$$w_{(u,v)} = \frac{\sum_{i \in I} (r_{u,i} - \bar{r}_u)(r_{v,i} - \bar{r}_v)}{\sqrt{\sum_{i \in I} (r_{u,i} - \bar{r}_u)^2} \sqrt{\sum_{i \in I} (r_{v,i} - \bar{r}_v)^2}} \tag{3}$$

$$T_{(u,i)} = \bar{r}u + \frac{\sum_{u \in U} (r_{u,i} - \bar{r}_u) w_{(u,v)}}{\sum_{u \in U} w_{(u,v)}} \tag{4}$$

Here, $w_{(u,v)}$ is the adjusted cosine similarity between user u and user v, whereas $r_{u,i}$ and $r_{v,i}$ is the ratings of user u and user v for the movie i respectively. In the same way, $\bar{r}_u$ and $\bar{r}_v$ are the average ratings of user u and user v. $T_{(u,i)}$ is the intention prediction for a target user u for a movie i computed over a set of similar users U. Hence, a user-item intention matrix is generated $(T_{m \times n})$ for all the users n and movies m in the dataset.

3.3 Location-Oriented Recommendations

LIOR employs preferences of spatial users for non-spatial items to produce location-oriented recommendations. Three attributes *locality*, *intentions*, and *ratings* are used to compute recommendations. The rating tuple $(user, ulocation, item, rating)$ is adaptively clustered into different regions on the basis of user *location* attribute. We use the item-based collaborative filtering technique for computing recommendations on the remaining three attributes $(user, item, rating)$ at each partitioned subset of users. Movielens dataset's zip code information has been used to trace the user's location. In Movielens dataset, zip code consists of 5 digits where different digit sets represent distinct locations in the USA. Hence, users can be divided into multiple spatial locations based on their zip code information.

Algorithm 1 shows the pseudo code for location and intention-oriented recommendations that takes the input of $(user, ulocation, uintention, item, rating)$ tuple and training set S_{train} and outputs top-k recommendations list. Algorithm 1 includes the user clustering strategy which hierarchically partitions users into three groups based on their location. This is achieved by sequentially comparing each user's zip code information with the target user u. The first cluster is extracted where the first digit of the zip code is the same as of the target user u. In the same way, the second cluster is obtained where the first three digits of the zip code are the same as of the target user u. The third cluster contains all the users in the training set. For each partitioned set, item-based collaborative filtering is applied to generate separate location-aware hierarchical recommendation lists: $R_{itemCF}L1$, $R_{itemCF}L2$, $R_{itemCF}L3$ respectively. To compute recommendations list for a target user u, all the recommendations lists are aggregated.

$$R_{locCF} = R_{locCF}L_1 + R_{locCF}L_2 + R_{locCF}L_3 \tag{5}$$

Algorithm 1. LIOR top-k items computation

Require: Tuple-$(user, rating, ulocation, uintention, item)$, training set (S_{train}) with zip code
Ensure: R_{LIOR} top-k recommendations
1: Generate sub-$train$ 1 from S_{train} based on zip code[0]
2: Apply item-based CF method on sub-train 1
3: Get recommendation list $R_{locCF}L_1$
4: Generate sub-$train$ 2 from S_{train} based on zip code[0-2]
5: Apply item-based CF method on sub-$train$ 2
6: Get recommendation list $R_{locCF}L_2$
7: Apply item-based CF method on S_{train}
8: Get recommendation list $R_{locCF}L_3$
9: $R_{locCF} = \sum_{R_{locCF[i=1]}}^{R_{locCF[i=3]}} R_{locCF}L_i$
10: Get intention values from equation 4
11: Get recommendation R_{locCF} from equation 5
12: Aggregate $R_{locCF}, T_{u,i} = R_{LIOR} = R_{locCF} + T_{u,i}$
13: select top-k items
14: **return** R_{LIOR} top-k recommendations

3.4 LIOR Recommendations

After computing location-aware predictions list R_{locCF} for a target user u and intention values $T_{u,i}$ for each user in the training set, the predicted ratings of top-k items of R_{locCF} for a target user are aggregated with the intention values of these items in the user-item, intention matrix, $T_{u,i}$ to get R_{LIOR} recommendation as given in the Eq. 6. Finally, top-k items from the aggregated R_{LIOR} list are presented to the target user u. LIOR effectively provides recommendations to the cold start users who have not previously rated any item. In this situation, the location-based user clustering is employed and spatial preferences at a particular location are recommended to the user.

$$R_{LIOR} = R_{locCF} + T_{u,i} \tag{6}$$

4   Experimental Evaluation

This section elaborates the experimental setup and evaluation of LIOR using the actual implementation in python. We perform experiments on a popular location-aware rating big dataset Movielens [8].

4.1   Dataset Description

The Movielens dataset consists of 1 million ratings for 6040 users who have rated 3900 movies. The dataset was taken from the famous movie rating recommender system Movielens at the University of Minnesota. In the Movielens dataset, each user's rating has been associated with the zip code which makes it as a real-world dataset comprising of location-aware rating records for non-spatial items.

We compare LIOR with three state-of-the-art location-aware recommendations techniques:

- State of the art location-oriented recommender system MLTRS [20] which employs Latent Dirichlet Allocation method to recommend items. The recommendations are produced according to the ratings provided by the querying user at a specific location along with item tag information.
- Location-aware recommendations technique LARS [16] which uses adaptive pyramid structure-based user clustering strategy to partition users and produce recommendations.
- A probabilistic generative model ULA-LDA [22] which utilizes user location-aware ratings for modeling profile of users and generate recommendations.

4.2   Evaluation

To measure the quality improvement, we perform experiments from the perspective of the two most important evaluation metrics: Mean Absolute Precision $MAP@k$ and $accuracy@k$. The evaluation was performed by splitting all the rating records randomly into 80% training and 20% test rating items, hence, the training and test set have no overlap. For each target user u having location as $ulocation$ and intention as $uintention$ his/her rating records have been split into 80% to S_{train} in order to learn the model whereas 20% to S_{test} to evaluate the model. The purpose of this is to ascertain the accuracy with which test set items S_{test} have been recommended by LIOR method to each target user. Users usually like the items to be ranked in an ordered list therefore, a top-k list has been generated for each user and $accuracy@k$ is computed for every test case in the test set S_{test} by the following conditions:

- Ranking values of not rated items by a user u.
- An ordered list is generated according to the generated ranking values.
- A top-k list is computed for each user, if the item proposed to the current user also falls in the S_{test} then it is termed as a $hit@k$, otherwise it is denoted as a $miss$.

Evaluation metrics of $accuracy@k$ is selected to demonstrate the effectiveness of LIOR and has been proposed by [21, 23] computed by using the Eq. 7.

$$Accuracy@k = \frac{\#hit@k}{|S_{test}|} \tag{7}$$

Where $\#hit$ corresponds to the total number of hits for every target user in the test set. In the same way, $|S_{test}|$ denotes the count of all test cases in the test set. We also utilize MAP to evaluate LIOR which is given in the Eq. 8.

$$MAP = \frac{AP}{|U|} \tag{8}$$

Here, AP denotes average precision which is calculated by using $Accuracy@k$ and is divided by the total number of users $|U|$. In our experiment, we compute AP using the accuracy values at k ranked items. The evaluation results have been presented in Fig. 3.

4.3   Evaluation Using $Accuracy@k$

The result of $Accuracy@k$ has been shown in Fig. 3a, on the items range of $\{2, 4, 6,\ 8, 10, 12, 14, 16, 18, 20\}$. The comparison is performed with LARS, MLTRS, and ULA-LDA. It can be observed that LIOR perform exceptionally well in computing top-k recommendations and the values of $accuracy$ were the highest among all the other techniques on all the values of k.

Analysis of the figure shows that the $accuracy$ value of LIOR was 0.231 at $k = 8$ and 0.307 at $k = 20$ which is higher than all the compared techniques. It is also pertinent to note that intention values are playing a vital role in improving the recommendation accuracy which can be observed by analyzing the significantly improved results of LIOR as compared to LARS, MLTRS, and ULA-LDA.

4.4   Evaluation Using MAP

The result of MAP evaluation on top-k recommendations is shown in Fig. 3b. It can be observed that MAP values of LIOR outperformed all the compared techniques which demonstrate the consistency of LIOR on producing effective recommendations. MAP has also been computed on the set of top-k items where $k = \{2, 4, 6, 8, 10, 12, 14, 16, 18, 20\}$. The MAP values of LIOR, MLTRS, ULA-LDA, and LARS at $k = 10$ were 0.181, 0.161, 0.135, and 0.102 respectively. This improvement demonstrates that locality preferences and similar user-based intentions are playing a positive role in producing recommendations. It can be observed that MLTRS and ULA-LDA perform better than LARS because as compared to LARS, MLTRS and ULA-LDA also employs latent tag information along with the location to produce personalized recommendations.

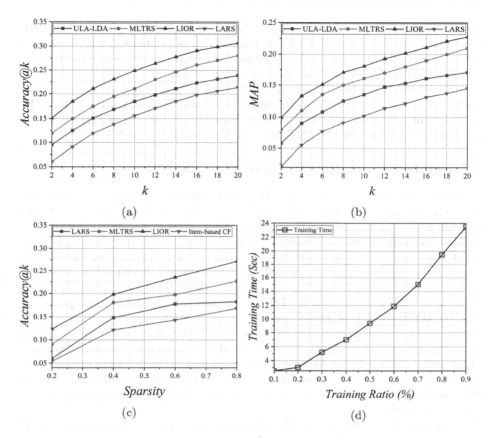

Fig. 3. Evaluation of LIOR method using different measures.

4.5 Dealing with Sparsity

We evaluate LIOR by varying different data sparsity levels (e.g., 0.2, 0.4, 0.6, 0.8) on Movielens dataset at $k = 10$. Figure 3c shows the accuracy of all the techniques on different data sparsity levels. The accuracy values increase with the increase of sparsity in all the approaches. LIOR still provides better results on all the sparsity levels. The accuracy values decrease with the decrease in data sparsity however, the accuracy values in LIOR decrease smoothly as compared to other techniques which shows the positive impact of hierarchical clustering strategy on reducing sparsity problem. The improved accuracy of LIOR is also evident that user intentions have a positive impact on increasing recommendations accuracy and decreasing the sparsity problem.

4.6 Scalability on Larger Datasets

We perform the experiments to evaluate the scalability of LIOR using different percentages of data. Training time is observed on each percentage of the data as a metric for scalability evaluation. As can be observed from Fig. 3d which demonstrate that the time required for training the model increases in a linear way with the increase in the amount of training data. This experiment demonstrates the feasibility of LIOR to be applied to larger datasets.

The above results proclaim that LIOR outperformed novel location-oriented recommendation techniques including LARS, MLTRS, and ULA-LDA. The results signify that user location and intention information positively affect the accuracy of recommendations and alleviates the sparsity problem.

5   Related Work and Comparison Analysis

There is a recent trend to incorporate user and items latent information along with the ratings to generate personalized recommendations. Social networks provide access to the personalized information of users which can be utilized to increase recommendation accuracy [13,17]. Wang et al. [10] use trust-based similarity, whereas zhang et al. [24] use auxiliary information from social networks to increase recommendation accuracy. Recently, location-based recommendations have gained immense popularity, these techniques mainly employ location information associated with the user and/or item to produce personalized recommendations [4,11,12]. Lian et al. propose an implicit feedback-based location recommendation technique to deal with the cold start users [6]. Chen et al. present explicit semantic analysis and deep neural networks-based personalized news recommendations system [3]. Stepan et al. utilize spatial, temporal, and social information for location recommendations. However, the drawback of these techniques is that they do not consider location-based ratings for computing recommendations [18].

Sarwat et al. [16] propose LARS which partitions users into multiple clusters and compute recommendations by only considering ratings of the same cluster users. However, they did not consider user intentions for computing personalized recommendations. Yin et al. [22] propose a location-oriented probabilistic mixture prediction model which utilizes user interest and the influence of locality preference to compute recommendations. Wang et al. [20] propose Memetic algorithm which considers *rating*, *location*, and *tag* information to produce recommendations. However, most of the times item tags are incomplete and ambiguous which lead to misinterpretation of the user's interests. As compared to these techniques, LIOR employs locality preferences along with intentions to produce high-quality recommendations.

Intention-oriented recommendations help in producing recommendations based on user underlying motivations of doing a business activity. User intentions are highly affected by the preferences of similar users [25]. Zhao et al. [26] link users on Weibo social network with ecommerce website JingDong to provide recommendations to cold start users however, they did not consider the problem of user location preferences on producing recommendations. Meng et al. [7] propose aspect2vec a user query intention extraction approach in which query aspects are represented as vectors and nodes by employing users latent information from their social networks. Still, authors did not observe spatial preferences of users which strongly affect user search intentions. Bhattacharya et al. [2] proposed a recommendation system that monitors user browsing patterns on the web to extract user intention and produce recommendations. They used an indirect method to infer user intentions however, location impact on these intentions have not been considered by the authors.

6 Discussion

The results and comparison analysis demonstrate the need for intention and location-aware recommendations and prove that ratings, location, and intentions are vital information sources to improve recommendations accuracy. Although, we achieve higher accuracy on top-k items recommendations, however, there is still a need to incorporate contextual information to produce personalized recommendations. Similarly, user-based similarity provides an estimate of the user intentions of buying a product or doing an activity, though realistic information can be extracted from the user's social media data to generate more accurate recommendations.

7 Conclusion and Future Work

In this research, we presented LIOR, a location and intention-oriented recommendation method to increase recommendations accuracy. We propose that ratings, location-based similarity, and user intentions strongly influence user preferences. For a target user, LIOR sequentially clusters all the users into multiple regions based on their location similarity with the target user. It then computes item-based collaborative filtering on each cluster to generate predictions. Afterward, the user's intentions are extracted by employing the user-based collaborative filtering technique. Finally, location-aware predictions and intentions are aggregated to compute LIOR recommendations. We performed comprehensive experiments on real-world location-aware Movielens big dataset. Our results reveal that LIOR outperformed state-of-the-art location-based recommendation techniques including LARS, ULA-LDA, and MLTRS in terms of MAP, $accuracy$, and reducing the sparsity problem. The experiments also proclaim that LIOR is highly scalable for larger datasets.

For the future work, we will extend LIOR by extracting user's intention-oriented data on multiple user-interaction platforms like location, IoT, user demographics, and integrating temporal impacts to develop a diverse intention-oriented service recommendation system. We intend to provide personalized recommendations by incorporating user's social network information and analyzing the impact of spatial-temporal-aware ratings using contextual information from social media.

Acknowledgments. This research is supported by the National Science Foundation of China under Grant No. 61672276 and 61702277 and the Collaborative Innovation Center of Novel Software Technology and Industrialization, Nanjing University.

References

1. Amazon. http://www.amazon.com/
2. Bhattacharya, B., Burhanuddin, I., Sancheti, A., Satya, K.: Intent-aware contextual recommendation system. In: 2017 IEEE International Conference on Data Mining Workshops (ICDMW), pp. 1–8 (2017)
3. Chen, C., Meng, X., Xu, Z., Lukasiewicz, T.: Location-aware personalized news recommendation with deep semantic analysis. IEEE Access **5**, 1624–1638 (2017)
4. Geng, B., Jiao, L., Gong, M., Li, L., Wu, Y.: A two-step personalized location recommendation based on multi-objective immune algorithm. Inf. Sci. **475**, 161–181 (2019)
5. Guo, G., Zhang, J., Yorke-Smith, N.: A novel recommendation model regularized with user trust and item ratings. IEEE Trans. Knowl. Data Eng. **28**(7), 1607–1620 (2016)
6. Lian, D., et al.: Scalable content-aware collaborative filtering for location recommendation. IEEE Trans. Knowl. Data Eng. **30**(6), 1122–1135 (2018)
7. Meng, Z., Shen, H.: Scalable aspects learning for intent-aware diversified search on social networks. IEEE Access **6**, 37124–37137 (2018)
8. MovieLens. http://grouplens.org/datasets/movielens/
9. Netflix. http://www.netflix.com/
10. Parvin, H., Moradi, P., Esmaeili, S.: TCFACO: trust-aware collaborative filtering method based on ant colony optimization. Expert Syst. Appl. **118**, 152–168 (2019)
11. Parvin, H., Moradi, P., Esmaeili, S., Qader, N.N.: A scalable and robust trust-based nonnegative matrix factorization recommender using the alternating direction method. Knowl. Based Syst. **166**, 92–107 (2019)
12. Qian, T., Liu, B., Nguyen, Q.V.H., Yin, H.: Spatiotemporal representation learning for translation-based POI recommendation. ACM Trans. Inf. Syst. (TOIS) **37**(2), 18 (2019)
13. Rafiq, W., Khan, S.A., Sohail, M.: Sociology study using email data and social network analysis. Information Technology: New Generations. AISC, vol. 448, pp. 1053–1061. Springer, Cham (2016). https://doi.org/10.1007/978-3-319-32467-8_91
14. Resnick, P., Iacovou, N., Suchak, M., Bergstrom, P., Riedl, J.: GroupLens: an open architecture for collaborative filtering of netnews. In: Proceedings of the 1994 ACM Conference on Computer Supported Cooperative Work, pp. 175–186 (1994)
15. Sarwar, B.M., Karypis, G., Konstan, J.A., Riedl, J., et al.: Item-based collaborative filtering recommendation algorithms. In: WWW'01, vol. 1, pp. 285–295 (2001)
16. Sarwat, M., Levandoski, J.J., Eldawy, A., Mokbel, M.F.: LARS*: an efficient and scalable location-aware recommender system. IEEE Trans. Knowl. Data Eng. **26**(6), 1384–1399 (2014). https://doi.org/10.1109/TKDE.2013.29
17. Shi, C., Hu, B., Zhao, W.X., Philip, S.Y.: Heterogeneous information network embedding for recommendation. IEEE Trans. Knowl. Data Eng. **31**(2), 357–370 (2019)
18. Stepan, T., Morawski, J.M., Dick, S., Miller, J.: Incorporating spatial, temporal, and social context in recommendations for location-based social networks. IEEE Trans. Knowl. Data Eng. **3**(4), 164–175 (2016)
19. Su, X., Khoshgoftaar, T.M.: A survey of collaborative filtering techniques. Adv. Artif. Intell. **2009**, 19 pages (2009)
20. Wang, S., Gong, M., Li, H., Yang, J., Wu, Y.: Memetic algorithm based location and topic aware recommender system. Knowl. Based Syst. **131**, 125–134 (2017)

21. Wang, W., Yin, H., Chen, L., Sun, Y., Sadiq, S., Zhou, X.: Geo-SAGE: a geographical sparse additive generative model for spatial item recommendation. In: Proceedings of the 21th ACM SIGKDD International Conference on Knowledge Discovery and Data Mining, pp. 1255–1264 (2015)
22. Yin, H., Cui, B., Chen, L., Hu, Z., Zhang, C.: Modeling location-based user rating profiles for personalized recommendation. ACM Trans. Knowl. Discov. Data 9(3), 1–41 (2015). https://doi.org/10.1145/2663356
23. Yin, H., Sun, Y., Cui, B., Hu, Z., Chen, L.: LCARS: a location-content-aware recommender system. In: Proceedings of the 19th ACM SIGKDD International Conference on Knowledge discovery and Data Mining, pp. 221–229 (2013)
24. Zhang, T.w., Li, W.p., Wang, L., Yang, J.: Social recommendation algorithm based on stochastic gradient matrix decomposition in social network. J. Ambient Intell. Humanized Comput., 1–8 (2019)
25. Zhao, G., Qian, X., Xie, X.: User-service rating prediction by exploring social users' rating behaviors. IEEE Trans. Multimedia 18(3), 496–506 (2016). https://doi.org/10.1109/TMM.2016.2515362
26. Zhao, W.X., Li, S., He, Y., Chang, E.Y., Wen, J., Li, X.: Connecting social media to e-commerce: cold-start product recommendation using microblogging information. IEEE Trans. Knowl. Data Eng. 28(5), 1147–1159 (2016)

Noise Sensing Calibration Under Different Phone Context

Min Huang[(✉)] and Lina Chen

South China University of Technology, Guangzhou, China
minh@scut.edu.cn

Abstract. Noise pollution severely threatens human well-being. Constructing a noise map based on crowd-sensing can help city planners better understand environmental noise at lower cost. Based on the strict sampling method limitation of state-of-the-art techniques, we build a new calibration model aimed at the pocket situations and the scenarios happened more frequently in actual life. The proposed model consists of a Activity Recognition Model (ARM) and a Signal Processing Model (SPM). Three types of data are taken into consideration, which are sitting, standing, and walking. In ARM, we collect 3-axis accelerometer data to identify current sampling context based on the convolutional neural network. SPM mainly implements noise level measurement and calibration according to the corresponding output of ARM under different phone context. The average errors after calibration are controlled to be within ±3 dB (A), and the classification precision reaches 99.2%. Finally, we display the noise map adopting different criteria based on the building types, which is more scientific and meaningful. The final results show that our proposed calibration model is feasible and can improve the data quality under different situations.

Keywords: Mobile sensors · Noise sensing · Phone context

1 Introduction

Urban noise pollution is increasingly serious along with the development of the industrial era and it becomes another unignored environmental problem following air pollution and water pollution. In 2017, Ministry of Ecology and Environment (MEE) of China received a total of 550,000 environmental noise complaints, accounting for 42.9% of the total environmental complaints [1]. Given that long-term disturbance of noise will greatly affect human health and raise the risk of tinnitus, heart disease and cardiovascular disease [2], establishing a noise map can effectively monitor urban sound level.

Building up a noise map is very expensive for the government to deploy dense sensor networks covering the whole city. Recently, thanks to the diverse and advanced sensors embedded in smartphones, crowd-sensing technology seems to be a promising solution by leveraging massive amount sensing data contributed by a large number of users [3] and provides opportunities for citizens to interact with the ambient environment [4, 5]. Most of today's smartphones are equipped with many powerful sensors, such as gyroscopes, accelerometers, microphones, proximity sensors, GPS, and digital

© ICST Institute for Computer Sciences, Social Informatics and Telecommunications Engineering 2019
Published by Springer Nature Switzerland AG 2019. All Rights Reserved
Y. Yin et al. (Eds.): MobiCASE 2019, LNICST 290, pp. 18–31, 2019.
https://doi.org/10.1007/978-3-030-28468-8_2

compasses, which makes mobile phones not only phones but also tools. Some papers have researched and implemented noise mapping based on this technology [6–8] and proved its feasibility and precision [9]. However, most of them require users to hold phones in their hands, which greatly limits the available conditions because only 6.27% people choose to hold phones in their hands instead of putting them in their bags or their pockets [10]. In this paper, we consider the pocket situation and use activity recognition techniques to study the effects of different behaviors on mobile phone measurements and how to correct them. Human activity recognition (HAR) can automatically detect human behavior and has been studied for a long time in many fields. Unlike conventional HAR, mobile phones play the role of sensing nodes in this paper, so only the equipped sensors can be utilized to identify users' behaviors and the 3-axis accelerometers are most commonly used to detect activity information.

We study the relationship between the measurements of mobile phones and the readings of sound level meters (SLM) in different phone context and propose a calibration model. This model can automatically adjust the corresponding sub-model according to the user's current activity to improve the data quality when the mobile phone is placed in the pocket. The proposed architecture consists of two models, Activity Recognition Model (ARM) and Signal Processing Model (SPM). ARM takes 3-axis accelerometer data as input and processes it by activity recognition technology based on convolutional neural network (CNN). ARM can identify three daily activities, walking, standing, and sitting by directly leveraging time series input without any manual operation. By adopting corresponding calculation sub-models in SPM, we can improve the accuracy of sensing data in previously unavailable situations, so we can get more data to analyze and construct a noise map.

The rest of this paper is organized as follows. In Sect. 2, we give an overview of relate work. In Sect. 3, the proposed noise sensing method is described in detail. In Sect. 4, we conduct the experiments and analyze the experimental results. Finally, Sect. 5 concludes this paper and discusses the future work in this field.

2 Related Work

As for noise sensing in intelligent terminals, microphones play a vital role in the system implementation. But the hardware differences between mobile phones and standard SLMs make it challenged to sense noise accurately. Mobile phones adopt Dual-Mic Noise Suppression technology to reduce the impact of background sound while SLMs equip a windshield to capture as much sound as possible [11–13]. Therefore, calibration is inevitable to make mobile phones work as SLMs. For improving data quality under different phone context, many researchers choose to use some extra devices. In [14], an additional microphone with foam windscreen was installed into the mobile phone so that no matter how the users moved the measurements reached relative stable and accurate results after avoiding the influence of wind and friction. The study [15] proved that using additional microphones installed into mobile phones could greatly improve measurements accuracy and suggested using them. However, It is obviously not so easy and convenient for everyone to get such an external microphone. So researchers try to introduce context-aware and HAR technologies into noise sensing.

In [16], they proposed a new architecture mainly including call detection module, signal processing module, speech detection module, and context discovery module. Sensing context was divided into hand and pocket or bag using a k-nearest neighbor algorithm, and the samples were adopted only when the phone was in the hand. In [17], a coarse-grained data analysis method was presented to classify collecting situations. The author made a set of criteria for evaluating every situation identified by accelerometer, gyroscope, proximity sensor and GPS. Each collection situation would be scored and data was filtered according to that. Only the qualified data would be adopted, which could effectively avoid the influence of friction and vibration caused by user movements.

In order to fully use any possible data, HAR technologies are non-trivial to identify and understand human performance. Differing from conventional methods requiring high computing power for data fusion and image processing, HAR based on mobile sensors embedded in smartphones must take low power and limited sensor types into consideration. The accelerometers can determine the phone direction and are most commonly used in HAR of mobile phones. WISDM Lab [18] collected six daily activities and classified them using traditional machine learning classification algorithms like J48, Logistic Regression, and Multilayer Perceptron. However, this kind of classification algorithms needs to manually extract features, which requires domain knowledge. Therefore, deep learning booms. The deep learning approaches can directly use sensing data as input and reduce much pre-work. CNN is the most frequent and effective-proven model of deep learning approaches used in HAR [19]. Once we solve the input adaption problem caused by the difference between our input time series data and images, using CNN in HAR will become relatively easy. In [12, 13], the 3-axis time series data was considered as the 3-channel input like RGB images and conducted the 1D convolution operation to them. However, the study in [20] argued that 1D kernel could not capture the dependency between different sensors in different positions. Therefore they present a CNN model with a 2D kernel to handle this. They concluded two types of modalities including sensors in different positions and different types. For the first model, they grouped the data according to positions, and for another model, they used padding zeros to avoid disturbance.

3   Noise Sensing Approach

3.1   The Proposed Architecture for Noise Sensing

In this paper, we propose a method for improving the data quality and for relieving data sparsity for noise evaluation and map construction. The hand-hold phone context is not the focus of this paper, so how to distinguish between hand hold and pocket context will not be discussed here, as there are already some papers solved this problem [21, 22]. What we try to do is to leverage sensing data even though the phones are put into the trouser pockets (front and right) in an upside-down way and that's the premise of our architecture. Because of that, the mobile phone is closely attached to the user's leg, and the current activity of the user can be predicted by using an accelerometer to sense the direction of the mobile phone and its changing law.

In this section, we describe the proposed architecture of the whole system in detail and give an overview of how it works. As we can see from Fig. 1, the architecture composes of two major models, Activity Recognition Model (ARM) and Signal Processing Model (SPM).

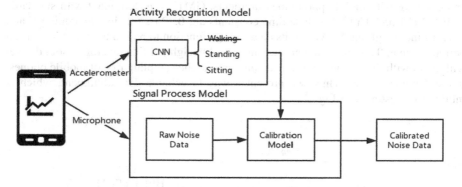

Fig. 1. The proposed architecture for noise sensing when mobile phones are in trouser pockets

There are two embedded sensors we will use, accelerometer and microphone. Firstly, the ARM detects the current activity of the user according to the accelerometer data based on CNN. When the user is in a correctable state (namely standing or sitting), the microphone is started to collect the acoustical signals, and the SPM module is started to calculate the decibel value of the surrounding environment, then the corresponding calibration sub-module is called to correct the initial measurements and output the calibrated values.

3.2   The Basis of Noise Level Measurement

We usually use the sound pressure level (SPL) to express the noise level and the A-frequency weighting sound level is the main standard for noise assessment today because it can reflect the loudness perceived by humans [14]. For evaluating the noise level in mobile phones, we must do a series of processing to compute these indicators. Since the frequency range that the human ear can sense is up to 20000 Hz, in our experiments, we collect audio signals at the rate of 44100 Hz for preserving all the audio signals information according to the Nyquist sampling theorem. We use the Android API of AudioRecord to collect the acoustic signals, whose parameter settings are displayed in Table 1.

Table 1.   Android AudioRecord API parameters

Parameters	Value
Sampling rate	44100 Hz
Sample size	16 bit
Buffer size	4410 byte

The mobile phone collects samples at a frequency of 44.1 kHz, that is, 44100 samples are collected per second. Following the settings in Table 1, each sample has 16 bit thus one buffer can store 2205 samples and there will be 20 buffers produced with no overlapping per second.

In this paper, we use BENETECH GM1356 SLM to measure the actual noise level and compare with mobile phone measurements. GM1356 is compliant with standards of IEC PUB 651 TYPE2, whose time constants are 0.125 s for time-weighting F and 1 s for time-weighting S. We use its data storage function to record the noise level for a period of time. This function can measure the A-weighted, time-averaged sound level within 1 s with time-weighting S. But compared to the sampling rate of mobile phones, it's still much slower. Thus, we present a way to achieve data alignment, which is intuitively illustrated in Fig. 2.

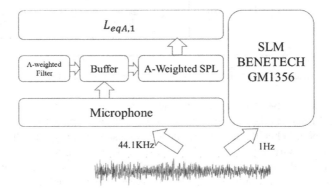

Fig. 2. Date alignment for solving different sampling frequency of SLM and mobile phone

After microphone collects audio signals at the rate of 44.1 kHz, the samples are stored in buffers temporally, we use an A-weighted filter [23] to obtain the A-weighted SPL in each buffer and calculate the A-weighted equivalent continuous sound level ($L_{eqA,T}$) [14] of the 20 buffers within 1 s. In this way, we can compare the measurements with the SLM readings by means of point to point of every second.

4   Experiments and Analysis

In this section, a series of experiments are carried out under different phone context. The mobile phones we used are MEIZU M5 Note, REDMI NOTE 5A and COOLPAD C106-9, and the standard SLM is BENETECH GM1356. Sensitivity is an important indicator of microphones, which is the ratio of the analog output voltage or digital output value to the input pressure [24] and the difference of microphones between mobile phones and SLM makes us have to do a series of processing and correction. In this paper, we define the hand-hold situation as the standard situation because it has been proven the feasibility and accuracy in many studies. All of our experiments are under the conditions of trouser pockets during sitting, standing or walking, except for the experiment in the standard situation.

4.1 Experiments for Constructing Calibration Sub-models

The experiments in this section are mainly for constructing calibration sub-models in our architecture, which will be integrated into SPM presented in Fig. 1.

Experiments in the Standard Situation. This experiment is carried out in the standard situation for proving mobile phones can accurately measure noise level in an acceptable range and comparing with the following experiments. In the experiment, we hold the phone and SLM closely and play the audio of traffic noise that was manually recorded before 1 m in front of them. This setting is for guaranteeing that both of them can simultaneously receive the acoustical signals.

The raw time series data collected from the mobile phone and SLM are described as Fig. 3.

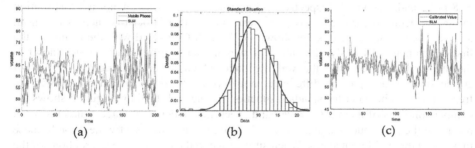

(a)   (b)   (c)

Fig. 3. (a) Time series data collected by the mobile phone; (b) Normal distribution fitting of the differences between measurements and SLM readings; (c) Time series data of standard SLM and mobile phone after linear model calibration (Color figure online)

In Fig. 3(a), it's obvious that there exists a certain distance between SLM (orange line) and mobile phone (blue line), and SLM readings are always larger than mobile phone readings. For further analyzing the differences between them, we plot the histogram of original errors and investigate the data distribution. We can see that the errors are intensive in the range of 5–10 and basically conform to the normal distribution. Its normal distribution fitting is plotted with the blue line in Fig. 3(b) and the related parameters of the fitting result can be found in Table 2. Also, we try to do linear fitting between them and the coefficients of the obtained linear model is $y = 0.7534x + 22.29$. We adopt this model to calibrate the raw measurements, the calibration result can be intuitively seen from Fig. 3(c). The two lines generally overlap and the average error is about ± 2.32 dB(A). It's a satisfying result within an acceptable range because the 3 dB difference is imperceptible to the human ear [25], thus we decided to use the linear model to do the calibration.

Experiments in Other Situations. The ideal hand-hold phone context is not always available, in many situations, most people will choose to put phones in their trouser pockets. Considering that people are actionless and there is no friction between the phone and the pocket when they are standing or sitting, there may exist a slightly different calibrated model from the standard one because the microphone is in an enclosed space.

In this section, for verifying our assumption, we carry out a series of experiments under different phone context, sitting, standing, and walking when the phone is in the pocket. The experimental materials used in experiments are always kept the same, jeans pocket covered by the plaid shirt. The experimental results are intuitively depicted in Fig. 4.

The Fig. 4(a) and (c) are the raw time series signals collected by the mobile phone. We can directly see from them that there also exits a certain difference between them like the previous experiment and SLM readings are always larger than mobile phone readings. Thus, we calculate the differences between measurements and SLM readings whose histogram is plotted in the Fig. 4(b) and (d). The distributions of standing and sitting data fit with normal distribution better according to the log likelihood of -1806.52 and -2055.19, respectively. Furthermore, the lines of normal distribution fitting are depicted for better observing results and other indicators such as the mean and variance of fitting results are shown in Table 2. Compared with the results of the first experiment, obviously, the values of standing and sitting data are much closer to the standard situation than the walking data, which means the high possibility of correction. We analyze the differences not only in the time domain but also in the frequency domain under the standard situation, sitting and standing. Figure 5 shows the comparison lines of their 1/3 octave band spectrums under these three situations when receiving the same audio signals. These three figures are not exactly the same because they are in three different states. When sitting, due to the posture, the microphone of the mobile phone in the pocket is blocked, and the measurements are obviously lower than the other two cases. When standing, the difference is not so obvious, just because the mobile phone is in a closed space, slightly different from the standard situation. Although like this, the trends of sitting and standing are basically the same as the standard situation, which is consistent with the normal distribution fitting results.

Thus, we do the linear fitting to standing and sitting data similar to Sect. 4.1 and obtain respective coefficients. After linear fitting ($y = 0.8316x + 17.15$) of standing data, we get the result depicted in Fig. 4(e) whose average error is about ± 2.90 dB(A). The raw data in Fig. 4(c) after the linear fitting ($y = 0.7911x + 20.02$) looks like Fig. 4(f) and the calibration model whose average error is within ± 3.06 dB(A) is available. As for walking data, unfortunately, as we can see from its time series plot and scatter plot in Fig. 4(g–h), we can't find a suitable relation and fitting model between walking data and SLM readings. The reason may be that the friction caused by users' periodical motion when the phone is put in the pocket leads to deviant readings. And that's why we decide to discard the walking data in our system architecture.

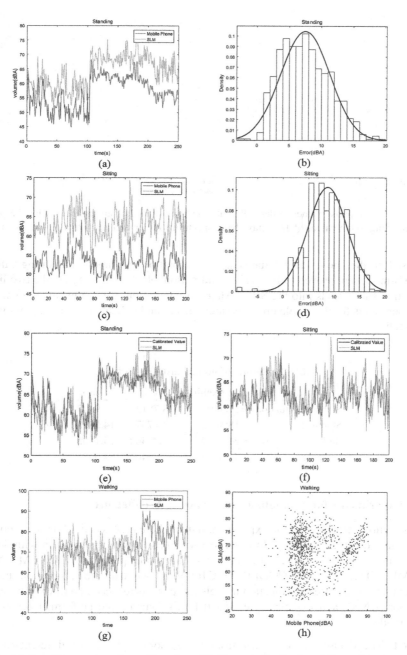

Fig. 4. (a) Raw time series of standing data; (b) Normal distribution fitting of raw errors of standing data; (c) Raw time series of sitting data; (d) Normal distribution fitting of raw errors of sitting data; (e) Time series of standing data after calibration; (f) Time series of sitting data after calibration; (g) Raw time series of walking data; (h) Scatter plot of SLM readings and raw data calculated by the mobile phone;

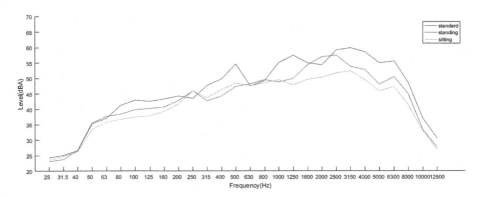

Fig. 5. The comparison lines under different situations (the lines are connected by the points corresponding to the values of 1/3 octave band spectrums under different situations, respectively)

Based on the above results, the standing calibration sub-model and sitting calibration sub-model are proved to be feasible and reasonable. So we integrate the two linear calibration sub-models into the SPM. After the integration, we can eventually conduct the experiments for the whole proposed architecture and validate its effectiveness in the next section.

Table 2. Results of normal distribution fitting

	Log likelihood	Mean	Variance
Standard situation	−1780.94	8.78134	17.9977
Standing	−1806.52	7.47372	14.5815
Sitting	−2055.19	8.71402	15.1505
Walking	−4146.17	5.20406	164.998

4.2 Experiments for Validating the Proposed Architecture

In this section, we carry out the experiment in the whole process based on the proposed architecture depicted in Fig. 1. In order to verify that there is no problem with device dependencies, we use three different types of mobile phones, MEIZU M5 Note, REDMI NOTE 5A, and COOLPAD C106-9 to validate the calibration model. Meanwhile, we use the classification models, support vector machine (SVM), k-nearest neighbor (KNN), and logistic regression (LR) to compare the performance with our CNN model.

Dataset. The dataset we collected from three mobile phones of different models includes 3-axis accelerometer data of x, y, and z sampled at 25 Hz and the raw original audio signals sensed by microphones at 44.1 kHz. The number of each type is shown in Table 3.

Table 3. The number of samples

	xyz-axis accelerometer	Audio signal
Sitting	24775	114357442
Walking	19371	197102180
Standing	17794	199931457
Total	61940	511391079

We collected 511391079 time series signal samples and 61940 3-axis accelerometer data in x, y, and z axis separately as the input data for training and testing the model. Firstly, we process the input 3-axis time series signals by our proposed CNN model and use it to classify and identify current user behaviors. Then, we leverage the calibration model obtained in the previous section to correct raw data and analyze the experimental results. More details will be explained in the next sub-sections.

The Proposed CNN Structure. Convolutional neural network (CNN) is one of the representative algorithms of deep learning. Since CNN can extract features from signals well and has the advantages of local dependency and scale invariance [26, 27]. We adopt the CNN model to process the raw time series accelerometer data following the idea of [26, 27] where the 3-axis data will be treated as the 3-channel input like RGB images. Given that we will integrate the classification model into mobile phones in the future, there is a tradeoff between computation and accuracy. In this paper, a relatively simple and classical CNN structure is adopted and the specific parameters are shown in Fig. 6.

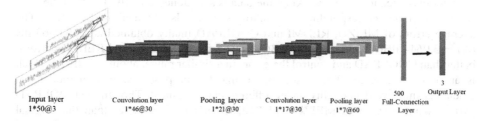

| Input layer | Convolution layer | Pooling layer | Convolution layer | Pooling layer | Full-Connection | Output Layer |
| 1*50@3 | 1*46@30 | 1*21@30 | 1*17@30 | 1*7@60 | 500 Layer | 3 |

Fig. 6. The structure of CNN model used for classifying user activities, including the input layer, 6 hidden layers (between input layer and output layer), and output layer.

Due to the obvious numerical feature differences among these three activities walking, sitting and standing, the architecture we leveraged is quite simple but the classified result is very satisfying. The structure consists of 1 input layer, 2 convolution layers, 2 max-pooling layers, 1 full connection layer and 1 output layer. In our model, we directly take the time series data as input differing from traditional image input, so some transformations must be done before inputting. We set a sliding window with the length of 50 to segment the raw time series accelerometer readings. The window size is the sample length of 2 s, which is long enough to capture the repeated walking motion. The sliding window moves forward in a half-overlapping manner (namely 25 samples per step). Then segments are input into the input layer in 3-channel way. In the following convolution layer, a 1*5 filter (stride = 1) is adopted to conduct a one-dimensional convolutional operation. In pooling layer, we use max-pooling (size = 1*5, stride = 2) to reduce the dimensionality of feature maps in the previous layer. The operations and parameters in the next convolution layer and pooling layer are the same as these two's. The flattened last pooling layer is connected to a full-connection layer with 500 hidden units and the output layer will give the final classified result standing, sitting or walking.

Experimental Results. We use the 10-fold cross validation method to perform the classification model. The performance comparison of different classifier results is shown in Table 4. The precision, recall, and F1 of CNN classification results are the highest of all, which reach 99.2%, 99.1% and 99.1%, respectively. In conventional classifier of machine learning, KNN performs better than the other two and its precision is very close to CNN's.

Table 4. Performance comparison of different classifier results

	Precision	Recall	F1
CNN	0.99170	0.99140	0.99141
LR	0.98735	0.98710	0.98713
KNN	0.99083	0.99054	0.99057
SVM	0.98625	0.98538	0.98554

After classification, if it's walking, the data is abandoned directly. For the other two cases, we adopt corresponding calibration sub-models obtained in Sect. 4.1. The average errors of MEIZU, REDMI and COOLPAD finally obtained are ±3.0563 dB (A), ±3.0644 dB(A) and ±4.8252 dB(A), respectively. MEIZU and REDMI perform better than COOLPAD and control the errors in a similar range, about ±3 dB(A) which is an acceptable value. The results prove that the proposed calibration model can efficiently improve data quality under different phone context. Though the COOLPAD performs not as well as MEIZU and REDMI, it's already better than the original average error (±13.6740 dB(A)). More intuitively, let's take 120 samples before and after calibration as the example. The raw data of mobile phones and SLM are shown in Fig. 7(a). In the raw time series data, the first 60 samples are recorded during sitting while the following 60 samples are standing data.

In Fig. 7(a), all the lines of the three phones deviate from the SLM readings (blue line) at different levels and are smaller than the blue line, this is consistent with our previous experiments. As how the designed system architecture works, the three different lines are calibrated by sitting calibration sub-model and standing calibration sub-model, respectively. As we can see from the corrected result shown in Fig. 7(b), most points of MEIZU and REDMI are very close to the SLM readings and the orange and red lines generally overlap blue line. Although the purple line still has a small distance, it is much closer than Fig. 7(a). The differences among them after calibration mainly caused by the hardware configuration differences. The hardware configuration of

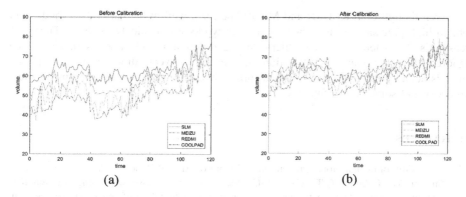

Fig. 7. Time series data, the first 60 samples are sitting data and the remaining is standing data (**a**) The raw series data before calibration; (**b**) The series data after calibration (Color figure online)

different brands and different models of mobile phones is quite different, and it will certainly affect the accuracy of the measured values to a certain extent. This is something we have no way to overcome at present but we will continue to study and solve it in the future work.

5   Conclusions

Noise pollution has obtained increasing attention in recent years with much more realization of its harm. But it's limited for us to know the specific sound strength, which is bad for monitoring ambient noise level. The previous work leveraging mobile sensors of mobile phones requires strict sampling conditions leading to little available data. The sparse data makes it difficult to reconstruct data for building up a noise map which can make people know the noise situation from a macroscopic perspective and provide much useful and meaningful information for the government.

In this paper, we conduct a sequence of experiments for validating feasibility in the standard situation and digging out the relations between phone readings and SLM readings during sitting and standing. The results show that linear fitting can reduce the differences between them and control the errors in the desirable range, ± 2.09 dB(A) and ± 3.06 dB(A) respectively. In Sect. 4.2, the calibration model and the CNN-based activity recognition classification are integrated into one to perform the whole noise sensing process. To avoid device dependent problem, we use three mobile phones of different models to conduct the experiments. In the first classification model, we leverage the 3-axis accelerometer data only but the accuracy reaches 99.2%. Then, output the classified result and choose a corresponding calibration sub-model to modify the raw noise data. Finally, we get the average error of ± 3.06 dB(A), ± 3.06 dB(A) and ± 4.8252 dB(A), respectively. The results prove that the proposed noise sensing calibration model can fully leverage noise data under different phone context which is unavailable in previous work and relieve the data sparsity problem in some way.

Even though both REDMI and MEIZU perform well in the calibration model and obtain high-precision results, the COOLPAD works not as nicely as them. The main reason is the heterogeneous problem among different mobile phones that can't be ignored. The hardware configuration differences between different mobile phone models actually influence the model accuracy, and this is the major problem we must consider and solve in our future work.

References

1. China Environmental Noise Prevention and Control Annual Report (2017)
2. Zamora, W., Calafate, C.T., Cano, J.-C., Manzoni, P.: Noise-sensing using smartphones: determining the right time to sample. In: 15th International Conference on Advances in Mobile Computing and Multimedia, MoMM 2017, Salzburg, Austria, 4–6 December 2017, pp. 196–200. Association for Computing Machinery (2017)
3. Huang, M., Bai, Y., Chen, Y., Sun, B.: A distributed proactive service framework for crowd-sensing process. In: IEEE International Symposium on Autonomous Decentralized System, pp. 68–74 (2017)
4. Unsworth, K., Forte, A., Dilworth, R.: Urban informatics: the role of citizen participation in policy making. J. Urban Technol. 21(4), 1–5 (2014)
5. Radicchi, A., Henckel, D., Memmel, M.: Citizens as smart, active sensors for a quiet and just city. The case of the "open source soundscapes" approach to identify, assess and plan "everyday quiet areas" in cities. Noise Mapping 4(1), 1–20 (2017)
6. Picaut, J., et al.: Noise mapping based on participative measurements with a smartphone. Acoust. Soc. Am. J. 141(5), 3808 (2017)
7. Aiello, L.M., Schifanella, R., Quercia, D., Aletta, F.: Chatty maps: constructing sound maps of urban areas from social media data. R. Soc. Open Sci. 3(3) (2016)
8. Li, C., Liu, Y., Haklay, M.: Participatory soundscape sensing. Landsc. Urban Plan. 173, 64–69 (2018)
9. D'Hondt, E., Stevens, M., Jacobs, A.: Participatory noise mapping works! An evaluation of participatory sensing as an alternative to standard techniques for environmental monitoring. Pervasive Mob. Comput. 9(5), 681–694 (2013)
10. Cui, Y., Chipchase, J., Ichikawa, F.: A cross culture study on phone carrying and physical personalization. In: Aykin, N. (ed.) UI-HCII 2007. LNCS, vol. 4559, pp. 483–492. Springer, Heidelberg (2007). https://doi.org/10.1007/978-3-540-73287-7_57
11. Al-Saloul, A.H.A., Li, J., Bei, Z., Zhu, Y.: NoiseCo: smartphone-based noise collection and correction. In: 4th International Conference on Computer Science and Network Technology, ICCSNT 2015, Harbin, China, 19–20 December 2015. Institute of Electrical and Electronics Engineers Inc. (2015)
12. Liu, L.: The design and implementation of a real-time fine-grained noise sensing system based on participatory sensing. Master, Shanghai Jiao Tong University (2015)
13. Liu, L., Zhu, Y.: Noise collection and presentation system based on crowd sensing. Comput. Eng. 41(10), 160–164 (2015)
14. Zuo, J., Xia, H., Liu, S., Qiao, Y.: Mapping urban environmental noise using smartphones. Sensors 16(10), 1692 (2016)
15. Kardous, C.A., Shaw, P.B.: Evaluation of smartphone sound measurement applications (apps) using external microphones - a follow-up study. J. Acoust. Soc. Am. 140(4), EL327–EL333 (2016)

16. Rana, R., Chou, C.T., Bulusu, N., Kanhere, S., Hu, W.: Ear-Phone: a context-aware noise mapping using smart phones. Pervasive Mob. Comput. **7**(PA), 1–22 (2015)
17. Huo, Z.: Research and implementation of a crowdsensing-based noise map platform. Master, China University of Geosciences, Beijing (2016)
18. Kwapisz, J.R., Weiss, G.M., Moore, S.A.: Activity Recognition using Cell Phone Accelerometers. ACM SIGKDD Explor. Newsl. **12**, 74–82 (2011)
19. Wang, J., Chen, Y., Hao, S., Peng, X., Hu, L.: Deep learning for sensor-based activity recognition: a survey. Pattern Recogn. Lett. **119**, 3–11 (2017)
20. Ha, S., Yun, J.-M., Choi, S.: Multi-modal convolutional neural networks for activity recognition. In: IEEE International Conference on Systems, Man, and Cybernetics, SMC 2015, Kowloon Tong, Hong Kong, 9–12 October 2015, pp. 3017–3022. Institute of Electrical and Electronics Engineers Inc. (2015)
21. Rana, R., Chou, C.T., Bulusu, N., Kanhere, S., Hu, W.: Ear-Phone: a context-aware noise mapping using smart phones. Pervasive Mob. Comput. **17**, 1–22 (2015)
22. Miluzzo, E.., Papandrea, M., Lane, N.D., Lu, H., Campbell, A.T.: Pocket, bag, hand, etc. - automatically detecting phone context through discovery. In: First International Workshop on Sensing for App Phones at Sensys (2010)
23. Zamora, W., Calafate, C., Cano, J.C., Manzoni, P.: Accurate ambient noise assessment using smartphones. Sensors **17**(4), 917 (2017)
24. Lewis, J.: Understanding Microphone Sensitivity, 12 June 2018. https://www.analog.com/en/analog-dialogue/articles/understanding-microphone-sensitivity.html
25. Rana, R.K., Chou, C.T., Kanhere, S.S., Bulusu, N., Hu, W.: Ear-phone: an end-to-end participatory urban noise mapping system. In: 9th ACM/IEEE International Conference on Information Processing in Sensor Networks, IPSN 2010, Stockholm, Sweden, 12–16 April 2010, pp. 105–116. Association for Computing Machinery (ACM) (2010)
26. Zeng, M., et al.: Convolutional Neural Networks for human activity recognition using mobile sensors. In: 2014 6th International Conference on Mobile Computing, Applications and Services, MobiCASE 2014, Austin, TX, USA, 6–7 November 2014, pp. 197–205. Institute of Electrical and Electronics Engineers Inc. (2015)
27. Yang, J.B., Nguyen, M.N., San, P.P., Li, X.L., Krishnaswamy, S.: Deep convolutional neural networks on multichannel time series for human activity recognition. In: 24th International Joint Conference on Artificial Intelligence, IJCAI 2015, Buenos Aires, Argentina, 25–31 July 2015, pp. 3995–4001. International Joint Conferences on Artificial Intelligence (2015)

Mobile App for Text-to-Image Synthesis

Ryan Kang[1], Athira Sunil[2], and Min Chen[3(✉)]

[1] Tableau Software, Seattle, WA 98103, USA
rkang@tableau.com
[2] eBay Inc., San Jose, CA 95125, USA
atsunil@ebay.com
[3] University of Washington Bothell, Bothell, WA 98011, USA
minchen2@uw.edu

Abstract. Generating visual representation of textual information is a challenging yet interesting topic with many potential applications. In this paper, we propose a novel approach to visualize natural language sentences using ImageNet to enhance language education. Currently the focus is to assist English language learners in building their vocabulary of common nouns and developing an in-depth understanding of the various prepositions of locations. To achieve this goal, real-world images representing nouns are obtained from ImageNet and their foreground objects of interest are extracted using image segmentation. The objects are then re-arranged on a canvas based on their spatial relationship specified in the sentence. To demonstrate the effectiveness of the proposed approach, we have developed a mobile application that uses the RESTful API to retrieve the images from the web service that operate the image generation program. The prototype mobile application can create visual representations of natural language sentences and a text description of the spatial relationship of objects to assist in learning new vocabulary and spatial prepositions during language education.

Keywords: Text-to-Image · Image-to-Text · Mobile application · ImageNet · WordNet · RESTful API · Speech recognition · English language education

1 Introduction

Creating the visual representation of natural language sentences is a challenging task with the potential to spark new and innovative applications. For instance, the technology can be used for automatic generation of text illustration, language translation using images as intermediaries, and more descriptive and intuitive sentence-based image search. Recently, there have been significant efforts to study the relationship between natural language sentences and their image representations. This study is generally done in two directions: an image can be given as input and a sentence can be produced as output; or an animation or scene can be generated from a textual description. In this paper, we propose an approach to visualize natural language sentences or a text representation that describe the spatial relationship between two objects to assist in language education.

Y. Yin et al. (Eds.): MobiCASE 2019, LNICST 290, pp. 32–43, 2019.
https://doi.org/10.1007/978-3-030-28468-8_3

Several studies have shown that multimedia visual aids can be effectively used in English language learning to enhance and facilitate the comprehension of grammar and language [1]. Visualization of textual information can also help in memorizing new vocabulary and structures. The objective of this study is to assist English language learners in studying common nouns and prepositions of location through automatic illustration of sentences or automatic text generation to describe the spatial relationship between two objects. Our mobile application enables speech recognition to generate text from an English spoken sentence consisting of common nouns and prepositions of location. Then, it sends a RESTful API request to the web service for images to illustrate the spatial relationship of the two noun objects in the sentence. The generated images are based on the real-world images containing the nouns from the ImageNet [2] database. The mobile application also enables users to select, drag, drop, and move two random images, on which it produces text descriptions of the spatial relationships between the two images accordingly.

The contributions of our work can be summarized as follows. Firstly, the system uses ImageNet [1], a large-scale image database organized according to the nouns in the WordNet [2] hierarchy with an average of over five hundred images per node of the hierarchy. By using ImageNet, the system can illustrate a rich set of common nouns in real-world contexts to build the vocabulary of users in a more meaningful manner. WordNet is also used for word tokenization and to collect the *Synset*: a set of synonyms that share a common meaning. Secondly, the mobile application integrates the iOS speech recognition engine to enhance the user's experience in language learning by converting the user's voice to text and then use the text as a parameter to send the request to the web service to generate images. When the mobile application receives the images, it shows the visual representation of the sentence to the user. Thirdly, the system allows the users to select noun images they prefer to be used in visualization to make the learning experience more engaging. Our mobile application provides two different approaches that can be used in English language learning.

2 Literature Review

Several studies have focused on learning the relationship between images and their sentence based semantic descriptions. Many works have studied the task of generating textual descriptions of images. Significant works have been also made in the multi-media and computer vision communities to improve image search using textual queries. Many papers have explored the visual meaning of different parts of speech. Comparatively fewer studies have addressed the idea of scene creation from natural language sentences.

One study [4] proposed an application to improve the user experience when reading news articles through automatic generation of an audio-visual presentation of the article. The application focused on retrieving an image from Flickr to illustrate a given sentence in the news article through the relation of neighboring sentences and image tags. Another study [5] proposed a system that can automatically add objects to an image when the background image and labels of objects (e.g. car) to be added are provided as input. The system estimated the position, scale, and appearance of objects and automatically added them to images without direct user input. The study in [6] focused on learning the visual features that correspond to semantic scene phrases derived from sentences. The work used abstract scenes generated from clip art to study semantic scene understanding. WordsEye [7] is an online application for converting text into representative 3D scenes. The system relies on its collection of 3D models and poses to depict entities and actions. All the models have associated shape displacements, spatial tags, and functional properties to be used in the scene generation process. Another work [8] proposed a system to create scenes from natural language sentences with a focus on the development of a hierarchical syntactic parser for sentence analysis and the correlation of words in the sentences with an image patch of the closest concept within a small number of choices.

3 Implementation

3.1 System Architecture

Figure 1 shows the high-level architecture of the system. Our system consists of the following four major components:

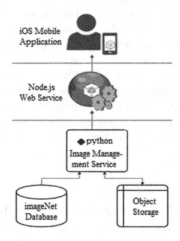

Fig. 1. Architecture diagram

- The ImageNet dataset: it contains the URLs to download the images and their annotations, and to obtain the set of cognitive synonyms (synsets) from the WordNet dataset for the nouns in the sentence.
- The image management component: it builds a database containing the attributes of the images in ImageNet, word tokenization, image segmentation, and output image generation.
- The web service component: it handles the request to start a job to generate the image and send back the generated image.
- The mobile application: it handles all the interactions with the user.

3.2   Data Set

The real-world images of nouns used in the visualization of sentences are obtained from the ImageNet database. A noun may have different meanings in different contexts. The WordNet database is used to obtain the specific meaning of a noun in a given sentence and retrieve images from ImageNet that visually represent the concept.

ImageNet. ImageNet is a large-scale image dataset organized according to the WordNet hierarchy. Currently, 21841 synsets of nouns in WordNet are indexed in ImageNet with an average of over 500 images per synset. ImageNet provides URLs of web images for each synset to download and all images in ImageNet are quality-controlled and human-annotated. ImageNet also provides annotations of object bounding boxes for each unique image in over 3000 popular synsets. Our system uses images with annotated and verified bounding boxes.

WordNet. WordNet is a large lexical database for English in which nouns, verbs, adjectives, and adverbs are grouped into sets of synonyms called synsets, each of which expresses a distinct concept. In our study, we focus on the synsets of nouns in WordNet. The synsets are ordered by their estimated frequency of use. Each synset has an associated synset offset which is the byte offset of the synset in the WordNet database file called data.noun. The synset offset of a synset is an 8 digit, zero-filled decimal integer which can be used to uniquely identify the synset. Table 1 shows the different synsets in WordNet containing the noun *table*.

Table 1. Synsets containing the noun *table* with the corresponding concepts and synset.

Synset	Concept	Synset offset
{table, tabular array}	A set of data arranged in rows and columns	08266235
{table}	A piece of furniture having a smooth flat top that is usually supported by one or more vertical legs	04379243
{table}	A piece of furniture with tableware for a meal laid out on it	04379964
{mesa, table}	flat tableland with steep edges	09351905
{table}	A company of people assembled at a table for a meal or game	08480135

3.3   Image Management Component

Database. We first built the database with image IDs, URLs to download the images, and object bounding box annotations for all the images available on the ImageNet. An image ID is a concatenation of POS (Part of Speech) tag and synset offset of WordNet ID followed by the underscore character (_) and a number which is unique for each image.

For example, the image ID of the image of *table* (see Fig. 2) is n04379243_17932, where 'n' is the POS tag for nouns, 04379243 is the WordNet ID (wnid), and 17932 is the unique number for the image. ImageNet provides the URLs to download the images as a text file and the annotations of object bounding boxes of images as XML files.

Fig. 2. Sample real-world image of *table* from ImageNet

The XML file contains the image ID, image dimensions (width, height, and depth) and bouning box coordinates of each foreground object in the image (see Fig. 3). We deserialized the XML files to extract the image ID, image dimensions (width and height) and coordinates of the top left corner and bottom right corner of the object bounding box. Then, we stored all the information we gathered from the ImageNet into a SQL database to improve the performance of the system and keep the system highly available even if the ImageNet website doesn't respond.

```xml
<?xml version="1.0"?>
- <annotation>
    <folder>n04379243</folder>
    <filename>n04379243_11010</filename>
  - <source>
      <database>ImageNet database</database>
    </source>
  - <size>
      <width>448</width>
      <height>265</height>
      <depth>3</depth>
    </size>
    <segmented>0</segmented>
  - <object>
      <name>n04379243</name>
      <pose>Unspecified</pose>
      <truncated>0</truncated>
      <difficult>0</difficult>
    - <bndbox>
        <xmin>0</xmin>
        <ymin>26</ymin>
        <xmax>447</xmax>
        <ymax>255</ymax>
      </bndbox>
    </object>
  </annotation>
```

Fig. 3. Sample XML file containing object bounding box annotations

Pre-download Images. We download 10 random real-world images for each unique image ID from the ImageNet in order to minimize the waiting time for the end user as image downloading time can vary from 2 to 8 s. Additionally, we also extract the object image from the original image using the bounding box coordinates and the GrabCut algorithm and store the processed images in the local file storage of the machine that runs the web service.

Word Tokenization. During the word tokenization process, the system tokenizes the input sentence that contains two common nouns and a preposition of location. In this step, the system will extract main noun, dependent noun, and preposition in the sentence using the tokenization, word singularization, and POS tag detection features from the Natural Language Toolkit [9]. The POS tag determines which object becomes the main noun or the dependent noun and which word is the preposition.

Image Segmentation. Our system extractsthe objects of interest from the images. To achieve this, the system uses the GrabCut algorithm proposed by Rother, Kolmogorov, and Blake in [10]. GrabCut is an interactive foreground extraction tool where the user drags a rectangle around the foreground region. The foreground region must be completely inside the rectangle since everything outside the rectangle will be taken as sure background. The algorithm then segments the image iteratively till the foreground/background classification converges. Our system automates the algorithm without the user having to select the region of interest by using the bounding box information. Figure 4 shows the image of a cat from ImageNet with a rectangle drawn using the object bounding box coordinates and the output from the GrabCut algorithm with a transparent background.

Fig. 4. (left) Original image of a *cat* from ImageNet (middle) The bounding box containing the *cat* (right) Output of GrabCut algorithm with transparent background

Create the Image Illustrating the Sentence. We create the output image visualizing the sentence by placing the images of the objects obtained from the previous step on a canvas according to the preposition of location. The sizes of the images obtained from ImageNet can vary greatly from 75×75 pixels to 1024×768 pixels. Therefore, the system resizes the images of the objects to a suitable and consistent size keeping the aspect ratio. After the images are resized, alpha blending is used on both main and dependent noun object images as foreground image to combine it with a background image to create the appearance of transparency and smooth out the boundaries.

The alpha blending uses the alpha channel of the image encoding and the following equation is used to overlay the image of the object on the canvas:

$$I_A = \alpha I_F + (1 - \alpha)I_B$$

In the equation, I_A is the alpha blended image, I_F is the foreground image of the object, and I_B is the background canvas image. The created image would not look as natural without the alpha blending (see Fig. 5).

Fig. 5. (left) Image created without alpha blending (right) Image created with alpha blending [11]

3.4   Web Service

Our Web Service component is built on the Node.js platform with Express.js web framework. This component starts an HTTP server and listens on the specific requests. When the web service receives the request, it creates a child process to start a job on the Image Management component to perform the image generation or image retrieval. When the job is completed, the child process will callback with either success or error. If the Image Management component has successfully completed, the web service will send the response back to the client with HTTP status code 200 (OK) and the image. Alternatively, the web service will send HTTP status code 500 (Internal Server Error) and error message when the child process fails.

3.5   Mobile Application

For the mobile application, we focused on the usability and performance as it is the end user facing application. Our mobile application is designed to target the English language learners and we tried to use as much visualization as possible to assist the users in understanding how to use the mobile application. We also added speech recognition and a drag and drop interaction that would help in making language education more engaging.

Speech Recognition. Apple supports speech recognition framework for the iOS 10 and above [11] and our mobile application uses this framework to recognize spoken words in live audio. The user will be seeing his/her voice translated into text on the mobile screen in live and uses the spoken words as input parameter to generate an image visualizing the sentence. Network connectivity is required for this feature as the speech recognition framework relies on Apple's server.

URL Sessions. Our mobile application uses Apple's URLSession APIs to download the image data from the web service [12]. This functionality has been written to support asynchronous calls to allow the main UI thread to continue to run smoothly while the data is being fetched in the background.

User Interaction. We have added drag and drop gesture support on our mobile application for Image-to-Text conversion feature. This feature is only available in the mobile application as the user has to use drag and drop gesture to move around the two images within the mobile screen. Once the user has finished moving the images, the 'Generate' button will become enabled and the user will see the text describing the spatial relationship between the two objects in the images.

Spatial Relationship Description Based on Images Location. Our mobile application calculates the distance between the location of the two object images to generate the text representing the scene on the mobile screen. It is currently supporting six different prepositions to show the spatial relationship between the two objects. The prepositions we support are 'On', 'Under', 'Beside', 'Above', 'Below', and 'Near'.

Text-to-Image Use Case Sequence Diagram. Figure 6 shows the use case of the Text-to-Image API from the mobile application. The mobile application first receives the voice command from the user and convert the audio input to text. Then, the mobile application sends GET request to the web service which starts a job in Image Management component. Upon successful call back to the web service with image location, the web service responds back to the mobile application with image file. Finally, the mobile application displays the image on the screen. The three components of the system work together as a single service for creating visual representations of natural language sentences.

4   Results

We have developed an educational application to demonstrate the effectiveness of the proposed approach to visualize natural language sentences. Our mobile application has been designed to help the English language learners with usability in our mind. The GUI of the mobile application for visualizing the spoken words on the mobile screen is shown in Fig. 7. As we can see, the main mobile application UI displays the tab bar buttons to switch between the Text-to-Image conversion view and Image-to-Text view on the bottom. The 'START'/'STOP' button for voice recognition is also visually appealing to the user for the interaction. The live text feedback on the center of the mobile screen helps the user to know if the voice recognition API has successfully converted the spoken words to text or not. The user can use this button to re-try if needed as the tapping on the 'STOP' button will clear the text. We used bright and high contrast colors and large font sizes for the usability and design purpose.

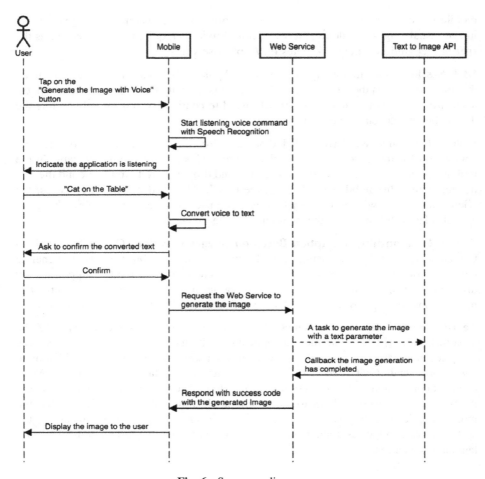

Fig. 6. Sequence diagram

The user interface of the converting the two images on the screen to a text describing the spatial relationship between two objects (see Fig. 8) is similar to Text-to-Image view. This view follows the same theme from the Text-to-Image conversion view and re-use the button with the font, font size, and color for consistency and usability. Although the drag and drop gesture to move around the images are not obvious, enabling the 'GENERATE' button only when the user interact with the mobile application suggest interaction is required.

The following Table 2 gives a summary of the performance measureswe collected. It took an average of 1.0594 s to extract the foreground object from the image using the GrabCut algorithm with bounding box annotations. An average number of the bytes the mobile application downloaded from the web service was 558502.875 bytes and the elapsed time to fetch the image was 3.78247 s.

Fig. 7. Text-to-Image conversion user interface

Fig. 8. Image-to-Text conversion user interface

Table 2. Elapsed time taken to fetch image created via Text-to-Image API.

Experiment count	Elapsed time to execute the GrabCut algorithm	Downloaded data bytes	Elapsed time to fetch the created image
1	2.0129 s	567736 bytes	3.89415 s
2	1.7314 s	585643 bytes	4.52450 s
3	0.8248 s	524609 bytes	3.39177 s
4	1.2437 s	563855 bytes	3.67760 s
5	0.5785 s	586443 bytes	4.52157 s
6	1.8266 s	561345 bytes	3.29475 s
7	0.8926 s	517657 bytes	3.37896 s
8	0.3305 s	560735 bytes	3.57648 s
Average	**1.0594 s**	**558502.875 bytes**	**3.78247 s**

5   Conclusion and Future Works

Visualization of natural language sentences has the potential to spark innovative applications. In this paper, we have proposed a novel approach to visualize natural language sentences using a large online image dataset called ImageNet. We have also developed an educational application to demonstrate the effectiveness of the proposed approach. The developed mobile application shows that the proposed approach can be effectively used to create illustrations of sentences containing common nouns and prepositions of location to assist in building new vocabulary and structures during language education.

One of the unique features of our approach is the use of a large online hierarchical image database. This helps in obtaining real-world images of a rich set of nouns in different contexts without the overhead of creating and maintaining an image database. By using the mapping between WordNet and ImageNet to automatically label images, the proposed approach eliminates the need to manually tag images.

The method proposed in this paper to illustrate natural language sentences can be used in many other applications. It can be used in language learning to assist learners enriching their vocabulary and developing a detailed understanding of the various grammatical structures of the language such as using the prepositions. The method can be also used for automatic illustration of language worksheets.

Currently, ImageNet provides annotations of object attributes like color (black, blue, brown, gray, green, orange, pink, red, violet, white, yellow), pattern (spotted, striped), shape (long, round, rectangular, square), and texture (furry, smooth, rough, shiny, metallic, vegetation, wooden, wet) for about 400 synsets. Examples of attributes provided by ImageNet for various objects is shown in Fig. 9. This information can be integrated into the system to use sentences that also contain adjectives for the nouns. For example, 'The *black cat* is *on* the *round table*.' The sentences can also include the number of objects like 'There are *three black cats on* the *table*.'

Fig. 9. Annotations of object attributes provided by ImageNet (Color figure online)

References

1. Omaggio, A.C.: Pictures and second language comprehension: do they help? Foreign Lang. Ann. **12**(2), 107–116 (1979)
2. Deng, J., Dong, W., Socher, R., Li, L.-J., Li, K., Fei-Fei, L.: ImageNet: a large-scale hierarchical image database. In: IEEE Conference on Computer Vision and Pattern Recognition (2009)
3. Miller, G.: WordNet: a lexical database for English. Commun. ACM **38**(11), 39–41 (1995)
4. Delgado, D., Magalhaes, J., Correia, N.: Assisted news reading with automated illustration. In: Proceedings of the International Conference on Multimedia – MM 2010 (2010)
5. Inaba, S. Kanezaki, A., Harada, T.: Automatic image synthesis from keywords using scene context. Ibn: Proceedings of the ACM International Conference on Multimedia – MM 2014 (2014)
6. Zitnick, C., Parikh, D., Vanderwende, L.: Learning the visual interpretation of sentences. In: 2013 IEEE International Conference on Computer Vision (2013)
7. Coyne, B., Sproat, R.: WordsEye. In: Proceedings of the 28th Annual Conference on Computer Graphics and Interactive Techniques – SIGGRAPH 2001 (2001)
8. Mano, T., Yamane, H. Harada, T.: Scene image synthesis from natural sentences using hierarchical syntactic analysis. In: Proceedings of the 2016 ACM on Multimedia Conference – MM 2016 (2016)
9. Bird, S., Loper, E., Klein, E.: Natural Language Processing with Python. O'Reilly Media Inc., Sebastopol (2009)
10. Rother, C., Kolmogorov, V., Blake, A.: GrabCut. ACM Trans. Graph. **23**(3), 309 (2004)
11. Efros, A.: Image Compositing and Blending, Carnegie Mellon University (2007). http://graphics.cs.cmu.edu/courses/15-463/2007_fall/Lectures/blending.pdf. Accessed 4 Feb 2019
12. Apple Developer Documentation Web Page. https://developer.apple.com/documentation/speech. Accessed 4 Feb 2019
13. Apple Developer Documentation Web Page. https://developer.apple.com/documentation/foundation/urlsession. Accessed 4 Feb 2019

Transformer Based Memory Network for Sentiment Analysis of Chinese Weibo Texts

Junlei Wu$^{(\boxtimes)}$, Jiang Ming, and Min Zhang

Institute of Software and Intelligent Technology, Hangzhou Dianzi University,
Hangzhou 310018, China
171050047@hdu.edu.cn, jmzju@163.com, hz_andy@163.com

Abstract. Weibo has already become the main platform of mobile social and information exchange. Therefore, the sentiment feature extraction of Weibo texts is of great significance, and aspect-based sentiment analysis (ABSA) is useful to retrieval the sentiment feature from Weibo texts. Now, context-dependent sentiment feature is obtained by widely using long short-term memory (LSTM) or Gated Recurrent Unit (GRU) network, and target vector is usually replaced by average target vector. However, Weibo texts has become increasingly complex and feature extraction with LSTM or GRU might cause the loss of key sentiment information. Meanwhile, average target vector might be wrong target feature. To correct drawbacks of the old method, a new Transformer (a new neural network architecture based on self-attention mechanism) based memory network (TF-MN), is introduced. In TF-MN, the task is migrated into question answering process in which context, question and memory module is modified optimally. The text is encoded by Transformer in context module, question module transfer target into sentiment question, memory module eliminates the effect of unrelated words by several extractions. The result of the experiment proves that our model reaches better accuracy than the state-of-the-art model.

Keywords: ABSA · Transformer · Memory network · Weibo texts

1 Introduction

Recently, rapid development has been witnessed in mobile social which has fully infiltrated into the global user communities. As one of the most important mobile social applications, Weibo contains entertainment, social, marketing and so on [1]. It has gradually evolved from a social demand that satisfies people's "weak relationship" to a popular public opinion platform, becoming one of the most important realtime information sources and the center of spreading public opinion. Viewpoints and proposals in Weibo are universal and adaptive due to large amounts of users along with the differences of their standpoints

© ICST Institute for Computer Sciences, Social Informatics and Telecommunications Engineering 2019
Published by Springer Nature Switzerland AG 2019. All Rights Reserved
Y. Yin et al. (Eds.): MobiCASE 2019, LNICST 290, pp. 44–56, 2019.
https://doi.org/10.1007/978-3-030-28468-8_4

and knowledge they have. Consumers or businesses can understand most users' emotional attitudes toward the relative products by means of sentiment analysis technique which can provide policy-making references for consumers and the evidence for enterprises to improve product quality. The recognition of the subjective information in Weibo is the main purpose of Weibo sentiment analysis, which means to analysis users' viewpoints and proposals toward products, news and hotspots.

Various aspects are included in viewpoints expressed in Weibo. For example, the text, "Nice Service but the food was too bad!", expresses the emotions of two different goals. With the approach of aspect level sentiment analysis, we can analyze the opinions and emotions expressed by Weibo in a more fine-grained manner. As to the above instance, the polarity is positive when target is "service", but it turns negative if "food" is seen as target.

Traditional methods focus on characteristic rule such as sentiment vocabulary and word bag feature for aspect-level sentiment analysis. These features are utilized to train a classifier [2]. However, the manual features are concentrated labor force and are highly relied by these methods. Different from previous methods, neural network models extract text feature in a labor-saving and scalable way.

Learning text feature is mainly by means of sequence transduction models in neural network models. The mainstream of sequence transduction models are based on complicated recurrent neural network (RNN) or convolutional neural networks (CNN) which consist of an encoder and a decoder. The models that connect the encoder and decoder through attention cells give the best combined properties [3]. Long short-term memory (LSTM) [4] and gated recurrent (GRU) [5] neural networks have been attained the best result in sentiment analysis domain. However, Weibo texts has become increasingly complex and it is quite difficult to extract context-dependent text feature. LSTM and GRU are the best sequence transduction models at present, which can't process long text. Reference [6] puts forward that text could be separated into four parts to ensure no key information lost. But, context-dependent text feature may be unable to be extracted.

Besides, target may consist of several words, and target feature can be learned directly by sequence transduction models. Experiment shows that average target vector is the best method to get target feature [7], however this method has certain weaknesses. For example, in text "Nice macarons in France are not good at all.", the target is "Nice macarons", consists of two words. Due to the limited number of words, vocabulary only contains "Nice", and thereby "macarons" will be assigned to a set of minimal random feature. Then, the average target feature of "Nice macarons" equals approximately the feature of "Nice", which leads to wrong results of classification.

Based on the two problems analyzed above, we propose a memory network model that combines Transformer. Transformer is a novel network architecture, based solely on attention mechanisms without recurrent and convolutional structure entirely. Its basic unit is self-attention mechanism which can obtain better context-dependent text representation using interactive calculation in each part of sequence whether the size of sequence.

And we utilize the memory network to capture sentiment information of given target. It contains four modules: the context module for encoding Weibo texts, the question module for storing knowledge from previous steps, the question module for conversion target and encoding questions, and the answer module for evaluating sentiment polarity by data from memory module.

The memory network is proposed for the question answering task, however, the aspect-based sentiment classification doesn't have an exact question. The original MN handles this by initializing the problem vector generated by the problem module with a zero or offset vector, while we argue that every target in the text could be converted into a question. We propose the Transformer based memory network (TF-MN) to realize our ideas, the question module of TF-MN treats each target in the text as implicitly asking a question "What is the emotion tendency of target in the text?". Figure 1 is the overview of TF-MN architecture.

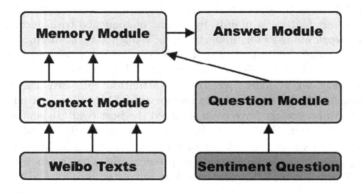

Fig. 1. The architecture diagram of TF-MN.

The following is a summary of our work:

- In sentiment analysis task, we extract long text feature by using Transformer for the first time. Our model effectively solves the problem of inaccurate long text feature extraction by using LSTM and GRU.
- The problem module does not average the target word vector, but is responsible for designing the corresponding target problem to handle the case where the target consists of multiple words.
- On our dataset, our model achieved the best accuracy, and the experimental results further show that using Transformer and adding implicit question can actually improve the performance of the model.

2   Related Work

ABSA is a subdomain in sentiment analysis which focuses on fine-grained sentiment information [8]. There are two main approaches to solve ABSA problem.

The first one is the traditional method using lexicons and rules. Reference [9] compute sentiment word score using the weight sum method. Reference [10] proposed a holistic lexicon-based method involving both explicit and implicit opinions. The method improves performance to identify the aspect level relations by multiple kernels [11].

The second one is the machine learning method. Reference [12] employed hingeloss Markov random fields to tackle ABSA in MOOC. Reference [13] put forward a emotion-aligned model for to predict aspect rate. Reference [14] combined vocabulary-based method and characteristics-based Support Vector Machine (SVM), and detect sentiment towards aspect words in SemEval 14 competition at first time. Reference [15] constructed binary phrase dependency tree of target to build the feature of aspect words. Reference [16] solved the problem using recurrent neural network, and suggested two approaches TD-LSTM and TC-LSTM. Reference [17] proposed an attention-based LSTM method. It is the best method that deal with abstractive context memory information. Reference [18] introduced a deep memory network method to solve ABSA task. It used hierarchical structure model in which the text was fully connected with target for final classification by using attention cell [19]. Reference [20] processed average target and context-dependent vector from LSTM with attention method. Reference [6] introduced a method of dividing each sentence into three parts, and the context-dependent feature was extracted using bidirectional GRU. LSTM and GRU are widely used by the models mentioned above without considering how to extract the long text feature. Meanwhile, they never consider the situation of lacking target in vocabulary when getting target by average target vector.

Different from above models, we are enlightened by self-attention mechanism. We resolve the problem of long text by Transformer. In addition, The way of solving the wrong target aims to convert target into the form of sentiment question. At last, we eliminate the influence of sentiment-irrelevant words by multiple extractions in memory module.

3   The Proposed Model

We presents TF-MN model for ABSA in this section. The task of ABSA concluded as follows: given a text consisting of n words $C = \{w_1^C, w_2^C, \cdots, w_{n-1}^C, w_n^C\}$ that is named context, a target $T = \{w_1^T, w_2^T, \cdots, w_{i-1}^T, w_i^T\}$ in which several adjacent words appear in the context, and the aim is predicting the sentiment polarity of the specified target in the given context.

Figure 2 shows the TF-MN architecture, which converts context into a consecutive low dimensional sequence with pretrained word embeddings in the context module. And Transformer processes context sequence to preserve sequential information in memory module. In question module, target is converted into sentiment question. The question is in the form of "What is the emotion tendency

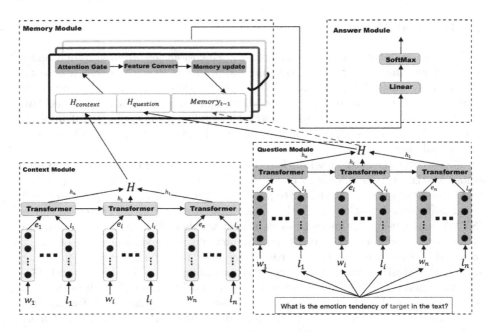

Fig. 2. The architecture of TF-MN model.

of target in the text?". Then, Transformer is also operated upon the question. In memory module, we eliminates the effect of unrelated words by several extractions. Finally, softmax layer outputs sentiment polarity. Each step of our model are showed as follows.

3.1 Context Module

The context module includes the following layers: the context encoder, the location encoder and the fusion layer. The context and the location encoder layer encode each context and location information into a vector separately, while the fusion layer exchange information between these encoded vectors using Transformer.

Context Encoder Layer. Specified a context $C = \{w_1^C, w_2^C, \cdots, w_{n-1}^C, w_n^C\}$, every word in C is converted into a k-dimensional vector $e_i^C \in \mathbb{R}^k$ with a pretrained word embedding matrix $E \in \mathbb{R}^{k*|V|}$, such as Tencent AI Lab Embedding [21]:

$$e_i^C = E(w_i^C) \tag{1}$$

where "$|V|$, k" are the size of vocabulary and word vector respectively.

Location Encoder Layer. We establish a context location word embedding matrix $L =\in \mathbb{R}^{k*n}$, which maps word location into a k-dimensional vector $l_i^C \in \mathbb{R}^k$:

$$l_i^C = L(w_i^C) \tag{2}$$

where n is the dimension of row vector in L. To provide rich location information for context, row vector of L is a k-dimensional vector consisting of k location information. Matrix L is a set of parameters to be trained, in which every row vector will be assigned a sequence of location information with random normal $U(-0.02, 0.02)$.

Fusion Layer. The fusion layer processes the context vector E_C and context location vector L_C which contain exchanged information among vectors. We generate context representation $H_C \in \mathbb{R}^{k*nc}$:

$$H_c = Transformer(E_C, L_C) \tag{3}$$

where nc denotes the max size of context (If the length is not enough, fill it with 0).

3.2 Question Module

The question module further also contains these layers: the question encoder layer, the location encoder layer and the fusion layer. The question encoder layer converts target into sentiment question firstly, and then encodes question into vector. The location encoder layer encodes location information into a vector. The fusion layer fuses these vectors into more specific features through the Transformer.

Question Encoder Layer. Given a question $T = \{w_1^T, w_2^T, \cdots, w_i^T\}$, T consists of one or more words, which can be included in C or doesn't appear in C. If T is embedded in sentiment question, you will get the question as "What is the emotion tendency of target in the text?". Every word in question is converted into a k-dimensional vector $e_i^Q \in \mathbb{R}^k$ with a pretrained word embedding matrix E:

$$e_i^Q = E(w_i^Q) \tag{4}$$

Location Encoder Layer. We also establish a question location word embedding matrix L, which maps word location into a k-dimensional vector $l_i^Q \in \mathbb{R}^k$:

$$l_i^Q = L\left(w_i^Q\right) \tag{5}$$

where the location information matrix of Q is the same as context module.

Fusion Layer. The fusion layer generates the sentiment question representation $H_Q \in \mathbb{R}^{k*nq}$:

$$H_Q = Transformer\,(E_Q, L_Q) \tag{6}$$

where nq denotes the max size of question.

3.3   Memory Module

The memory module has three components: the attention gate, feature conversion and the memory update gate, which is used to combine information from context with target and purify of the target vector from the given context.

The output F from context module, the question q^* from question module and the acquired knowledge stored in the memory vector m_{t-1} from the previous step.

The three inputs are transformed by:

$$u = [F * q^*; |F - q^*|\,; F * m_{t-1}; |F - m_{t-1}|] \tag{7}$$

where ";" is concatenation. "$*$, $-$, $||$" are element-wise product, subtraction and absolute value respectively. F is a matrix of size $(1, H_C)$, while q^* and m_{t-1} are vectors of size $(1, H_Q)$ and $(1, H_m)$, where H_m is the output size of the memory update gate. To allow element-wise operation, H_C, H_Q and H_m are set to the same shape. In Eq. (7), the first two terms measure the similarity and difference between facts and the question. The last two terms have the same functionality for context and the last memory state.

Let the i-th element in α to be the attention weight for w_i^C. α is obtained by transforming u using a two-layer perceptron:

$$\alpha = softmax\,(tanh\,(u \cdot W_{m1}) \cdot W_{m2}) \tag{8}$$

where W_{m1} and W_{m2} are parameters of the perceptron and we omit bias terms.

The feature conversion takes F and α as input and then get the updated F:

$$F = F \cdot \alpha \tag{9}$$

The memory update gate outputs the updated memory m_t using question q^*, previous memory state m_{t-1} and the updated F:

$$m_t = relu\,([q^*; m_{t-1}; F] \cdot W_u) \tag{10}$$

where W_u is the parameter of the linear layer.

The memory module could be iterated several times with a new α generated for each time. This allows the model to attend to different parts of the facts in different iterations, which enables the model to perform complicated reasoning across sentences. The memory module produces m_t as the output at the last iteration.

3.4   Answer Module

In answer module, we regard the memory module outputs as the final representation, and put it into a softmax layer for aspect-based sentiment analysis task. To minimize the cross entropy error of sentiment classification, we train the model in a supervised method in which loss function is described as follows:

$$loss = - \sum_{(c,q) \in T} \sum_{lb \in LB} P_{lb}^{g}(c,q) \cdot \log\left(P_{lb}(c,q)\right) \qquad (11)$$

where T is all training items, LB is the set of sentiment polarities, (c, q) is a context-question pair. Our system outputs the probability of class lb by computing the item (c, q). $P_{lb}^{g}(c, q)$ means zero or one, expressing whether the item is positive or not. In the module, We calculate the gradients of the overall parameters by using back propagating and update them in a stochastic gradient descent manner.

4   Experiment

4.1   Dataset and Experiment Setup

Dataset. In most recent ten years, a lot of Chinese Weibo competitions have been held, and many excellent datasets have been produced such as NLPCC 2013 and 2014 training dataset. Unfortunately, Most datasets only analyze the overall sentiment polarity of the entire sentence. So we try to construct a new dataset for ABSA. We collect weibo data from Weibo, and each the weibo may contain multiple target entities. Each target can be an entity that appears in weibos or an abstracted entity in weibos. The emotional polarity of the goals we mark includes positive, negative, and neutral. If the target has a divergence between these three polarities, we will ignore this target entity. We mainly build dataset in the fields of restaurant which contains four aspects: traffic, service, price and environment. Then, we randomly selected 18480 Weibo items (a total of 22821 Weibo items) as training set, and the rest 4341 items as test set. Table 1 is the detail of the dataset. Finally, it is noted that the text length of our dataset is generally more than 200 words, which belong long texts.

Evaluation. We validate our model with the accuracy, and remove the label from test dataset before training the model. If the output label of the model answer module matches the label by manual method, it will become the right classification result.

Parameter Setting. In the model, the word embeddings matrix of the contexts and targets in the dataset are assigned 200-dimensional vectors from Tencent AI Lab Embedding [21]. All words out of the vocabulary are randomly assigned a vector that obeys uniform distribution $U(-0.01, 0.01)$. To prevent data overfitting, we set the loss rate to 0.1. Our optimizer is Adam whose batch size and

Table 1. Statistics of dataset

Type	Aspect	Negative	Neutral	Positive
Train	Traffic	629	629	629
	Service	1929	1929	1929
	Price	2197	2097	2097
	Environment	1505	1505	1505
Test	Traffic	88	88	88
	Service	871	871	871
	Price	280	280	280
	Environment	208	208	208

learning rate is 8 and 6.25e−5 respectively. We use jieba [22] to do Chinese phrase segmentation and generate the word vector matrix of our experiment. It is noted that the results of the experiment will change with each randomly assigned word vector even if we set up the seeds of the experiment. In order to solve this problem, the experimental data are obtained through average 10 experimental results.

4.2 Experiment Setting

In order to test the performance of our model, we did the following set of experiments: SVM, LSTM, TD-LSTM [17], AT-LSTM [23], IAN [24], BILSTM-ATT, MENNET [16].

Firstly, for the SVM experiment, we directly call the svm class inside sklearn [25]. Then, since the number of samples is much larger than the number of features, we use a nonlinear kernel rbf. As for the optimal parameters of the model, we search for parameters in a large-range and large-step grid by the grid search method.

Secondly, we use the LSTM and BILSTM module in tensorflow, where we regard Webo text as input. Then, we output the results of the classification through the softmax layer.

Finally, we use the open source TD-LSTM and AT-lSTM [26], IAN [27], MENNET [28] code on github to do experiment. Some parameters and settings of the experiment are as close as possible to the original author's paper.

4.3 Model Comparisons and Analysis of Results

In these models, SVM belongs to the traditional machine learning field; LSTM and TD-LSTM are general neural network model methods; AT-LSTM, IAN, BILSTM-ATT, MEMNET are mainly apply the attention mechanism.

We compared the TF-MN model with the correctness of other models, and the results of this comparison are listed in Table 2.

In this table, we can observe that the performance difference between SVM performance and TF-MN model is the largest. We suggest it is caused by two reasons: the SVM training model does not use aspect; the SVM model only classifies the text, and does not mine deep text features.

The effect of the LSTM model on this data set is also not very good, because LSTM can cause the loss of key sentiment information due to the mechanism of forget-door when processing long text.

The accuracy of TD-LSTM is much better than the single LSTM model because it combines ASPECT and text.

Unlike TD-LSTM, AT-LSTM uses a attention mechanism to effectively extract important emotional information from text with aspect, which greatly enhances the final classification result.

BILSTM-ATT is derived from the improvement of the AT-LSTM model, which uses a bidirectional LSTM model. Bidirectional LSTM can significantly improve the performance of the model for sequence classification problems.

The above models mainly focus on the impact of ASPECT on text, but the IAN model also uses the influence of text on ASPECT as a basis for classification. It believes that ASPECT and text should be mutually influential and not just one-way connections.

Based on the above models, MENNET proposes that the attention mechanism should directly affect the process of LSTM coding. Therefore, this model abandon the LSTM model and uses a simpler memory module to encode information. This memory model repeatedly uses the local attention mechanism to extract information and achieves good results.

Although MENNET is good enough, we found that the separate memory module does not encode the text information well during the experiment, and it is as bad as the LSTM model for longer text encoding. At the same time, we also feel that the previous treatment of ASPECT is too rough. Based on these two problems, we improve the MENNET model and achieve better model results.

Table 2. 3-way experimental results in accuracy. 3-way represents the three polarities of positive, negative, neutral. Best scores in each group are in bold.

Model	3-way restaurant
SVM	51.55
LSTM	52.45
TD-LSTM	55.26
AT-LSTM	56.34
BILSTM-ATT	57.47
IAN	58.33
MEMNET	60.78
TF-MN	**61.67**

4.4   Memory Network Optimization

To improve the effect of the memory module to extract emotional information, we conducted a number of experiments to optimize and adjust the number of our memory updates. We found that when the updated hop count is set to 5, the model classification works best. The results of these groups of experiments are shown in Table 3. We believe this is due to excessive update operations that cause the local attention mechanism to repeatedly operate on the same block of text.

Table 3. The result of Memory network hop count comparison.

Hops	Restaurant accuracy
1-hop	58.78
2-hop	59.40
3-hop	60.55
4-hop	60.99
5-hop	**61.67**

5   Conclusion

In this work, we explore the use of memory network architecture to model sentiment classification into the question answering task. The key is to frame the goal as an emotional question. Therefore, we believe that memory networks can be replaced by other more efficient network architectures. We believe that the attention gate in the memory module of TF-MN can add syntactic information. Other tasks with context but no clear issues may also benefit from this work. In the paper, the TF-MN model is proposed, which uses the memory network model to model the Weibo sentiment analysis to the question answering task. We turn the goal into an emotional question. We have done 3-way experiments in the field of restaurant on the Weibo dataset. The results show that this way of modeling improves the accuracy of classification.

Acknowledgements. This work is supported by Zhejiang Provincial Technical Plan Project (No. 2018C03039, 2018C03052).

References

1. Chen, X., et al.: Degree of integration into social networks (DISN) evaluation model based on micro-blogging platforms and information dissemination prediction. In: 2016 IEEE International Conference on Computer and Information Technology (CIT). IEEE (2016)
2. Pontiki, M., Galanis, D., Papageorgiou, H., et al.: SemEval-2016 task 5: aspect based sentiment analysis. In: Proceedings of the 10th International Workshop on Semantic Evaluation, SemEval-2016, pp. 19–30 (2016)

3. Vaswani, A., et al.: Attention is all you need. In: Advances in Neural Information Processing Systems (2017)
4. Hochreiter, S., Schmidhuber, J.: Long short-term memory. Neural Comput. **9**(8), 1735–1780 (1997)
5. Chung, J., et al.: Empirical evaluation of gated recurrent neural networks on sequence modeling. arXiv preprint arXiv:1412.3555 (2014)
6. Zheng, S., Xia, R.: Left-center-right separated neural network for aspect-based sentiment analysis with rotatory attention. arXiv preprint arXiv:1802.00892 (2018)
7. Do, H.H., et al.: Deep learning for aspect-based sentiment analysis: a comparative review. Expert Syst. Appl. **118**, 272–299 (2018)
8. Liu, B.: Sentiment Analysis and Opinion Mining. Synthesis Lectures on Human Language Technologies, vol. 5, no. 1, pp. 1–167 (2012)
9. Hu, M., Liu, B.: Mining and summarizing customer reviews. In: Proceedings of the 10th ACM SIGKDD International Conference on Knowledge Discovery and Data Mining. ACM (2004)
10. Ding, X., Liu, B., Yu, P.S.: A holistic lexicon-based approach to opinion mining. In: Proceedings of the 2008 International Conference on Web Search and Data Mining. ACM (2008)
11. Nguyen, T.H., Shirai, K.: Aspect-based sentiment analysis using tree kernel based relation extraction. In: Gelbukh, A. (ed.) CICLing 2015. LNCS, vol. 9042, pp. 114–125. Springer, Cham (2015). https://doi.org/10.1007/978-3-319-18117-2_9
12. Ramesh, A., et al.: Weakly supervised models of aspect-sentiment for online course discussion forums. In: Proceedings of the 53rd Annual Meeting of the Association for Computational Linguistics and the 7th International Joint Conference on Natural Language Processing. Long Papers, vol. 1 (2015)
13. Wang, H., Ester, M.: A sentiment-aligned topic model for product aspect rating prediction. In: Proceedings of the 2014 Conference on Empirical Methods in Natural Language Processing (EMNLP) (2014)
14. Kiritchenko, S., et al.: NRC-Canada-2014: detecting aspects and sentiment in customer reviews. In: Proceedings of the 8th International Workshop on Semantic Evaluation, SemEval 2014 (2014)
15. Nguyen, T.H., Shirai, K.: PhraseRNN: phrase recursive neural network for aspect-based sentiment analysis. In: Proceedings of the 2015 Conference on Empirical Methods in Natural Language Processing (2015)
16. Tang, D., et al.: Effective LSTMs for target-dependent sentiment classification. arXiv preprint arXiv:1512.01100 (2015)
17. Wang, Y., Huang, M., Zhao, L.: Attention-based LSTM for aspect-level sentiment classification. In: Proceedings of the 2016 Conference on Empirical Methods in Natural Language Processing (2016)
18. Tang, D., Qin, B., Liu, T.: Aspect level sentiment classification with deep memory network. arXiv preprint arXiv:1605.08900 (2016)
19. Cheng, J., et al.: Aspect-level sentiment classification with heat (hierarchical attention) network. In: Proceedings of the 2017 ACM on Conference on Information and Knowledge Management. ACM (2017)
20. He, R., et al.: Effective attention modeling for aspect-level sentiment classification. In: Proceedings of the 27th International Conference on Computational Linguistics (2018)
21. Song, Y., Shi, S., Li, J., Zhang, H.: Directional skip-gram: explicitly distinguishing left and right context for word embeddings. In: NAACL 2018. Short Paper (2018)
22. Sun, J.: Jieba' Chinese word segmentation tool (2012). https://github.com/fxsjy/jieba. Accessed 10 May 2019

23. Wang, Y., Huang, M., Zhao, L.: Attention-based LSTM for aspect-level sentiment classification. In: Proceedings of the 2016 Conference on Empirical Methods in Natural Language Processing (2016)
24. Ma, D., et al.: Interactive attention networks for aspect-level sentiment classification. arXiv preprint arXiv:1709.00893 (2017)
25. sklearn.   https://scikit-learn.org/stable/modules/generated/sklearn.svm.SVC.html. Accessed 5 Mar 2019
26. TD-LSTM and AT-LSTM. https://github.com/jimmyyfeng/TD-LSTM. Accessed 5 Mar 2019
27. IAN. https://github.com/lpq29743/IAN. Accessed 5 Mar 2019
28. MENNET. https://github.com/Humanity123/MemNet_ABSA. Accessed 5 Mar 2019

The Feasibility of Repurposing Recycled Cell Phones as Sensors in a Smart Campus Shuttle Monitoring System

Shamar Ward[(✉)] and Mechelle Gittens

Department of Computer Science Mathematics and Physics,
The University of the West Indies Cave Hill Campus,
Wanstead, Barbados TO Cave Hill, Barbados
shamar.ward@mycavehill.uwi.edu,
mechelle.gittens@cavehill.uwi.edu

Abstract. Information updates on the current location of public buses and shuttles are necessary to everyday commuter life and plays a vital role in their efficiency. Some current approaches to providing this information involve installation of stand-alone GPS modules and others involve user-driven participatory sensing. In this paper, we present a low-cost approach to providing information on a vehicle's location by repurposing damaged mobile phones as sensors. This approach reduces the battery draining effect that users experience when using their personal cell phones to transmit the location of the vehicle (participatory sensing). Additionally, as small-island-developing states (SIDs), this concept reduces the need for the importation of new GPS devices by repurposing mobile devices that are already on island and will likely contribute to the landfill waste problem. We tested our repurposing approach with The University of the West Indies - Cave Hill Campus (UWICHC) student shuttle service in Barbados. Students access this system using any web-enabled device. The web application displays the shuttle's location on a Google™ map that also shows the route and direction of the shuttle. A student survey indicated that they found the system useful and are willing to donate retired cell phones to such a project. This result demonstrates the sustainability of the mobile phone repurposing concept.

Keywords: Smart campus · Cell phone · Transportation · GPS ·
Repurpose cell phone · Recycled cell phone

1 Introduction

Most approaches to providing information and data on transportation systems to users involve the collection of data using new stand-alone GPS devices or user enabled participatory sensing. Mandal et al. [1] provide an example of the former with bus stop identification and visualization using GPS systems in the developing world. Their work requires the acquisition and installation of new hardware. It is, relevant since this was applied in a developing world scenario similar to the locale of UWICHC. Zhou et al. mention that their [2] participatory sensing method is less demanding and less energy

© ICST Institute for Computer Sciences, Social Informatics and Telecommunications Engineering 2019
Published by Springer Nature Switzerland AG 2019. All Rights Reserved
Y. Yin et al. (Eds.): MobiCASE 2019, LNICST 290, pp. 57–67, 2019.
https://doi.org/10.1007/978-3-030-28468-8_5

intensive since they do not use GPS. Thiagarajan et al. confirm in their work [3] that GPS' effect on the user's mobile phone battery is high which causes them to turn off this feature to preserve their battery. However, other cell phone features used in the work by Zhou and colleagues can also reduce the lifetime of the user's mobile. These features include the microphone and audio analysis that require CPU power. Additionally, crowd-participated approaches introduce battery effects and reduction in battery life for multiple users as opposed to one [6]. Additionally, the importation of new devices such as stand-alone GPS devices can contribute in the long term to landfill issues that currently affect countries as explained in work by Musson et al. in [2].

Cell phones and other mobile electronic devices contain toxins such as arsenic, mercury and lead. If these harmful metals enter the water supply due to improper disposal methods, they can be harmful to humans [2]. Additionally, the brominated flame retardant found in newer cell phones and other devices can cause organ dysfunctions [3]. Our recycling approach - demonstrated in [4] - shows that we can implement the repurposing concept to use mobile phones that are already available, and in our case on the island, are damaged and no longer used by owners. Such out-of-service phones will likely end up in the landfill and cause problems. Hence, we use them to perform the task of GPS sensors and Bluetooth beacons rather than acquiring new hardware.

Previously [6] we explained that it is simple to replace a failed repurposed cell phone (RCP) sensor with another since the applications can run on any compatible device. Therefore, the failed repurposed mobile phone can be properly disposed of and another one can be repurposed. In this work, we repurpose a damaged cell phone as a sensor, in this case for its GPS, Bluetooth and Wi-Fi capabilities, to perform a task without human interaction. We then deployed a repurposed damaged mobile phone on the UWICHC shuttle independent of a user to collect and report GPS data on the location of the shuttle to help shuttle users to plan their time. We also show that acquiring retired cell phones on a university campus for such applications is sustainable.

2   System Requirements

To gather requirements and design a system that caters to students' needs, we asked a convenience sample of 78 students from UWICHC if a mobile application that indicates that the shuttle is entering the campus compound, or has already arrived, would assist them. Ninety-six percent (96%) of respondents answered in the affirmative. This confirmed the need for the application.

We also asked students if they preferred a voice indicator or a visual indicator to identify the shuttles' location when they are in class. Most - 69% - of respondents preferred visual indication rather than voice indicator for the shuttles' arrival at the shuttle stop. Additionally, Zhou et al. [5] stated that bus users indicated that they would like to be able to track the arrival time of the bus instantly on arrival at the stop. Hence, the visual indicator also needed to track arrival time instantly.

Based on the requirements identified by respondents to our survey we decided to investigate if a system that will visually display the location of the campus shuttle and its estimated arrival time using an RCP will assist students. Additionally, we realized that using RCPs for such systems must be sustainable.

3   Collection, Testing and Selection

Ward and Gittens [20] developed three models to identify suitable devices for building smart campus applications using cell phones. They considered the attributes outlined by Shye et al. [16] and Ahmad et al. [17]. The authors of the work in [16, 17] identified the following attributes: battery, input mechanism, data/power interface, mobile phone services, SIM card, antenna, microphone, speaker, and a CPU. Additionally, most smartphones carry an accelerometer and GPS capability.

After applying the models outlined in [20] we classified all donated cell phones into the following groups:

Group 0: Either these cell phones do not power on or they have touch response and USB port problems. They cannot be repurposed in their current state.

Group 1: Cell phones in this group do not respond to touch commands. However, they can still be repurposed because they can be controlled via USB.

Group 2: In this group, cell phones respond to touch but have no functioning USB ports. These can be repurposed since they are touch controlled but they cannot connect to a computer.

Group 3: These cell phones are preferred because they have passed all tests. They are easier to work with since the basic hardware works.

After classifying the devices into groups, we applied the features test introduced [20] to identify donated devices with GPS, GPRS and Bluetooth.

4   Case Study

In this section, we discuss the system design based on the primary system requirement elicited from students in the previously mentioned survey, that is, to provide a visual indicator that would instantly track the arrival of the shuttle.

4.1   System Design

In order to meet the visual indicator requirement, we assessed the hours of operation of the shuttle. The hours range from 7 am to 11 pm Monday to Friday. Our solution needed to be operational within these hours. However, we recall from the work of other researchers [2, 3] and from our own experience that the GPS capabilities that enable the necessary tracking are battery intensive and drain the cell phone battery. We mitigated battery depletion by installing a cell phone on the campus shuttle and in the first instance; the five (5) volt lighter socket in the vehicle powered the mobile phone directly. In the second instance, if there is no functioning lighter socket, an alternative installation method is used for the bus sensor.

In order to describe how the system operates we will describe the system components and their interaction to provide GPS real-time information and detection of the shuttle at the shuttle stops. We will then discuss the additional installation method of the bus sensor.

4.2 System Components

The system has six (6) components were two (2) are optional, these are (Table 1):

Table 1. Six core components of the RCPs configurations for tracking

Component name	Function
Reused cell sensors:	
Bus sensor (recycled cell phone)	A Group 3 cell phone was used as a GPS sensor and also to constantly emit a Bluetooth signal which would be detected by the shuttle stop sensor when in range - The smartphone used was a BLU Life Play 2™
Shuttle stop sensor	A Group 3 cell phone was used as Bluetooth sensor which scanned and detected Bluetooth signals when the bus sensor is in the range - Alcatel POP C3™ housed in PVC box [6] at the shuttle stop powered by fixed 110 v outlets
Other components:	
Database server	The database server runs the Ubuntu 14.04.3 LTS and MYSQL server as in [6, 7, 13]
Processing and display engine	As in [6–8, 13] we used Google JavaScript API 3 maps to display the location of the shuttle. The information was first processed using a set of PHP scripts that filtered the GPS and Bluetooth data. The location was shown on a Google map using Google JavaScript API 3 via a web page accessible by students
Raspberry pi zero (Optional)	Used with a battery pack in the absence of a functioning cigarette lighter to keep the mobile phone continuously charged.
Battery pack (Optional)	The 10000-mAh battery pack is used in the second configuration to power the Raspberry Pi that then powers the mobile phone when the shuttle or bus does not have a working lighter socket

4.3 System Core Component Interconnection

We will now discuss how the components of our system connect. The bus sensor performs two functions in the system. Its first function is to emit a continuous Bluetooth signal. Bohonos et al. [9] show that Bluetooth can be used as a beacon. They used a Bluetooth device as a beacon to assist the blind in crossing busy intersections. We used this approach and treated the shuttle sensor as the beacon. When the shuttle arrives, the shuttle stop sensor, which is constantly scanning for Bluetooth device signals senses the bus sensor emitting the Bluetooth signal and sends it to the database. The shuttle stop sensor collects the MAC address of the device and its RSSI value emitting Bluetooth devices. Ghose et al. [10] developed a system called BlueEye that detects distances between individuals in crowds using the Bluetooth on their mobile phones. We used this approach in our system to determine if the shuttle was at the shuttle stop. We stored the MAC address of the bus sensor in our database so we could verify the shuttle in the Bluetooth data.

The second function of the bus sensor collected GPS location data for the shuttle and transmitted it to the database. Similar work by Anderson et al. [11] developed an SMS and GPS system to provide information to users of a transportation system in a developing country. However, their work [11] required the bus operator to enter the route using a keypad. However, in our work no interaction with the driver is necessary. The PHP scripts analyze the Bluetooth data every minute to determine if the shuttle is in proximity to one of the on-campus shuttle stops. The PHP scripts also display the current position of the shuttle by querying the database for the latest update using database time stamps aligned with the GPS data.

Bus Sensor Installation. The cigarette lighter in the bus is the primary source of power for the bus sensor; however, there may be some cases were the cigarette lighter is not functional. An alternative installation method requires the use of two additional components. These components are a 10000 mAh battery bank and Raspberry Pi Zero. In this alternate installation method, a battery pack powers the RCP. However, we noted that when the mobile phone became fully charged, the power bank would switch itself off. When the mobile phone needed an additional charge, the power bank remained off and the mobile phone died. To address this issue, we attached a Raspberry Pi Zero to the power bank and then connected the mobile phone to the Raspberry Pi Zero. This method keeps the power bank on as the Raspberry pi Zero constantly uses 80 mA [12] to keep the power bank on and available when more power is needed by the mobile phone.

Cost Reduction Using RCPs. The cost of implementing our system is reduced by RCPs. When compared with the work done by Anderson et al. in [11] who dismissed the possibility of using a mobile smartphone as opposed to their US $200 self-designed device due to the possibility of theft. Even with the additional components required for the alternative installation method shown in Table 2, the cost is reduced.

Table 2. Cost of Bus and Shuttle sensor

Sensor name	Cost
Reused cell sensors:	
Bus sensor (recycled cell phone)	$ 0 (Donated)
Shuttle stop sensor	$ 0 (Donated)
Supporting components:	
USB cable 5v charger	$ 5 US
USB vehicle charger	$ 8 US
Raspberry Pi Zero (Optional)	$ 17 US
Battery Pack (Optional)	$ 21 US
Total:	**$ 51 US**

4.4   Deployment of RCPs

We outline how the cell phones selected in as in Sect. 3.3 were deployed and tested before and in operation. We outline the process of developing the bus sensor application and shuttle-stop-sensor application on the RCPs.

Bus Sensor Application: The (onboard) bus sensor application is a native Android application designed using Android studio and the Java programming language. The Android application was designed as an Android service. The service listened for location updates and as the GPS update occurred, the application would send the GPS data to the database for storage. This service also controlled the beacon emitted from the shuttle. The service checks every minute to ensure the Bluetooth on the bus sensor is enabled and it has Bluetooth discover set to be constantly on.

Shuttle Stop Sensor Application: Like the (onboard) bus sensor application, the shuttle stop sensor application is a native Android application designed using Android studio and the Java programming language. The android application was designed as an Android service however, unlike the bus sensor application, which uses 3G data to submit the GPS data to our database, the shuttle stop sensor uses Wi-Fi on the UWICHC as done in similar work by Ward et al. [6, 13] where we designed an application to monitor and report on Wi-Fi in areas. The shuttle stop application connects to the Wi-Fi then constantly scans for Bluetooth devices in the area and transmits them to the database.

Application Development and Testing: The bus sensor and shuttle stop application were installed on the cell phones and run for 24 h. This testing ensured correct functioning. Subsequently, the cell phones were ready to be deployed.

4.5   Hardware Implementation and Deployment

This section presents the deployment of the hardware in various environments.

Bus Sensor Hardware: Figure 1 shows the configuration of the bus sensor. The Raspberry Pi Zero keeps the battery pack on even if the mobile phone is fully charged. This is unlike customary operation. The Raspberry Pi will keep the battery pack on as it requires constant power. Therefore, when the mobile phone requires additional charge it would be available via the USB port on the Raspberry Pi.

Fig. 1. Showing the bus sensor configuration comprising a Raspberry Pi Zero, 16750 mAh power bank and BLUE LIFE PLAY 2 with a damaged screen

Shuttle Stop Sensor Hardware: The shuttle stop sensor hardware adopts the same hardware implementation method used in [6]. The RCP is placed in a PVC box which contains a 110v outlet which powered the RCP as shown in Fig. 2.

Fig. 2. Showing the installation of the bus stop sensor.

Information Delivery: We displayed the shuttle information to students on a Google Map similarly to [6, 7]. As shown in Fig. 3 the green blimp indicates the current location of the shuttle and the red circle is a radius of five meters from that point. The four red blimps behind the circle indicate the direction that the shuttle came from. This is the trail. The trail is ascertained by selecting the last four points the bus sensor reported. The trails indicate to students the direction the shuttle is traveling since the shuttle travels the same route to and from the campus. This eliminates confusion. The trail can also be used to indicate if the shuttle is stationary or moving, since all red blimps would be in the circle if the shuttle were stationary or moving very slowly. The web application also displays the last updated time and the current route of the shuttle. The current route is determined based on the Bluetooth data collected using the shuttle-stop sensors. We can identify which stop the shuttle left from and this would indicate its current route. The (onboard) bus sensor application, the shuttle-stop sensor application is a native Android application designed using Android studio and the Java programming language. The Android application was designed as an Android service however, unlike the bus sensor application that uses 3G data to submit the GPS data to our database. The shuttle stop sensor uses Wi-Fi on the UWICHC as done in similar work [6, 13] with an application to monitor and report on Wi-Fi availability and strength in outdoor areas. The shuttle stop application connects to the Wi-Fi then constantly scans for Bluetooth devices in the area and transmits them to the database.

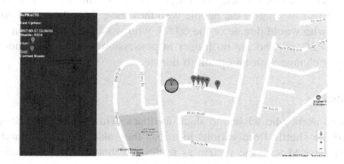

Fig. 3. Shows the students a visual application indicating the shuttles current location. (Color figure online)

5   Feasibility, Sustainability and Usefulness

In this section, we will discuss our findings from our survey of 175 randomly selected UWICHC students. We will examine the feasibility of the cell phone repurpose concept and its sustainability for building smart campus applications.

5.1   Feasibility

Our findings have shown 54% of respondents keep cell phones they do not use in their possession. Additionally, based on our responses 44% of the students indicated they retired their cell phone, not because of a fault or issue but because they simply wanted to upgrade. This coincides with what Geyer et al. [1] mentioned in their work that users mainly dispose of their cell phones just to get a newer version or model. As it relates to the repurposing of the cell phones this could be a good indication since these cell phones would more than likely still be in good working condition and capable of performing majority if not all of its capable task. In addition, our findings have shown 74% of students are willing to donate their old/retired cell phone to the repurposing research. This is also good for feasibility because the acquisition of these cell phones for repurposing would come at no additional cost where the cell phone could be repurposed to reduce cost in some systems. However, a few people not willing to donate their cell phones to research said they would however sell their cell phone. Although this is not favorable for feasibility it demonstrates that retired cell phones can be acquired, but there may be a cost. Our findings have also indicated 22% of students have retired their phones not because of a hardware issue but because the cell phone sticks and freezes. This shows that the cell phone still works and may be a candidate for RCP with some diagnosis.

5.2   Sustainability

The majority of persons indicated they would donate their current cell phone to research when upgrading. This is good for sustainably not only because of willingness to donate the cell phones for repurposing, but because over the collection period, no cost would be attached to the acquiring of the cell phones. Interestingly, the majority of the students who indicated that they no longer had their retired phone, indicated they gave it away. This can suggest the people who they gave it to also could possibly fall into the 73.7% who would donate or the 60.6% who would not donate but would sell. Additionally, 24.2% of who are no longer in possession of their cell phone threw it away. This may change with an option to donate.

5.3   Usefulness

We interviewed users who wished to share feedback. This totaled ten (10) users. The users boarded the shuttle from various locations they also boarded at random times. Students were pleased with the system as it allowed them to perform activities right until they needed to board the shuttle that helped them to use their time more efficiently. Some students indicated they would like to receive more information such as how long it would take the shuttle to get from its current location to where they are waiting. Additionally, some students stated they would like to be alerted when the shuttle is at one of the shuttle stops so they could make their way there. Overall we believe the user's comments were supportive and indicated we have a working and value-added system for its users.

6 Related Work

In this work, we were able to develop a low-cost shuttle tracking system using the Ward et al. cell phone repurposing concept originally shown in [6] for detecting the Wi-Fi signal strength and download speeds in study areas. Ward et al. [13] also showed it was possible to use a mobile phone without user interaction by using mobile applications installed on the phone.

The primary advantages of using these approaches are the reduction of battery power consumption which mobile phone users experience by contributing to participatory sensing as used by Zhou et al. in their work [2]. Zhou et al. developed a bus prediction system using participatory sensing by relying on users to enter information and using nearby resources such as cell towers and resources found on the bus such as transit IC card readers and accelerometers to determine the location of the bus. In this work by Zhou et al. they reference GPS as heavily draining the phone battery as opposed to bus tracking using cell towers which they used in their work. However, Zhou et al. did not include the other attributes of the user's cell phone such as accelerometer and microphone as also affecting the user's battery life. In our work, battery degradation and energy use of the user's device does not have to be considered, since our system features a stand-alone device that removes battery drainage and the privacy concerns mentioned in Zhou et al.'s research [2]. This also noted in work by Thiagarajan et al. [3].

In work by Anderson et al. [11] they mentioned disadvantages due to the cost associated with replacing a new mobile phone when deployed in a bus when it was stolen. Consequently, they decided to develop their own device. However, the development of this new device to perform GPS tracking of the bus requires the acquisition of new components that will eventually add to the E-waste in landfill problem mentioned earlier. Our approach also addresses these concerns mentioned by Anderson et al. since by employing the repurposing concept these mobile phones have no cost as they were no longer needed and were therefore donated. Since they were damaged, they also become less attractive and less likely to be stolen. Calabrese et al. [18] in their work mentioned that the high cost of GPS device implementation across a fleet of vehicles is a deterrent. However, Calabrese et al. [18] failed to mention the concern would not only be the cost of acquiring these new devices but also the implication it has on the environment. When these brand new devices are replaced, they will contribute to the e-waste problem.

On the other hand, if the repurposing or recycling of devices concept is used as mentioned in a report by AT&T [19], it indicated a reduction of one million cell phones in the landfills which would equate to the removal of 1368 cars off the road. We also saw work by Biagioni et al. [14] were they have developed an easy tracker system using a cell phone placed on transit vehicles to track its location and path. However, in their work, it was not clear how they installed and powered the phone or if the cell phone battery lasted throughout the entire period of operation of the transit vehicle. This is a concern since users of the system need to know where the shuttle is in real time. Additionally, Bagioni does not mention if interaction with the cell phone. Required user interaction is prone to faults since the driver may forget to engage the system. Other approaches to repurposing cell phones were found in work by Katsumoto and Inakage [15] where they designed toys from damaged cell phones. This confirms that the repurposing concept is also applicable in other contexts.

7 Conclusion

We have shown in this work it is possible to apply the repurposing concept to provide a service which can be used to determine the location of the shuttle and if it is at a shuttle stop. Additionally, the system is capable of displaying the shuttles' locations on visually on a map. Additionally, this concept not only shows its benefits to users in information delivery but also its benefits in comparison to other methods that provide vehicle location services to users, such as the mitigation of battery power depletion encountered in participatory testing. Furthermore, benefits can be seen in its sustainability as it is easy to replace one RCP and the software is interoperable. Benefits can also be seen environmentally as RCP after they have failed and need to be disposed of can be done correctly removing some of the cell phones that would otherwise be disposed of incorrectly. We have therefore shown repurposing cell phones for use in vehicle location tracking are beneficial financially, environmentally, and it is sustainable.

References

1. Mandal, R., et al.: A system for stoppage pattern extraction from public bus GPS traces in developing regions. In: Proceedings of the Third ACM SIGSPATIAL International Workshop on Mobile Geographic Information Systems. ACM, Dallas (2014)
2. Zhou, P., Zheng, Y., Li, M.: How long to wait?: predicting bus arrival time with mobile phone based participatory sensing. In: Proceedings of the Proceedings of the 10th International Conference on Mobile Systems, Applications, and Services. ACM, Low Wood Bay (2012)
3. Thiagarajan, A., et al.: VTrack: accurate, energy-aware road traffic delay estimation using mobile phones. In: Proceedings of the Proceedings of the 7th ACM Conference on Embedded Networked Sensor Systems. ACM, Berkeley (2009)
4. Musson, S.E., et al.: RCRA toxicity characterization of discarded electronic devices. Environ. Sci. Technol. **40**(8), 2721–2726 (2006)
5. Neira, J., Favret, L., Fuji, M., Miller, R., Mahdavi, S., Blass, V.D.: End-of-Life Management of Cell Phones in the United States UNIVERSITY OF CALIFORNIA Santa Barbara (2006)

6. Ward, S.A., Gittens, M.: Monitoring and analyzing wi-fi availability and performance on a university campus using recycled cell phones to aid students in selecting study areas. In: Proceedings of the Proceedings of the 2016 ACM on SIGUCCS Annual Conference. ACM, Denver (2016)
7. Kestranek, D., et al.: Spaces Without Faces. In: Proceedings of the Proceedings of the 13th International Conference on Human Computer Interaction with Mobile Devices and Services. ACM, Stockholm (2011)
8. Aloul, F., Sagahyroon, A., Al-Shami, A., Al-Midfa, I., Moutassem, R.: Using mobiles for on campus location tracking. In: Proceedings of the Proceedings of the 7th International iConference on Advances in Mobile Computing and Multimedia. ACM, Kuala Lumpur (2009)
9. Bohonos, S., Lee, A., Malik, A., Thai, C., Manduchi, R.: Universal real-time navigational assistance (URNA): an urban bluetooth beacon for the blind. In Proceedings of the Proceedings of the 1st ACM SIGMOBILE International Workshop on Systems and Networking Support for Healthcare and Assisted Living Environments. ACM, San Juan (2007)
10. Ghose, A., Bhaumik, C., Chakravarty, T.: BlueEye: a system for proximity detection using bluetooth on mobile phones. In: Proceedings of the Proceedings of the 2013 ACM Conference on Pervasive and Ubiquitous Computing Adjunct Publication. ACM, Zurich (2013)
11. Anderson, R.E., et al.: Experiences with a transportation information system that uses only GPS and SMS. In: Proceedings of the Proceedings of the 4th ACM/IEEE International Conference on Information and Communication Technologies and Development. ACM, London (2010)
12. Geerling, J.: Raspberry Pi Dramble. City https://www.pidramble.com/wiki/benchmarks/power-consumption
13. Ward, S.A., Gittens, M.: A real-time application to predict and notify students about the present and future availability of workspaces on a university campus. In: Proceedings of the Proceedings of the 2015 ACM Annual Conference on SIGUCCS. ACM, St. Petersburg (2015)
14. Biagioni, J., Gerlich, T., Merrifield, T., Eriksson, J.: EasyTracker: automatic transit tracking, mapping, and arrival time prediction using smartphones. In: Proceedings of the Proceedings of the 9th ACM Conference on Embedded Networked Sensor Systems. ACM, Seattle (2011)
15. Katsumoto, Y., Inakage, M.: Notori: design of wooden toys and mobile apps for reviving a worn-out smartphone. In: Proceedings of the SIGGRAPH Asia 2013 Symposium on Mobile Graphics and Interactive Applications. ACM, Hong Kong (2013)
16. Shye, A., Scholbrock, B., Memik, G., Dinda, P.A.: Characterizing and modeling user activity on smartphones: summary. SIGMETRICS Perform. Eval. Rev. 38(1), 375–376 (2010)
17. Ahmad, S., Haamid, A.L., Qazi, Z.A., Zhou, Z., Benson, T., Qazi, I.A.: A view from the other side: understanding mobile phone characteristics in the developing world. In: Proceedings of the Proceedings of the 2016 Internet Measurement Conference. ACM, Santa Monica (2016)
18. Calabrese, F., Colonna, M., Lovisolo, P., Parata, D., Ratti, C.: Real-time urban monitoring using cell phones: a case study in Rome. Trans. Intell. Transport. Sys. 12(1), 141–151 (2011)
19. Wireless, A.T.: Cell Phone Recycling Fact Sheet City (2013)
20. Ward, S., Gittens, M.: Building useful smart campus applications using a retired cell phone repurposing model. In: 2018 Third International Conference on Electrical and Biomedical Engineering, Clean Energy and Green Computing (EBECEGC), Beirut, pp. 43–48 (2018)

Edu-BUS Wi-Fi: An On-Board Wi-Fi Educational System Using a Raspberry Pi

Shamar Ward$^{(\boxtimes)}$ and Mechelle Gittens

University of the West Indies Cave Hill Campus, Cave Hill, Barbados
shamar.ward@mycavehill.uwi.edu,
mechelle.gittens@cavehill.uwi.edu

Abstract. Onboard transit systems are commonly used for commutes to and from home, work and other destinations. However, this is generally not productive time with commuters often gazing out of the window. Other systems have proposed a solution to this problem however, they are offline and would require each device on each vehicle to be updated manually. In this paper, we present an onboard educational Wi-Fi system that offers educational content which can be updated remotely as well as free internet access to particular commuters. Also, specific users can be allowed to browse the internet by connecting wirelessly while onboard. Additionally, Edu-Bus can be used as an educational tool, requiring persons to watch an educational video or read some educational content before gaining access to Edu-Bus services such as free Wi-Fi. Our system uses a Raspberry Pi which is converted into a wireless hotspot, as well as an optional USB or Wi-Fi modem to connect to the 3G/4G provider. Additionally, Edu-Bus can be powered directly from an adapter using the vehicle's cigarette lighter outlet or temporarily from its internal battery. We implemented this work on-board a fleet of four (4) buses at the University of The West Indies Cave Hill Campus. We analyzed student connections to the system generated by user activities. Our approach to this problem not only makes Edu-Bus extendable but also introduces the ability to deploy similar systems on varying vehicle types and modes of transportation.

Keywords: Raspberry pi · On-Board Wi-Fi · University campus ·
Educational content

1 Introduction

Many commuters use transit systems to travel to and from their destinations. For some, their trip may be lengthy in distance. However, others may have shorter trips but due to traffic congestion, they may have a long transit time to their destination. As discussed in the work done by Rahane et al. in [1] commuters may become bored during these journeys. To address this Rahane et al. in [1] proposed an entertainment service system that users could connect to and view content during their journey. Additionally, Rahane et al. in [1] also offered a recommendation system to persons who connected to their system. While the work done by Rahane et al. in [1] may address the issues faced by bored passengers, its major flaw is that the system is completely offline and only maintains a network in the bus. Therefore, the system has to be manually updated,

Y. Yin et al. (Eds.): MobiCASE 2019, LNICST 290, pp. 68–82, 2019.
https://doi.org/10.1007/978-3-030-28468-8_6

which does not cater to wide-scale implementation on a fleet of busses. Additionally, Rahane et al. in [1] introduced additional components such as a router to facilitate users connecting to the system. This incurs an additional cost when trying to develop a low-cost system. In this paper, we implement a similar concept to the one introduced by Rahane et al. in [1]. However, our system only uses the Raspberry Pi which reduces the cost of the system as well as it allows content to be uploaded remotely using the optional 3G/4G modem or via Wi-Fi when it becomes available. Most importantly, our system allows selected users to connect to the internet directly. Users can view educational content on select web pages. The Edu-BUS Wi-Fi system records the MAC address of each connecting user. This allows administrators to monitor the connection rate and time for each vehicle. Additionally, administrators can restrict persons from performing certain activities if necessary, based on their device's MAC address. The system is also capable of being implemented in any vehicle that has a functional cigarette lighter outlet but can also operate as a self-powered device for a limited time based on the internal battery storage capacity. Our approach lends to extensibility and the ability to offer various content types on various modes of transportation.

2 Related Works

In this section, we will discuss similar systems to our work. We will break down these works into sections which will focus on the core features of our work which are: onboard systems, Raspberry Pi systems, and Wi-Fi Captive portal systems.

2.1 On-Board Systems

We formerly mentioned work by Rahane et al. in [1], which developed a system that was capable of delivering entertainment content to passengers. They used a Raspberry Pi, router and a USB Wi-Fi dongle to provide content using a server which was installed on the Raspberry Pi, a block diagram illustrating their work is shown in Fig. 1.

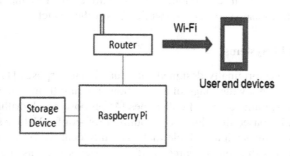

Fig. 1. Raspberry Pi block diagram [1].

The server delivered pages with static content, allowing users to select various media to view. Rahane et al. in [1] mentioned that this method reduced the data cost for users since the content was stored locally. From this work, we gathered that the Raspberry Pi could be used to serve web pages, as well as it could be used as a recommender system to suggest media content to users. However, this work has some limitations such as the ability to deploy new content remotely. This would have a serious impact if being deployed on a fleet of vehicles. Additionally, this system does not log or report user activity and does not allow access control of individual users. It is also unclear how the equipment is powered and the ease of deployment of such a system on multiple vehicles. We, therefore, performed a search for an easy deployment method of connecting such a system to a vehicle. We discovered the work done by Rathod et al. in [2] where they developed a vehicle tracking and air pollutant monitoring system. In their work, they were concerned about the air pollution poorly maintained vehicles would cause. Therefore, they developed a system which would monitor the air pollution emitted by the vehicle using an MQ-7 gas sensor. Based on the values which were generated by the sensor the system would notify the driver by sending an SMS message using a GSM module. The SMS received by the driver contained the status and emission level of their vehicle. Additionally, they used a 12 V supply from the vehicle and implemented a 5 V step-down module that would allow the ATmega328 microcontroller and sensor to receive power. From this work, we gathered the ability to use a 12 V supply from the vehicle. However, we also noted we must use a step-down module to allow the Raspberry Pi module to operate, since it needs a 5 V supply (Sect. 2.2).

We also found work by Shinde et al. [3] where they developed a vehicle monitoring system using a Raspberry Pi. The Raspberry Pi engaged a GSM, GPRS module SIM900A to transmit information to the server. They also added temperature and gas sensors to the Raspberry Pi to ensure students' safety on their journey. From this work, we learned how to connect the Raspberry Pi to the internet to transmit and receive information from a server using the SIM900A module. However, passengers on the vehicle who were interested in viewing this information would have to use their phones GPRS data, which is inefficient [1]. Our system allows passengers to view information whilst on-board using their cell phone. Our system eliminates the need to install additional software to use such features while aboard the vehicle.

2.2   Raspberry Pi Systems

The Raspberry Pi was originally designed for educational purposes [1]. However, the Raspberry Pi is used in a wide range of applications ranging from home automation to educational projects. Guravaiah and colleagues [4] propose an algorithm called River Formation Dynamics based the Multi-hop Routing Protocol for Vehicles (RFDMRPV) that addressed problems such as vehicle theft within a locality. To test this algorithm, they implemented it using open source platform systems such as the Raspberry Pi, Arduino and XBee which uses the ZigBee protocol. In their work, they described the details of the Raspberry Pi 3 B model which are shown in Fig. 2.

CPU	1.2GHz 64-bit Quad Core ARMv8 CPU
GPU	Video Core IV 3D Graphics Core
RAM	1GB LPDDR2 (900 MHz)
GPIO	40-pin header, Populated
Networking	802.11n Wireless LAN and 10/100 Wired LAN
Bluetooth	Bluetooth Low Energy (BLE), Bluetooth 4.0
Storage	Micro SD Card Slot
Ports	HDMI, 3.5mm analogue audio-video jack, 4 x USB2.0, Ethernet, Camera Serial Interface (CSI), Display Serial Interface (DSI)
Power	Micro USB. Requires 5V, 2.5Amp

Fig. 2. Details on Raspberry Pi 3 B device [4].

We learned that the Raspberry Pi requires 5 V power from a micro USB adapter. Additionally, we also discovered that the Raspberry Pi 3 B model has Wi-Fi capabilities that can be used to connect to wireless routers or as a Wi-Fi hotspot. This work by Rahane and colleagues is similar to the work done in [5] by Ward and Gittens where they developed a system using repurposed cell phones to monitor Wi-Fi signals.

Bhardwaj and associates [6] developed a system called Wi-Pi that used the Raspberry Pi and an additional Wi-Fi dongle to monitor Wi-Fi in an enterprise environment. They deployed various Raspberry Pis to store Wi-Fi performance. When a connection to the Wi-Pi server was established, the Raspberry Pis transmitted the performance data to the main Wi-Pi server. From this work, we learned how to use the Raspberry Pi to connect to access points. However, as previously identified, the Raspberry Pi 3 B model has built-in Wi-Fi, therefore, this is not necessary.

In addition to using a Wi-Fi dongle with the Raspberry Pi to enable network services, we can use a GSM 3G/4G modem to connect the Raspberry Pi to the cellular network as shown in [7]. Vujović in [7] proposed a system that provides a sensor node that is accessible all over the world using either a GSM/GPRS shield or a USB 3G/4G modem. This system would be useful in situations where sensors are deployed in dangerous or hazardous areas. This work demonstrates how to integrate the Raspberry Pi with the cellular GSM/GPRS network by using a GSM/GPRS shield or by connecting a USB GSM 3G/4G modem. Since the Raspberry Pi does not contain self-powering capabilities, we must consider instances where the vehicle is turned off. At this time, the vehicle may still have occupants that would rely on the Edu-BUS.

We therefore, need to identify a method to keep the Raspberry Pi powered even with additional attachments. Sakai and Sugano [8] developed a system that can track humans. Use cases for this work include small children and dementia patients. Sakai and Sugano used a Raspberry Pi, GPS module, battery, 3G modem and a Wi-Fi adapter. They used a battery to keep the Raspberry Pi powered. This allowed the device to be deployed wirelessly in a stuffed animal 30 cm in size. From this work we learned how to connect the Raspberry Pi to a battery that allowed it to be powered without a wired connected power source.

2.3   Wi-Fi Captive Portal Systems

Dabrowski et al. in their work in [9] introduced the concept of captive portals. In their work, they mentioned that captive portals are used worldwide in restaurants, airports and train stations, which offer Wi-Fi Hotspots. Captive portals allow administrators to set a display page that requires some action from the user before they are allowed Wi-Fi access. Dabrowski et al. [9], created a proof of concept to raise awareness that personal privacy could be at risk when using public Wi-Fi with captive portals implemented. To test this, they deployed a virtual machine that had a USB Wi-Fi adapter (TP-LINK TL-WN722 N) configured in access point mode. From this work we learned that captive portals could be used to control access to free Wi-Fi access points. Additionally, we recognized that USB Wi-Fi dongles, particularly the (TP-LINK TL-WN722N) could be configured to not only connect to Wi-Fi access points but could also be configured as an AP. Gatehouse [10] implemented a Wi-Fi network and captive portal gauging the multiple meanings of free and public Wi-Fi.

The interface requires users to navigate the interface which should prompt reflection. From this work, we gathered a captive portal could be used for more than just accepting user credentials but could also be used to display various types of information before users are allowed to connect.

2.4   Related Works Summary

From our survey of related works, we noted it was possible to use a Raspberry Pi with a router to provide Wi-Fi access to resources on the Raspberry Pi. However, we noted that the Raspberry Pi 3 B has onboard Wi-Fi and therefore is suited to replace the external router mentioned in the work by Rahane et al. in [1]. We also found that it is possible to use a captive portal to capture information from the user before they are provided with free Wi-Fi service. Additionally, from the work done by Rathod et al. in [2] we noted that a 5-V step-down module can be used in a vehicle system to connect microcontrollers. We, therefore, can use this approach to connect the Raspberry Pi to a vehicle which has a 12-V supply. Having identified similar systems, devices and approaches employed we will now define the Edu-Bus Wi-Fi system.

3   Edu-BUS Wi-Fi Implementation

In this section we will discuss the implementation of Edu-Bus Wi-Fi which seeks to address our research question: *Can a low-cost system be deployed onboard multiple vehicles to offer Free Wi-Fi to passengers and allow administrators to monitor and control user activities and authentication remotely.*

To implement the free Edu-BUS Wi-Fi we used the following:

- Raspberry Pi
- Battery
- USB 3G/4G modem

We will now discuss how we configure the devices mentioned previously to offer the Free Edu-Bus Wi-Fi which is illustrated in Fig. 3.

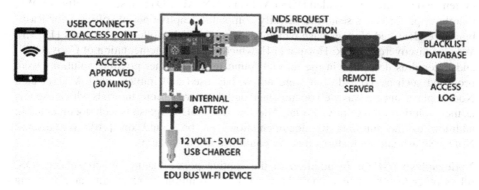

Fig. 3. Free Wi-Fi Edu-Bus

3.1 Wireless Configuration

In this section, we discuss how we configured the Raspberry Pi to offer Wi-Fi access to persons on-board. We recall the work done by Rahane et al. in [1] used a Raspberry Pi with a USB Wi-Fi dongle and a router to enable users to connect to their devices wirelessly while onboard. However, we also recall in the work done by Kataoka and Kumar in [6] mentioned the Raspberry Pi has built-in Wi-Fi capabilities. We also recognized in the work done by Dabrowski et al. in [9] some USB adapters can be converted into AP mode that allows users to connect their devices. We, therefore, investigated the possibility of using the Raspberry Pi as an access point which would remove the need to use a wireless router done in the work by Rahane et al. in [1].

Kim and Lee [11] used open source software to deploy APs. They identified HOSTAPD and OpenWRT as software that is useful to convert the Raspberry Pi into an AP. We, therefore, investigated the HOSTAPD and OpenWRT and recognized OpenWRT requires the Raspberry Pi to run on specific software where as HOSTAPD can be installed on the native Raspbian platform designed for the Raspberry Pi. This would allow us to install other native features to that operating system while having the Raspberry Pi configured as an AP. Additionally, Kim and Lee [11] identified DHCPD to allocate IP addresses to users after they connect to the AP. Having installed HOS-TAPD and used DNSMASQ, we have a functioning wireless AP that users can connect to using Wi-Fi enabled devices. We must now identify compatible software with the Raspbian operating system that would enable us to offer captive portal features as discussed previously in Sect. 2.3.

3.2   Captive Portal

In this section, we discuss how we integrate a captive portal with our Raspbian operating system and are already installed HOSTAPD and DNSMASQ open source software. We, therefore, performed a search to identify compatible captive portal software for Raspbian. We identified Nodogsplash which is suggested in the following tutorials [12, 13]. We also discovered Kupiki Hotspot [14], which was an implementation of CoovaChilli and Freeradius described in the tutorial found on [15]. Other possible solutions were proposed such as Tornado but were not widely used and implemented. We selected Nodogsplash since it was well documented and there are various tutorials which use this as their solution for a Captive Portal. Additionally, NoDogSplash is well documented in addition to the tutorials its documentation can be found on [16]. We discuss NoDogSplash and its features that we could use in our system.

Nodogsplash (NDS): In addition to the captive portal feature, Nodogsplash(NDS) offers other features which could be used in our solution by restricting and applying access control measures on users these include:

- Blocking all outgoing packets
- Performing Packet filtering
- Forwarding External Authentication Methods (FAS)

Blocks All Outgoing Packets: NDS intercepts all outgoing packets which have a destination of port 80. NDS will display its default page when a user attempts to access a webpage. In some cases, devices may be equipped with Captive Portal Detection (CPD) and will automatically display the NDS splash page. This function can be used to validate users before they are allowed to access the internet and other services provided by Edu-BUS Wi-Fi.

Performs Packet Filtering: By inserting rules into the iptables, NDS can filter incoming packets that contain certain marks and forwards matching ones. Packets coming through the router is one of the following types:

- **Blocked** – The MAC address of the transmitting device is in the BlockedMACList or the MAC address is not in the AllowedMACList or TrustedMACList. These packets are dropped [16].
- **Trusted** – The MAC address of the transmitting device exist in the TrustedMACList. These packets by default are automatically routed to their destination port [16].
- **Authenticated** – The IP address and MAC address has been authenticated using the NDS process and has not yet expired. These packets are routed to their destination [16].
- **Preauthenticated** - Packets which have a port destination or addresses not allowed by the NDS configuration are dropped except packets with a destination of Port 80. Packets addressed to Port 80 are redirected to Port 2050. NDS has an libhttpd-based web server that is listening on Port 2050 and displays the NDS splash page. The user is then authenticated by performing some defined activity.

Facilitates External Authentication Methods: We discussed the packet filtering capabilities of NDS that enables us to authenticate users. However, NDS has the ability to use an external method for validating users this could be done on an external server. NDS offers four methods of authentication using its Forwarding Authentication Service (FAS) these are:

- **Fasport** – The port number of the NDS is changed to a Port that another application is listening.
- **Fasremoteip** – NDS navigates to this address for authentication.
- **Faspath** – NDS will navigate to this path for authentication.
- **Fas_secure_enable** – When set to 1 the client token which is used for authentication is held and FAS has to request a token using NDSCTL. However, if this value is set to 0, NDS will provide the client token in clear text to FAS along with authentication and redir.

NDS Configuration: We selected the Fasremote method for authentication as this would allow us to remotely control the authentication of users. However, this requires us to have an internet connection on our Raspberry Pi to connect to our server since NDS FAS will navigate to http://[fasremoteip]:[fasport]/faspath?authaction=http://[-gatewayaddress]:[gatewayport]/nodogsplash_auth/?clientip=[clientip]&gatewayname=[gatewayname]&tok=[token]&redir=[requested_url] passing the above parameters. We, therefore, need to have an established internet connection on the Raspberry Pi to facilitate the connection.

3.3 Enabling Internet Connection

Since the system is being deployed on a moving vehicle the method of connecting to the internet needs to consider this factor. We recall in the work done by Vujović in [7], they proposed the use of a GSM/GPRS shield or a USB 3G/4G modem to connect Raspberry Pis to the internet using the cellular network. We selected the USB 3G/4G method as it was the most available method to us. We selected the Huawei E3372h-510 Unlocked 150 Mbps 4G LTE USB Stick shown in Fig. 4 after performing a search to identify modems which were both compatible with our 4G LTE bands and with the Raspberry Pi. The Huawei E3372h-510 adapter auto-configures to enable internet connection on the Raspberry Pi.

Fig. 4. Huawei E3372h-510

Additionally, we tested an alternative method that could be used in the event that a USB 3G/4G adapter is not available. This method was similar to the method employed by Rahane et al. in [1]. We attached a USB Wireless adapter to the Raspberry Pi similar to Rahane et al. in [1] however, the router which we connected to was a Huawei E5573C modem with 3G/4G connectivity the device is shown in Fig. 5.

Fig. 5. Huawei E5573C Modem

This required us to create a shell script which would ensure the Raspberry Pi remained connected to the Wi-Fi. However, we recognized this approach had a major flaw. When the vehicle is switched off for an extended period and the backup battery has no remaining charge the device will switch off completely. When the vehicle is switched back on the device will not automatically turn back on it will require the power button to be pressed. Whereas, with the USB 3G/4G approach as soon as the Raspberry Pi receives power again the USB 3G/4G will switch on and auto reconfigure itself to provide internet connectivity. This capability is important to avoid the need for human interaction. Additionally, to avoid human interaction with the Edu-Wi-Fi Bus system we need to develop a method of implementation which does not require an action from the vehicle operator after installation.

3.4   Vehicle Installation

We recall in the work done by Rathod et al. in [2] the authors used the 12 V power supply from the vehicle to power their device. Additionally, they employed the use of a 5 V step-down module since their microcontroller required a 5 V power supply. We also recall in the work done by Guravaiah, Thivyavignesh and Velusamy in [4] the Raspberry Pi also requires a 5 V power supply. We, therefore, investigated how we could power the Raspberry Pi from a vehicle employing a step-down module. We discovered the cigarette lighter port which is available in most vehicles and is used to charge phones and other devices. The USB adapter converts the 12 V power supply outputted from the cigarette lighter and converts it to a 5 V output that provides a USB male jack. By employing this installation method, it makes it easier to move the Edu-Bus Wi-Fi System to other vehicles if necessary. Figure 10 shows the USB 5 V adapter which is used to charge the Raspberry Pi. However, we recall when the vehicle is switched off no power is supplied from the cigarette lighter. Therefore, we have to implement a redundancy in the event that users wish to use the Edu-Bus Wi-Fi system for a limited time while the vehicle is switched off. We, therefore, recall the work done by Sakai and Sugano in [8] were they used a battery to power the Raspberry Pi which had various other modules connected to it. We, therefore, connected the Raspberry Pi to a battery and then connected the battery to the 5 V outlet in the USB adapter as shown in Fig. 3. This method would, therefore, allow us to connect the Edu-Bus Wi-Fi box to any vehicle which contained a functioning cigarette lighter and the system would remain functional for a limited time when the vehicle is switched off.

3.5 User Access Control Management

We now have an access point with NDS enabled and when a user connects to the access point, they will be presented with the NDS splash page shown in Fig. 6. When the image displayed in the center of the page is clicked the user is given access to free Wi-Fi. In answering our research question, we must have the ability to monitor and control users access to the free Wi-Fi resource.

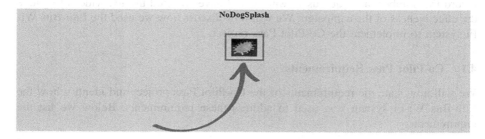

Fig. 6. NDS Page shown when a user connects to Edu Wi-Fi

We, therefore, need to implement a method that would allow us to configure the NDS splash page remotely. We recall NDS allows for external authentication (FAS). We also note using FAS we can configure NDS to redirect the splash page to a remote URL and port and pass it parameters. This would enable us to remotely control and update what is displayed to the user before they are authenticated.

Authenticate Users Remotely. We recall the FAS functionality of NDS allows NDS to be configured to direct users to a remote host for it to provide authentication. We, therefore, created a page using PHP and javascript on our remote server which NDS FAS would be forwarded to. NDS FAS has the ability to pass the mac-address of the user's device who is seeking to access the Edu Wi-Fi system. We recorded the mac-address of each user to perform authentication and monitoring. Before giving access to the user their mac-address is checked against the blacklist database. If their mac-address is found they are denied access.

Remotely Monitor Users Activity. We mentioned previously we attain the mac-addresses from NDS FAS as users attempt to connect. These mac-address are stored in our database along with the Gateway mac-address which is the mac-address of the Raspberry Pi they are connecting too which is the unique mac address of each Raspberry Pi on each vehicle as well as the time of the activity.

Having designed a system which answers our research question. We will now test our system design and implementation by applying it to a case study which has the requirements of our research question.

4   CASE STUDY – Co-Pilot Pass

Our case study is motivated by the 2018 Internet Society Chapterthon which focused on promoting the safe usage of the internet of Things (IoT) devices. The University of the West Indies Cave Hill Campus (UWICHC) offers a shuttle service to students that allow them to travel off and on campus. Our proposed approach was to use the Edu-Bus Wi-Fi system to educate students who boarded any four (4) of the UWICHC shuttles. To do this we provided free Wi-Fi access to students aboard however, before connecting they were presented with a captive portal that required them to watch an educational video based on safe usage of IoT devices. Additionally, we needed to record the number of unique users who would have watched the IoT videos to gauge the effectiveness of the campaign. We will now discuss how we used the Edu-Bus Wi-Fi system to implement the Co-Pilot Pass project.

4.1   Co-Pilot Pass Requirements

We will now state the requirements of the Co-Pilot Pass project and identify how the Edu-Bus Wi-Fi system was used to address these requirements. Below we list the requirements:

- Authenticate users remotely after watching educational videos.
- Display, edit and update educational video paths remotely.
- Record the number of unique users who watched the IoT videos.

Authenticate Users Remotely After Watching Educational Videos. We recall the FAS functionality of NDS allows NDS to be configured to direct users to a remote host for it to provide authentication. We, therefore, created a page using PHP and javascript on our remote server which NDS FAS would be forwarded to which is shown in Fig. 7. We placed an HTML 5 tag that linked to a video locally on the Raspberry Pi which maintained the benefit mentioned by Rahane et al. in [1] since the locally hosted video would not incur a cost. We then used JavaScript to listen for a video complete event. After this event was received, we used JavaScript to hide the video tag and display a button shown in Fig. 8. This button contains the link which is required for NDS to authenticate the user by placing the URL and Port to NDS mentioned in Sect. 3.3 and by passing the user token and redir parameter.

Display, Edit and Update Educational Video Paths Remotely. We stated in Sect. 4.1 that we insert a video link into the page that allows for the loading of the video locally hosted on the Raspberry Pi. However, we should be able to display multiple videos and update these videos remotely. We, therefore, implemented a bash script which contained an RSYNC function called by a Cron job which would sync the local folder with the remote folder on our server at 12:15 AM daily. This time was

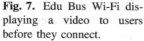

Fig. 7. Edu Bus Wi-Fi displaying a video to users before they connect.

Fig. 8. Edu Bus Wi-Fi displaying a button after users watched the video.

chosen based on operation times of shuttle and based on user connections by time analysis discussed in the section below. Additionally, we wished to randomize the videos being displayed we, therefore, included a JavaScript function that would allow us to check the contents of the remote directory through PHP and identify the videos that could be displayed. Additionally, we implemented a feature which allowed the script to randomize the selection of a video from the video folder in the event only one video should be displayed. However, our script accepted parameters from FAS and could, therefore, be used to further customize which video and how it is displayed.

Record the Number of Unique Users Who Watched the IoT Videos. We recall from Sect. 3.5 we recorded the mac-address of each user which connected to the Edu Bus Wi-Fi. This activity was also recorded with other parameters passed by NDS FAS which include the device gateway (Raspberry Pi mac-address). From this information, we can, therefore, ascertain the number of users which connected and viewed the videos which were 829 unique users and 2724 sessions. Figure 9 shows the number of sessions which occurred over the 3-week testing period per bus. We notice bus 1 sessions are much lower than the other busses having only 122 sessions during the test period. This occurred bus was having mechanical issues during that time and was removed from operation from time to time.

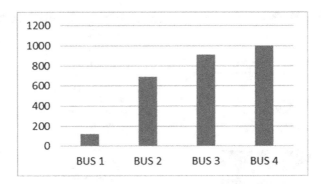

Fig. 9. A graph illustrating the number of connections and video views per bus

While we achieved the requirements of the Co-Pilot project by attaining the number of unique users and number of sessions were persons viewed the education videos we were also able to provide additional information which could be used to target users on particular days ant particular times. In Fig. 10 we show the user connections and sessions by day of the week and Fig. 11 by hour of the day.

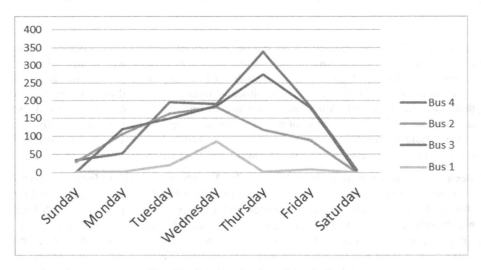

Fig. 10. Sessions by day of the week

The day of the week view of the data showed users on Sunday and Saturday had very few sessions. This is consistent with the operation days of the shuttle which is Monday to Friday. However, from time to time on Sundays the shuttles are mobilized to ferry students to various events we can, therefore, see a slight number of users connected on Sunday on Bus 2 and Bus 4 in relation to Saturday. Additionally, the same could be said about hours of the day since the shuttle operates from 6 AM until 11:00 PM. We can also see most connections occurred during the morning between the hours of 7 PM–9 PM.

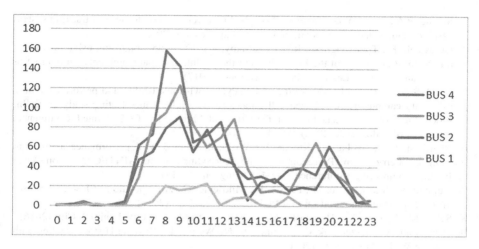

Fig. 11. Session per hour

5   Conclusions and Future Work

In this paper, we developed a system capable of providing internet enabled Wi-Fi onboard a vehicle using a Raspberry Pi and a USB 3G/4G modem. Additionally, we integrated NDS and used its FAS capabilities to perform validation and authentication of users seeking to use the onboard Wi-Fi. Our system is also capable of displaying content during the authentication process which must be viewed by a user before access is given. To reduce the data cost content is stored locally on the Raspberry Pi. However, the content is automatically synchronized with a remote server and therefore allows content to be uploaded remotely. Our system can be used on-board any vehicle which has a functioning cigarette lighter. It can also function when the vehicle is completely turned off for a limited period of time based on the battery capacity. We tested our system on-board four (4) UWICHC shuttles which has a ridership of 20,000 students per semester. We collected the connection time mac-address and default gateway mac-address of each user. We tested the system for three weeks and recorded 829 unique users and a total of 2724 sessions. We also presented information which could be used to determine the peak times when users connect to Wi-Fi onboard the vehicles and could be used to display special videos during that time.

References

1. Rahane, W.P., Anand Kabra, S., Ravindra Kore, P., Dipakkumar Pawar, A., Vijaykumar Gugale, A.: Onboard Entertainment Services using Raspberry Pi with Recommendation Engine (2018)
2. Rathod, M., Gite, R., Pawar, A., Singh, S., Kelkar, P.: An air pollutant vehicle tracker system using gas sensor and GPS, City (2017)

3. Shinde, P.A., Mane, Y.B., Tarange, P.H.: Real time vehicle monitoring and tracking system based on embedded Linux board and android application (2015)
4. Guravaiah, K., Thivyavignesh, R.G., Velusamy, R.L.: Vehicle monitoring using internet of things. In: Proceedings of the Proceedings of the 1st International Conference on Internet of Things and Machine Learning. ACM, Liverpool (2017)
5. Ward, S.A., Gittens, M.: Monitoring and analyzing wi-fi availability and performance on a university campus using recycled cell phones to aid students in selecting study areas. In: Proceedings of the Proceedings of the 2016 ACM on SIGUCCS Annual Conference, Denver, Colorado, USA, 2016). ACM
6. Bhardwaj, D., Kataoka, K., Kumar, V.: Wi-Pi: distributed wi-fi performance assessment using raspberry pi. In: Proceedings of the Proceedings of the AINTEC 2014 on Asian Internet Engineering Conference. ACM, Chiang Mai (2014)
7. Vujović, V., Maksimović, M., Perišić, B., Milošević, G.: A proposition of low cost Sensor Web implementation based on GSM/GPRS services. City (2015)
8. Sakai, M., Sugano, M.: Human tracking system embedded in stuffed animal. City (2016)
9. Dabrowski, A., Merzdovnik, G., Kommenda, N., Weippl, E.: Browser History Stealing with Captive Wi-Fi Portals. City (2016)
10. Gatehouse, C.: FreeAsInWifi (2015)
11. Junho, K., Sungwon, L.: Constructing Infrastructure wireless network using open source. City (2016)
12. Gus Setting up a Raspberry Pi Captive Portal. PiMyLifeUp, City (2018)
13. Guy, C.S.: Building a Raspberry Pi Captive Portal Wi-Fi Hotspot Cyber Security Guy, City
14. Server, R.P.H.: Kupiki-Hotspot-Script
15. Server, R.P.H.: Raspberry Pi, CoovaChilli and Freeradius for a Wifi Hotspot with captive portal. Raspberry Pi Home Server, City (2016)
16. Nodogsplash Nodogsplash. City (2018)

Mobile Application with AI

Fast Map-Matching Based on Hidden Markov Model

Shenglong Yan, Juan Yu$^{(\boxtimes)}$, and Houpan Zhou

Smart City Research Center, Hangzhou Dianzi University, Hangzhou, China
yujuan@hdu.edu.cn

Abstract. Map matching is the processing of recognizing the true driving route in the road network according to discrete GPS sampling datas. It is a necessary processing step for many relevant applications such as GPS trajectory data analysis and position analysis. The current map-matching algorithms based on HMM (Hidden Markov model) focus only on the accuracy of the matching rather than efficiency. In this paper, we propose a original method: Instead of focusing on a point-by-point, we consider the trajectory compression method to find the key points in the discrete trajectory, and then search for optimal path through the key points. The experiments are implemented on two sets of real dataset and display that our method significantly improve the efficiency compared with HMM algorithm, while keeping matching accuracy.

Keywords: Map matching · Efficiency · Trajectory compression · Key points

1 Introduction

With the popularity of electronic mobile devices with built-in GPS sensors, a large amount of driving tracks which contain rich traffic information and user behavior are generated every day. However, with limited satellite visibility and high-rise buildings, the satellite signal is blocked and refracted, and the positioning data we obtain through the GPS sensor is can be inaccurate and noisy, which means that GPS trajectories can not accurately reflect the location of moving objects. Therefore, map-matching is proposed to identify the actual road segment where the user (or vehicle) is/was driving. This process is useful in applications such as vehicle navigation [1], path planning and recommendation [2], traffic forecasting and management [3] and many other LBS (Location-Based Service).

Over the last decades, hundreds of map-matching algorithms were proposed by abundant researchers.

According to the information involved in the input data, Quddus et al. [4] divided the existing map-matching algorithms into four categories: geometric [5], topological [6], probabilistic and advanced. Geometric algorithm only considers the geometric information for identifying the real paths, such as distance, angle and shape, this type of algorithm can provide good accuracy and fast matching efficiency in the case of high sampling rate and accurate positioning, but it is not suitable for trajectory data with low sampling rate and large positioning error. Based on the geometric algorithm, topological algorithm considers the connectivity between road segments, so that the

Y. Yin et al. (Eds.): MobiCASE 2019, LNICST 290, pp. 85–95, 2019.
https://doi.org/10.1007/978-3-030-28468-8_7

accuracy can be improved to a certain extent. However, they are still susceptible to the influence of noise collection and sparse data, and cannot completely solve the complex urban road problems. In fact, we can classify probability algrthim as advanced algorithm which tends to incorporate comprehensive information and use more refined concepts, such as kalman filter [7] fuzzy logic model [8] hidden markov model [9–12] and so on, these advanced algorithms have generally higher accuracy, and the HMM matching algorithm has the highest accuracy. Although the advanced algorithm is better than geometry and topology in matching accuracy, it has poor matching efficiency.

QMM [11] (Quick Map Matching) is the first matching algorithm that emphasizes running time. The algorithm is designed to run on multi-core cpus, because the processing of road segments can be separated from each other during indexing, and each sample trajectory point is independent of each other during matching. The application of multithreading technology greatly reduces the running time of the algorithm. Furthermore, efficiency-based algorithms [13, 14] both consider parallel processing to speed up map matching computation. The above three methods are all based on the idea of processing multiple trajectories at the same time.

Different from the three efficiency-based algorithms, we propose a algorithm called FHMM(Fast map matching based on HMM) to speed up single track matching efficiency. Firstly, our algorithm employs the idea of trajectory compression to find a set of key points. Subsequently, riginated from HMM, we employs measurement probabilities and transition probabilities to measure the relationship between consecutive candidate points of key points in map-matching. Finally, to solve the HMM problem, we make use of dynamic programming Viterbi algorithm to search for optimal travel route.

This paper is organized as follows. Section 2 states the problem of map matching algorithm. The detail of the FHMM is introduced in Sect. 3. The experiment results are presented and analyzed in Sect. 4. Finally we summarize the paper in Sect. 5.

2   Preliminary

2.1   Map Matching Problem

To facilitate the description, we first define some basic concepts and symbols, and then formalize the map matching problem.

- **Definition 1 (GPS Trajectory)**: A GPS track $T : p_1 \rightarrow p_2 \rightarrow \cdots \rightarrow p_n$ is an ordered sequence composed of a series of GPS coordinate points, in which each GPS point $p_i = (t, lat, lon, heading, speed)$ contains information such as sampling time t, latitude and longitude coordinates, GPS real-time direction heading and speed.
- **Definition 2 (Road Network)**: road network is composed of a series of intersection and connection crossroads sections, can be represented as a directed graph G (V, E). V is a vertex set, which contains all the intersection in the road or the road end point. E is directed edge set, which represents sections of road network.

- **Definition 3 (Path):** A Path is a road segment sequence P: $r_1 \rightarrow r_2 \rightarrow \cdots \rightarrow r_n$, where $r_{i-1}.e = r_i.s$, $(1 \leq i \leq n)$. r.s and r.e represent the start point and end point of the road segment r respectively.

2.2 Candidate Points Selection

The preparation process of candidate sets is divided into two sub-steps. Step 1: to establish the r-tree index of road network data, which is mainly aimed at the road section to facilitate the quick search of candidate road sections. Step 2: based on the r-tree index of road segment, fast query all possible candidate road segments of each sampling point in the road network on track T, and then calculate the corresponding candidate points.

Specifically, for each sampling point $p_i(1 \leq i \leq n)$ in GPS track $T : p_1 \rightarrow p_2 \rightarrow \cdots \rightarrow p_n$, all sections within the search radius r of the road network with GPS point $(p_i.lon, p_i.lat)$ as the center of the circle are taken as candidate sections, denoted as $R_i = \{r_i^k | k = 1, 2, \cdots\}$, r_i^k represents the candidate section k of GPS point p_i, and the point closest to the sampling point on the candidate section is called the candidate point, denoted as c_i^k. Figure 1 gives an example of candidate points selection. After calculation, GPS point p_1 obtains four candidate sections, and the corresponding candidate points are c_1^1, c_1^2, c_1^3 and c_4^1.

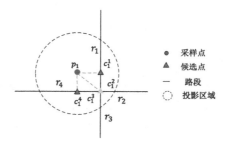

Fig. 1. Illustration of candidate sections and candidate points.

3 FHMM Algorithm

The proposed FHMM algorithm consists of four phases: trajectory preprocess, candidate preparation, HMM training, and result matching, of which candidate preparation has been introduced in Sect. 2. Figure 2 shows a framework of the FHMM algorithm.

3.1 Trajectory Preprocess

Generally speaking, the number of driving vehicle records with GPS acquisition devices is greater than the amount of data required by existing algorithms, such as HMM matching algorithm. The influences of intersections and signal controls mean that vehicles travelling on normal arterials often display a 'stop-and-go'pattern. In other

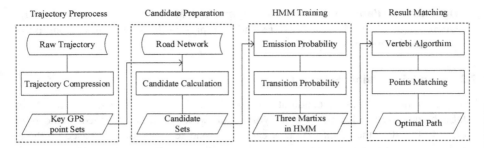

Fig. 2. Framework of the FHMM algorithm.

words, there will be lots of stop points in the raw trajectory. In addition, the vehicles tends to drive on the same road for a period of time, which means the driving route is close to a straight line. As a result, there is also a lot of GPS redundancy between the two ends of the line.

Our insight that compress a trajectory can remove stop points and redundant points that are between the key points. An example is illustrated in Fig. 3, obviously, the blue sampling points that can increase the computational cost in map matching are redundant. In the actual matching process, we only need the key sampling points (such as red sampling points) in the original trajectory to infer the entire driving route.

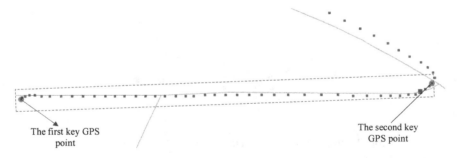

Fig. 3. An example to illustrate key points and the redundant. (Color figure online)

In this paper, we propose a method to compress trajectory by sliding window, which can be used for both online and offline compression. Our approach aims to describe the original trajectory with fewer key points by using the distance threshold which can be changed according to the required compression. We apply an example to describe the main ideas of our method. As Fig. 4 shows, there is a raw GPS trajectory $T : p_1 \rightarrow p_2 \rightarrow \cdots \rightarrow p_6$.we firstly put p_1, p_2 into sliding window, then as a new point arrives in the sliding window, it uses the new point and the first point to calculates the PED (Perpendicular Euclidean Distance) $(PED_{p_m|(p_i,p_j)})$ by Eq. 1 for all the points in the sliding window. If there is $PED_{p_m|(p_i,p_j)} > PED_{\text{threshold}}(i < m{<}j)$, the p_{j-1} is called key point. In Fig. 4, because $PED_{p_3|(p_1,p_4)} > PED_{\text{threshold}}$, we take p_3 as the key point and p_3, p_4 as the new starting point of the sliding window. $PED_{p_4|(p_3, p_6)} > PED_{\text{threshold}}$, so p_5 also is a key point. p_6 is the end point of trajectory, we also add p_6 to the key points sequence.

$$PED_{p_m|(p_i, p_j)} = \frac{\left|(y_j - y_i)x_m - (x_j - x_e)y_m + x_j y_i - x_i y_j\right|}{\sqrt{(y_j - y_i)^2 + ((x_j - x_e))^2}} \tag{1}$$

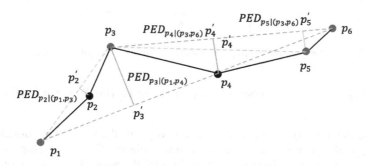

Fig. 4. An example to illustrate proposed method.

3.2 HMM Training

We give a brief description of the matching algorithm based on HMM [9]. For each GPS point, a group of candidate sections is determined first. Each candidate section is represented as a hidden state (vertex) in the markov chain, and has the probability of observation state, which is the feasibility of observing whether the GPS point matches the candidate section. If the GPS point is found to be very close to a section, assign a high probability value to that section. Then, the weight of each pair of adjacent vertices connected in the markov chain is calculated, that is, the state transition probability. Finally, the maximum likelihood path with the highest observed state probability and state transition probability is found on the markov chain. Fig. 5 illustrates a hidden markov chain of map matching.

Observation probability. Although it is simple to calculate the observation probability based on the gaussian distribution model, it has been proved to be effective in the previous work of [9–12] map matching. So the observation probability is as:

$$N(c_i^j) = \frac{1}{\sqrt{2\pi}\sigma_1} e^{\frac{\left(x_i^j - \mu_1\right)^2}{2\sigma_1^2}} \tag{2}$$

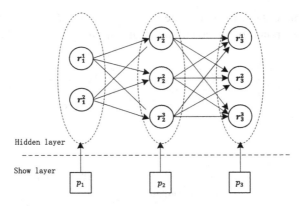

Fig. 5. An example to illustrate a hidden markov chain of map matching

Where c_i^j is a candidate point of sampling point p_i, and X_i^j is the Euclid distance from c_i^j to p_i.

Transition probability. Compared to circuitous paths, the true driving distance tends to be close to the euclidean distance between the adjacent GPS points, especially after trajectory compression. Based on the above insight, We adopt the transition probability method proposed by Lou et al. [10], which further improves the robustness of the algorithm based on HMM [9].

$$V\left(c_{i-1}^s \to c_i^t\right) = \frac{\text{Euclid}(i - 1 \to i)}{route\left(c_{i-1}^s \to c_i^t\right)} \tag{3}$$

Where $E(i - 1 \to i)$ is Euclid distance from p_{i-1} to p_i, and $route\left(c_{i-1}^s \to c_i^t\right)$ represents the driving path distance from c_{i-1}^s to c_i^t.

3.3   Result Matching

The most likely sequence of hidden states in a HMM is commonly found apply a DP (dynamic programming) algorithm known as the Viterbi algorithm, which can quickly find the optimal path in the road network to maximize the product of observation probability and transition probability.

Figure 6 shows an example of finding the optimal path by Viterbi algorithm. We consider candidate c_2^1, the weight of path($c_1^1 \to c_2^1$) is $1.36 = 0.8 + 0.8 \times 0.7$, and the path's $(c_2^1 \to c_2^1)$ weight is 0.61. Therefore candidate $c_2^{1'}s$ weight is 1.36, and its parent is c_1^1. We repeat the above process for all c_i^j. After completing the calculation we find that c_3^1 has the highest score, and its parent is c_2^1. the Viterbi algorithm finally output the matching path is $c_1^1 \to c_2^1 \to c_3^1$.

c_1^1	c_1^2	c_2^1	c_2^2	c_2^3	c_3^1	c_3^2
0.8	0.4	0.7	0.4	0.2	0.8	0.2

	c_2^1	c_2^2	c_2^3
c_1^1	0.8	0.5	0.2
c_1^2	0.3	0.5	0.6

	c_3^1	c_3^2
c_2^1	0.3	0.4
c_2^2	0.5	0.1
c_2^3	0.7	0.8

$$8 + 0.8 \times 0 \qquad 1.36 = \max\{0.8 + 0.8 \times 0.7, 0.4 + 0.3 \times 0.7\}$$

$$1.0 = \max\{0.8 + 0.5 \times 0.4, 0.4 + 0.4 \times 0.5\}$$

$$0.4 + 0.2 \times 0.6 \qquad 0.84 = \max\{0.8 + 0.2 \times 0.2, 0.4 + 0.2 \times 0.6\}$$

$$1.50 = \max\{1.36 + 0.8 \times 0.3, 1.0 + 0.8 \times 0.5, 0.84 + 0.8 \times 0.7\}$$

$$1.44 = \max\{1.36 + 0.2 \times 0.4, 1.0 + 0.2 \times 0.1, 0.84 + 0.2 \times 0.8\}$$

Fig. 6. An example of finding the optimal path by Viterbi algorithm.

4   Experiment

In this section, we use real-world trajectory data to evaluate our FHMM algorithm. We first describe the setting of experiment and then report the experiment results.

4.1   Parameter Selection

In our experiment, we set k = 6 as the maximum number of candidates for each sampling point. and the query radius is r = 100 m. In the trajectory compression stage, in order to ensure that the travel path between two adjacent GPS points after compression is close to a straight line, we set PED threshold as 20 m. For observation probability calculation, we use a normal distribution with $\mu = 0$ and $\sigma = 4.61$ estimated by Eq. 4 [9]. In addition, the algorithms are implemented in python 2.7, on an Intel i5-7200u PC with memory 8 GB on windows10 operating system.

$$\sigma = 1.4826 \; \text{median}\left(\parallel p_i - c_i^j \parallel_{Euclid}\right) \tag{4}$$

4.2   Experiment Datasets

We evaluate the performance of our proposed algorithm using two real-world trajectory datasets, and the details of the dataset are as follows:

- **Dataset 1**: The dataset [9] was collected by Krumm et al. to test HMM matching algorithm and its sampleing rate, number of sampling points et al. are showed in Table 1. Moreover, the dataset provides the road network and ground truth data for comparsion with matching result.
- **Dataset 2**: The dataset [15] was used for map matching in the ACM SIGSPATIAL CUP 2012, and the details are also shown in Table 1. Besides, the dataset also provides the ground true.

Table 1. Description of experimental datasets

Dataset	Trips	Sampling	Size	Time	Length
Dataset 1	1 trip	1 s	7531	∼2 h	∼80 km
Dataset 2	10 trips	1 s	14436	∼4 h	∼228 km

4.3   Evaluation Approach

The FHMM is an improved algorithm based on the HMM [9], so we compared the matching accuracy and efficiency of the FHMM with the HMM. The accuracy is the correctness of matching the road, and the efficiency is to compare the running time of the algorithm on the same platform. We use matching precision (MP) to evaluate the accuracy of the algorithm.

$$MP = \frac{|correct\ matched\ road\ segments|}{|road\ segments\ to\ be\ matched|} \times 100\% \tag{5}$$

4.4   Result and Analysis

Figure 7 present the visualized compressing result using the GPS trajectory of dataset 1. In this picture, the blue dots represent raw sampling GPS points, and the red dot represents the GPS sampling points in the compressed trajectory. Figure 7(a), (b) and (c) represent global compression results and local compression results respectively. Obviously, the trajectory obtained by our method of compression can completely describe the original trajectory to the maximum extent. The original trajectory has 7,351 trajectory points. After compression, there are 167 key GPS points left, with a compression rate of 97.3%. A large number of redundant GPS points are removed, which greatly reduce the calculation cost in the subsequent matching process. The dataset 2 has similar compression results as dataset 1.

Tables 2 and 3 shows the matching accuracy and running time of HMM and FHMM algorithms. We compare the performance of the algorithms on the same platform. We can see that the FHMM algorithm is about faster 2 to 3 times than the HMM algorithm, while keeping matching accuracy.

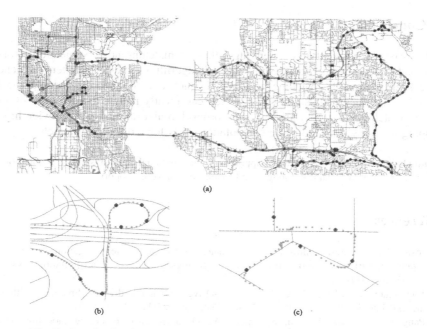

Fig. 7. Result of trajectory compression of Dataset 1. (Color figure online)

Table 2. Comparsion of two algorithms on accruracy

Dataset	Method	
	HMM	FHMM
Dataset 1	99.30%	99.30%
Dataset 2	99.45%	98.61%

Table 3. Comparsion of two algorithms on efficiency

Dataset	Track	HMM		FHMM	
		Size (raw)	Running time/s	Size (compressed)	Running time/s
Dataset 1	Track1	7351	131.6	167	46.1
Dataset 2	Track1	2356	29.4	47	14.7
	Track2	1070	13.6	39	6.6
	Track3	1566	17.4	52	5.8
	Track4	1177	21.5	50	10.0
	Track5	885	7.4	19	3.7
	Track6	1017	9.1	35	4.2
	Track7	2368	26.5	54	7.9
	Track8	1135	13.2	53	5.9
	Track9	1543	21.4	60	9.7
	Track10	1320	9.7	40	4.3

5 Conclusion

In this paper, we present an efficient algorithm for matching nosiy vehicle trajectories onto road network. Experiments show that our algorithm achieves excellent efficiency, while keep reasonable matching accuracy. In fact, our compression method can be applied to the track acquisition stage, which can greatly reduce the difficulty of subsequent matching. In the future, we plan to develop algorithms which provide higher mapping accuracy with moderate computation costs for more noisy datasets.

Acknowledgment. This study was supported by the national natural science foundation of China(61702148). We thank the judges and thank you for your support.

References

1. Joshi, R.R.: A new approach to map matching for in-vehicle navigation systems: the rotational variation metric. In: 2001 Proceedings Intelligent Transportation Systems, pp. 33–38 (2001)
2. Jing Yuan, Y., Zheng, X.X., Sun, G.: T-Drive: enhancing driving directions with taxi drivers' intelligence. IEEE Trans. Knowl. Data Eng. **25**(1), 220–232 (2013)
3. Pang, L.X., Chawla, S., Liu, W., Zheng, Y.: On detection of emerging anomalous traffic patterns using GPS data. Data Knowl. Eng. **87**(9), 357–373 (2013)
4. Quddus, M.A., Ochieng, W.Y., Noland, R.B.: Current map-matching algorithms for transport applications: state-of-the art and future research directions. Transp. Res. Part C: Emerg. Technol. **15**(5), 312–328 (2007)
5. White, C.E., Bernstein, D., Kornhauser, A.L.: Some map matching algorithms for personal navigation assistants. Transp. Res. Part C: Emerg. Technol. **8**(1), 91–108 (2000)
6. Velaga, N.R., Quddus, M.A., Bristow, A.L.: Developing an enhanced weight-based topological map-matching algorithm for intelligent transport systems. Transp. Res. Part C **17**(6), 672–683 (2009)
7. Obradovic, D., Lenz, H., Schupfner, M.: Fusion of sensor data in siemens car navigation system. IEEE Trans. Veh. Technol. **56**(1), 43–50 (2007)
8. Quddus, M.A., Noland, R.B., Ochieng, W.Y.: A high accuracy fuzzy logic based map matching algorithm for road transport. J. Intell. Transp. Syst. **10**(3), 103–115 (2006)
9. Newson, P., Krumm, J.: Hidden markov map matching through noise and sparseness. In: Proceedings of the 17th ACM SIGSPATIAL International Conference on Advances in Geographic Information Systems,, pp. 336–343. New York, NY, USA (2009)
10. Lou, Y., Zhang, C., Zheng, Y., Xie, X., Wang, W., Huang, Y.: Map-matching for low-sampling-rate GPS Trajectories. In: Proceedings of the 17th ACM SIGSPATIAL International Conference on Advances in Geographic Information Systems, pp. 352–361. New York, NY, USA (2009)
11. Song, R., Lu, W., Sun, W., Huang, W., Chen, C.: Quick map matching using multi-core CPUs. In: Proceedings of ACM-GIS, pp. 605–608 (2012)
12. Ozdemir, E., Topcu, A.E., Ozdemir, M.K.: A hybrid HMM model for travel path inference with sparse GPS samples. Transportation **45**(1), 233–246 (2018)
13. Tiwari, V.S., Arya, A., Chaturvedi, S.: Framework for horizontal scaling of map matching: using map-reduce. In: 2014 International Conference on Information Technology, Bhubaneswar, pp. 30–34. India (2014)

14. Huang, J., Qiao, S., Yu, H., Qie, J., Liu, C.: Parallel map matching on massive vehicle GPS data using MapReduce. In: 2013 IEEE 10th International Conference on High Performance Computing and Communications & 2013 IEEE International Conference on Embedded and Ubiquitous Computing, Zhangjiajie, pp. 1498–1503. China (2013)
15. Ali, M., et al.: ACM SIGSPATIAL GIS cup 2012. In: Proceedings of the 20th International Conference on Advances in Geographic Information Systems, SIGSPATIAL 2012, Redondo Beach, pp. 597–600. California. New York: ACM (2012)

VDIF-M: Multi-label Classification of Vehicle Defect Information Collection Based on Seq2seq Model

Xindong You[1], Yuwen Zhang[1], Baoan Li[1], Xueqiang Lv[1(✉)], and Junmei Han[2]

[1] Beijing Key Laboratory of Internet Culture and Digital Dissemination Research, Beijing Information Science & Technology University, Beijing, China
lxq@bistu.edu.cn
[2] Laboratory of Complex Systems, Institute of Systems Engineering, AMS, PLA, Beijing, China

Abstract. Classification and treatment of vehicle defect complaint data is an important link in the process of vehicle recall. Traditionally, the complaint data is classified by keyword matching method based on defect label library during the process of dealing with vehicle complaint data, which heavily relies heavily on the quality of the vehicle defect label library. The speed of traditional classification methods is rapid, but the accuracy is low. We transform the classification task of vehicle complaint data into a multi-label classification problem. Multi-label classification of vehicle defect information collection based on seq2seq model named VDIF-M is proposed in this paper. Firstly, a synonymous vehicle defect description label library is constructed based on the vehicle defect description data and vehicle domain corpus collected from various channels. Then a seq2seq model is proposed to solve the problem of multi-label classification of vehicle complaint data, which fuses the distribution relationship between labels. Substantial experimental results show that the proposed method outperforms previous methods in multi-label classification of vehicle complaint data.

Keywords: Multi-label classification · Seq2seq · Label generation · Deep learning

1 Introduction

With the continuous development of the vehicle industry, vehicles have become a necessity in people's lives. Data show that China is the largest country of vehicle production and sales country in the world. At the same time, the quality defects of vehicle products have also aroused people's concern and the complaints about vehicle quality defects appear on the Internet. In recent years, the recall system of defective vehicle products in China has been gradually improved. A large number of consumer complaints are collected in the vehicle quality defect complaint system, which named the defect information collection system of Defective Product Administrative Center [1]. Most of these complaints contain one or more defect description information. The Defective Product Administrative Center needs to investigate and verify the vehicle

© ICST Institute for Computer Sciences, Social Informatics and Telecommunications Engineering 2019
Published by Springer Nature Switzerland AG 2019. All Rights Reserved
Y. Yin et al. (Eds.): MobiCASE 2019, LNICST 290, pp. 96–111, 2019.
https://doi.org/10.1007/978-3-030-28468-8_8

defects reflected in these complaints to determine whether to initiate a recall. But because different users have different understanding of the vehicle, the same kind of vehicle defect may be expressed in different ways, which brings great difficulties to the defective product management center for the analysis and processing of these complaints data. It is a feasible solution to classifying these complaints with multi-bale using the multi-label classification technology in Artificial Intelligence and natural language processing and according to the corresponding defect classification system. In this paper, we transform the classification task of vehicle complaint data into a multi-label classification problem employed with seq2seq model.

Multi-label classification is an important problem in the field of natural language processing. Multi-label classification is a concept relative to single-label classification. Traditional single-label classification associates instance X with a single label L from a previously known finite set of labels L. A single label data set D consists of n instances $(x_1, L_1), (x_2, L_2), ..., (x_n, L_n)$. The multi-label classification task associates a subset of labels S with each instance. Thus, the multi-label data set D is composed of n examples $(x_1, S_1), (x_2, S_2), ..., (x_n, S_n)$. In a practical application scenario, an instance is usually associated with multiple labels in most cases. In this paper, a piece of vehicle complaint information may contain two or more kinds of vehicle defect information. Considering the great achievements of neural networks in natural language processing in recent years, we transform the multi-classification problem into a label generation method in this paper. Solving the multi-classification problem with sequence-to-sequence model (seq2seq) is popular in machine translation and generative text summarization. The seq2seq model used in this paper consists of an encoder and a decoder with attention mechanism. The encoder uses Bi-directional Long Short-Term Memory (Bi-LSTM) to read the semantic information of the vehicle complaint information on the one hand, and compares the complaint text with the vehicle defect description label library on the other hand, and extracts the defect description features. The decoder generates a label sequence through the LSTM based on the previously predicted label. Because different words in the complaint information contain different amount of defect information, the attention mechanism can distribute different weight to different parts. Therefore, this kind of neural network model can capture the feature of the complaint text better.

As a whole, the main contributions of this paper are listed as follows:

(1) *Two vehicle complaint datasets are constructed through utilizing web crawler technology. The constructed datasets contain descriptions of all kinds of complaints in the process of vehicle recall.*

(2) *We firstly employ the seq2seq neural network model to solve the multi-label classification on vehicle complaint data. And the defect label features and defect label distribution are added to the basic seq2seq model, which makes the model more suitable for multi-label classification of vehicle complaint data.*

(3) *Substantial experiments are conducted on the two constructed dataset with different deep learning models, the experiment results demonstrate that the proposed method outperforms current existing methods in multi-label classification of vehicle complaint dataset.*

The following sections are organized as follows. Section 2 introduces the relevant work. We describe our methods in the Sect. 3. In Sect. 4, we present the experiments and make analysis and discussion. Finally in Sect. 5 we conclude this paper and explore the future work.

2   Relate Work

Multi-label classification mainly includes three types of solutions, they are problem transformation methods, algorithm adaptation methods and neural network-based methods.

The idea of problem transformation is to transform multi-label problem into single-label classification problem in some way, a mature single label classification method is used to solve the problem. Binary Reliance (BR) algorithm proposed by Boutell [2] transforms each label into a single label classification problem, which is independent of each other. The disadvantage of this method is that the relationship between labels is ignored. Similar algorithms include LIFT algorithm [3], which improves the classification effect by clustering the positive and negative instances to construct the characteristics of each label in the multi-label. Label Powerset (LP) [4] algorithm transforms the multi-label classification problem into a single-label multi-classification problem by treating each label set as a new independent label. The Classifier Chain (CC) algorithm [5] transforms the multi-classification tasks into a series of binary classification problems. The author combines the multi-labels into a sequence, and adds the predicted labels into the feature vector when predicting the new labels in the sequence, which can introduce the global information into the fusion of labels and the relationship between labels. However, CC algorithm is inefficient in solving the problem of more labels or more samples.

The algorithm adapts to multi-label data after modifying and extending the traditional single-label classification algorithm. Clare [6] extends the definition of information entropy to multi-label problem, and then uses improved decision tree algorithm to classify multi-label. Elisseeff [7] proposes Rank-SVM algorithm by introducing loss function to support vector machine (SVM). Zhang and Zhou [8] proposed an improved ML-KNN algorithm based on k-nearest neighbor algorithm to solve the multi-label classification problem. Li [9] proposed a new joint learning algorithm, which propagates the feedback of the current label to the classifier of the subsequent label, and achieves good results in text multi-label classification.

With the successful application of deep learning in image and speech fields in recent years, some neural network models are also applied to multi-label learning tasks. Zhang and Zhou [10] proposed BP-MLL model, which uses a new loss function in the fully connected neural network. Experiments show that the neural network model can capture the characteristics of multi-label tasks. Chen [11] uses a combination of CNN and RNN to represent the semantic information of the text and the higher-order features between the labels. Baker [12] will map to the rows of co-occurrence labels to initialize the final hidden layer of the CNN to improve the model effect. Yang [13] put forward that multi-label classification task should be regarded as sequence generation problem, and used a new sequence generation model with a new decoder structure to solve the multi-label classification problem, and achieved good results.

3 VDIF-M: Multi-label Classification of Vehicle Defect Information Collection Based on Seq2seq Model

This section will introduce the details of the method used in this paper to solve the problem of multi-label classification of vehicle complaint data. An overview of the method used in this paper is given in Subsect. 3.1. In Subsect. 3.2, some preparatory work is described, including word vector training, data preprocessing and the extension of vehicle defect label library. Finally the details of seq2seq model structure used in this paper are present in Subsect. 3.3.

3.1 Model Architecture of VDIF-M

In the task of multi-label classification, we use L to represent the defect label library corresponding to the vehicle complaint text, which contains h class defect labels. The task of multi-label classification is to generate a set Y of corresponding labels for each complaint text x containing n words. Y is a subset of the label library L, and Y contains one or more labels like Ln.

An overview of our proposed model is Fig. 1. Firstly, in the embedding layer, we use the pre-trained word vector v_i to join the coding vector b_i in the defect label library to form x_i as the input of the seq2seq model. In the encoder layer, we use bi-directional LSTM to read x_i to get the hidden layer state vector h, and combine the attention mechanism to get the context vector c_t at time t. The decoder layer receives these vectors and predicts the label distribution vector v_l corresponding to the previous label, and then gets the distribution of the label sequence through softmax layer. According to the distribution, we can get the defect label sequence $L_1, L_2 \dots L_n$.

3.2 Defect Label Library Feature

The vehicle defect label library is composed of standardized vehicle defect names and corresponding typical defect descriptions. Since the embedding layer of the model used in this paper consists of two parts, one part is based on the word vector obtained by the pre-trained vehicle domain word vector model. And the other part reflects whether the key words in the defect description appear corresponding vehicle defect description directly. Considering that the complaint data come from different kinds of consumers of different cultural levels, different descriptions may appear for the same group of different users of the defect, we expands the synonym of the existing defect label library in this part. After analysis, the defect description is usually composed of secondary assembly and specific defect description, such as "door rust". The secondary assembly is mainly the name of the vehicle parts. We extend the nickname, abbreviation and common misnomer of vehicle parts by search engine. For the vehicle defect description part, we use the synonym extension tool synonyms [14] to extend this collection. We replace the word vector model of the toolkit with the pre-trained vehicle domain word

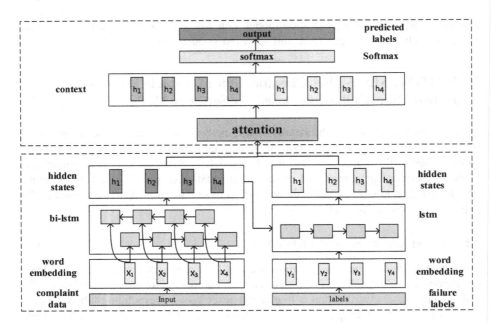

Fig. 1. VDIF-M model architecture

vector, that is to say, a group of synonyms is extended based on word2vec. Then the candidate words are selected by similarity of defect description. Finally, a defect label library with extended synonymous descriptions is obtained. In the embedding layer of the model, the representation of a word is divided into two parts, one is the word vector represented by the domain word vector model, and the other is the 32-bit defect coding feature bits transformed from the defect coding. For each word in the complaint text, if the current word belongs to the defect label library or the corresponding secondary assembly appears in the text, the word defect coding feature position of the complaint text is defect code, otherwise the defect coding bit of the word is '0000' (Table 1).

In order to capture the relationship between the defect labels corresponding to the vehicle complaint data, this paper first extracts the label data, each row corresponds to a set of defect labels of the complaint data, and converts the defect labels into codes according to the coding table of the vehicle defect label library. And then a vector v_1 which can reflect the distribution of defect labels is obtained by training word2vec word vector.

3.3   Seq2seq Model in Our Method

In this section, we introduce the seq2seq model used in this article in detail. The complete model includes the embedding layer, the encoder layer, the decoder layer, and the softmax layer. The basic idea of seq2seq is to use Bi-LSTM called encoder to read the input sentence, that is, the whole sentence is compressed into a fixed dimension of

Table 1. Vehicle defect label library code.

First assembly	Second assembly	Defect label	Defect code
车身	车门	车门生锈	5002
car body	doors	Rusting of doors	
车身	车门	车门缝隙	5007
car body	doors	doors gap	
发动机	进排气系统	排气管脱落	2104
engine	Intake and exhaust	pipes fall off	
发动机	点火与起动系统	喷油嘴故障	2205
engine	starting system	Injector fault	
制动系统	制动通用装置	回位不良	6310
brake	brake device	return fault	

the code, and then use another LSTM called decoder to read the code, the information of the sentence will be compressed into a vector. This model is also called the encoder-decoder model.

Embedding. In a deep learning task, the quality of the word vector determines the final effect of the neural network. Embedding layer mainly vectorize the complaint text S. That is, the words in the text S are represented by a real vector, which can reduce the input dimension and reduce the number of parameters of the neural network. On the other hand, the dense vector representation of the word vector layer can contain more semantic information. After using the word segmentation tool jieba [15] for the complaint text S, a sequence of n words is formed and denoted by w = (w_1, w_2 ... w_n). In the process of word segmentation, in order to improve the accuracy of word segmentation, the vehicle domain dictionary constructed in our previous published paper [16] is used as the user-defined dictionary. The word2vec model proposed by Mikolov [17] is used to construct a pre-trained word vector model based on the vehicle domain corpus. The model forms n*d embedding matrix, where n denotes the number of words in the dictionary and d denotes the dimension of the word vector. As described in the previous section, for the word w in complaint text, label feature vector $\vec{wd}_i$ is constructed by searching whether the word in the text is the keyword of the vehicle defect label library. The purpose of this process is to capture label library features at the word embedding. The expression of the i_{th} word x_i in the complaint text is as follows:

$$\vec{x}_i = \left[\vec{wv}_i; \vec{wd}_i \right] \tag{1}$$

Where $\vec{wv}_i$ is the word vector representation of the i_{th} word in the complaint text based on the pre-trained word2vec model, $\vec{x}_i$ is composed of $\vec{wv}_i$ and $\vec{wd}_i$ splices.

Encoder Layer. In the encoder layer, we use a recurrent neural network bidirectional LSTM [18] to read the text information in order from the front and back two directions, and calculate the hidden layer vector h_i for each word w in the text. Each word corresponds to the hidden state vector h, which includes the state vectors in the two directions $\vec{h}_i$ and $\overleftarrow{h}_i$ representing the semantic information centered on i^{th} word. The concealed state vector h is composed of the state vectors in the two directions. The calculation process is as follows:

$$\vec{h}_i = \overrightarrow{lstm}\left(\vec{h}_{i-1}, x_i\right) \tag{2}$$

$$\overleftarrow{h}_i = \overleftarrow{lstm}\left(\overleftarrow{h}_{i-1}, x_i\right) \tag{3}$$

$$h_i = [\vec{h}_i; \overleftarrow{h}_i] \tag{4}$$

Attention Mechanism. When predicting defect labels, the complaint text may contain information that is not relevant to the defect label. Considering that different words have different effects on prediction labels, we use seq2seq model with attention mechanism to find out the hidden state of encoder and decoder through attention connection. The decoder searches the hidden state of encoder at every step of decoding by using the hidden state of encoder as the input of query calculating a weight related to the query input at each location of the input, according to this weight, the hidden state of each position is weighted to obtain a context vector. In decoding the next word, the context vector and the pre-trained label distribution vector label stitching are used as additional information input to the decoder, which enables the decoder to read the information most relevant to the vehicle defect in the text rather than relying entirely on the hidden vector at the previous moment. The attention mechanism assigns the vector context$_i$ as follows:

$$e\left(h_i, s_j\right) = U_a tanh\left(V_a h_i + W_a s_j\right) \tag{5}$$

$$\alpha_{i,j} = \frac{\exp\left(e\left(h_i, s_j\right)\right)}{\sum_{k=1}^{m} \exp(e(h_i, s_k))} \tag{6}$$

$$context_i = \sum_{i=1}^{m} \alpha_{i,j} h_i \tag{7}$$

Where V_a, W_a, U_a are weight parameters and h$_i$ is the hidden state.

Decoder Layer. In a decode layer, in order to capture the relationship between defect labels, we use the vector representation of the previous label based on the pre-trained label distribution vector and the context vector, and use the LSTM in the recurrent neural network. The decoder receives the hidden layer state s_{t-1} at time-step t, the context vector c_{t-1} and the label distribution vector $l(y_{t-1})$ from the attention mechanism, respectively, and inputs them to the decoder. The vector $l(y_{t-1})$ reflects the overall distribution of labels. Adding this vector to the decoding process can integrate the relationship between labels. The decoder calculates the hidden state vector s as follows:

$$s_t = LSTM(s_{t-1}, [l(y_{t-1}); c_{t-1}]) \tag{8}$$

Softmax. The softmax layer is the final prediction layer, and a defect label y_t with the highest probability is generated by the output state vector s_t from the decoder.

$$y_t = \left[\frac{\exp(V_l)}{\sum_{p=1}^{L} \exp(V_p)} \ for \ l \ in \ L \right] \tag{9}$$

Where L represents the vehicle defect label library and m_t is the mask vector. y_t is the label probability distribution at time-step t predicted by the model.

4 Experimental Results and Analysis

In this section, we evaluate our proposed methods on datasets. First, we introduced the datasets, evaluation metrics and experimental details. Then we make analysis and discussions about the experimental results.

4.1 Experimental Datasets

DPAC Corpus. This dataset is provided by the defect information collection system of Defective Product Administrative Center. It contains more than 130,000 pieces of vehicle defect complaint information, of which about 22,747 pieces of data contain one or more defect labels marked by experts. These defect labels are from the Vehicle Defect Label Library of the Defective Product Administrative Center, which contains 934 defect labels. The number of defect label and data sample is listed in Table 2.

Table 2. DPAC corpus Statistical tables

The number of label	1	2	3	>=4
22747	16351	4991	1183	222
percent label	71%	23%	5%	1%

AUTO Corpus. We build a new large dataset form a vehicle complain website by crawler system. It contains more than 200,000 descriptions of complaints about defects in vehicles. All data is labeled by experts. These defect labels come from the vehicle defect classification label library of the vehicle complain website, with a total of 402 defect labels. The number of defect label and data sample is listed in Table 3.

Table 3. AUTO corpus Statistical tables

The number of label	1	2	3	>=4
200000	136701	44814	12871	5601
percent label	68%	22%	6%	4%

4.2 Evaluation Metrics

Following the previous work, we uses Hamming-loss [19] and Micro-F1 [20] which are the most commonly used indicators in multi-label classification tasks.

Hamming-Loss. You can evaluate the difference between the predicted result sequence and the actual label sequence for the data in the test set. The higher the similarity between the two sequences, the lower the value of Hamming-loss, which means the better the result.

$$hamming - loss(h) = \frac{1}{p} \sum_{i=1}^{p} \frac{1}{Q} |h(x_i) \Delta Y_i| \tag{10}$$

Where Δ represents the symmetric difference between two sets, which is used to measure the degree of difference between the two sets.

Micro-F1. This is a micro-average, based on the basic quantities in the binary classification problem including true negative number (TP), false negative number (FP), true positive number (TN), false positive number (FN) evaluation indicators. Firstly, we calculate the average of the basic quantities of all labels, and then use the average to calculate the performance indicators of the classification.

4.3 Experimental Details

In this paper, the most representative multi-label classification algorithms are selected as baseline, and the comparative experiments are carried out in large-scale corpora (AUTO corpus) and small-scale corpora (DPAC corpus).

This experiment uses the pre-trained vehicle domain word vector model as word representation, for words that are not in the vocabulary, replace them with 'unks'. In order to avoid the influence of the vehicle brand on the prediction result, this paper makes synonymous substitution of the description of the vehicle brand and the vehicle system, and also makes corresponding substitution of the figures in the complaint text. After statistical analysis, the first 600 words of the complaint text are intercepted as input, and the part exceeding the length of the complaint text will be discarded. Referring to the conclusion of paper [13], the frequency of the defect labels corresponding to the complaint text in the training data is sorted. The hidden state vector of the encoder and decoder is set to 300 and 600, and the number of LSTM layers of the encoder and decoder is set to 2. In the training phase, the loss function is the cross-entropy loss function. We use the beam search algorithm [21] to find the highest ranked prediction path at the inference time. This prediction paths ending with the 'eos' are added to the set of candidate paths. The length of the beam search is set to 5. In the training process, Adam optimizer is used to minimize the cross-entropy loss function.

4.4 Baselines

In order to compare the performance of different multi-label classification methods, the following five representative methods are implemented on the two dataset.

Binary Relevance (BR) [3]: transforms each label in multiple labels into a single label classification problem.

Classifier Chains (CC) [5]: transforms the multi-label classification problem into a single label classification problem, which introduces the relational information between labels in a chain structure of one label.

Label Powerset (LP) [6]: treats every possible label set combination as a new label, transforming the problem into a multi-classification problem with a single label.

CNN-RNN [11]: Global and local text semantics and label dependencies are captured using CNN and RNN, and label sequences are predicted using RNN.

The Sequence Generation Model (SGM) [13]: transforms the multi-label classification problem into a sequence generation problem, and generates a label sequence using a global-embedding decoder architecture.

We implement the BR and CC algorithms using the open source multi-label classification toolkit Scikit-Multilearn [22], and use Support Vector Machine (SVM) as the basic classifier in these algorithms.

4.5 Experimental Results and Analysis

Based on pre-trained vehicle domain word vectors, five typical multi-label classification methods are tested on two vehicle complaint datasets. The experimental results are shown in the following Table 4, Figs. 2 and 3, where BR stands for Binary Relevance algorithm, CC stands for Classifier Chains algorithm, BF stands for feature extraction based on vehicle defect labels, and LE stands for adding defect labels distribution vectors at the decoding layer.

Table 4. Label prediction results comparison

Corpus	AUTO		DPAC	
Metrics	Hamming loss	Micro-F1	Hamming loss	Micro-F1
BR-BF	0.0106	0.5996	0.0529	0.5517
BR-W2V	0.0038	0.6301	0.0319	0.6103
CC-BF	0.0087	0.6176	0.0473	0.5885
CC- W2V	0.0031	0.6565	0.0297	0.6237
LP-BF	0.0097	0.6028	0.0476	0.5904
LP-W2V	0.0032	0.6468	0.0415	0.6175
CNN-RNN	0.0031	0.6971	0.0178	0.6412
SGM	**0.0027**	**0.7203**	**0.0125**	**0.6563**
Seq2seq	0.0028	0.7195	0.0129	0.6511

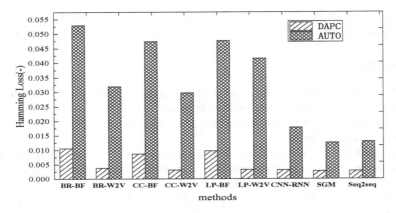

Fig. 2. Comparison of hamming loss

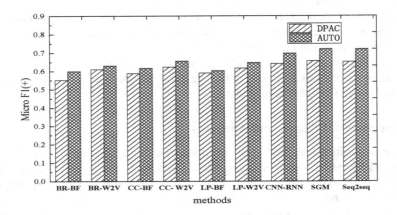

Fig. 3. Comparison of Micro-F1

In BR, CC, and LP algorithms, for a complaint text containing m words, the pre-trained domain word vector model is used to obtain the word representation vector of each word, and then the average value is obtained to represent the complaint text.

The following conclusions can be drawn from the above experiment results:

(1) Neural network based methods are better than those using traditional multi-label classification, which shows that the neural network can recognize text information better and improve the accuracy of classification in multi-label classification.

(2) In the traditional machine learning multi-label classification method, the selection of text features has a great influence on the prediction results. From the table, it can be seen that for the same method, the result of using pre-trained domain word vectors is better than that of using label-only database features to express the complaint text, which verifies the necessity of pre-trained domain word vector model.

(3) Compared with the BR algorithm and the CC algorithm, the Classifier Chains algorithm performs better because the multiple defect descriptions contained in the vehicle complaint data are generally related to each other, and the CC algorithm takes into account the relationship between the labels. Because LP algorithm transforms the problem of multi-label classification into the problem of multi-class classification in single-label learning, and there are many kinds of multi-label combinations in the data analysis and statistics, LP algorithm is not suitable to solve this problem, and the experimental results also prove this point.

(4) Compared with CNN-RNN model, seq2seq model performs better in multi-classification of Chinese complaint texts. The reason is that seq2seq model reads the semantic information before and after each word in the complaint texts through Bi-LSTM, and pays attention to the words related to the predicted failure results through attention mechanism. CNN-RNN focuses on the high-order relevance of labels, but the recognition of the semantic information of the text itself is insufficient.

(5) Comparing SGM model with seq2seq model with attention mechanism, the input of SGM model and seq2seq model is based on pre-trained vehicle domain word vector model, and the value of word vector is allowed to change during the training process, because SGM model is based on seq2seq model with mask module and global embedded information (global embedded) in the decoder part. Experiments show that the mask module and global embedding vector are equally effective in vehicle complaint dataset. In analyzing the classification results of seq2seq model, we also find that the prediction results of the same article text contain some duplicate labels.

Based on the above conclusions, we add the feature of extended vehicle defect label library (CF) to the input layer of seq2seq model with attention mechanism. Considering the diversity of vehicle defect label combinations, a label distribution vector (LE) of each vector is obtained by using the training method of word2vec based on the defect label text of all data. A comparative experiment was carried out in two datasets. The results are shown in Table 5, Figs. 4 and 5.

Table 5. Label prediction results comparison

Corpus	AUTO		DPAC	
Metrics	Hamming loss	Micro-F1	Hamming loss	Micro-F1
Seq2seq	0.0028	0.7195	0.0129	0.6511
SGM	0.0027	0.7203	0.0125	0.6563
Seq2seq+CF	0.0026	0.7212	0.0121	0.6532
Seq2seq+CF+LE (VDIF-M)	**0.0025**	**0.7363**	**0.0100**	**0.6624**

The experimental results in the table show that the label library features added have obvious effect on the auto dataset, and the reason may be that there are fewer defect categories in the vehicle quality network, but there are more defect labels in the dataset of DPAC corpus, so the effect of adding label library features is not obvious. After the

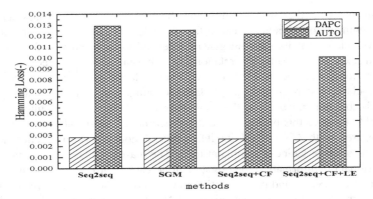

Fig. 4. Comparison of Hamming-loss

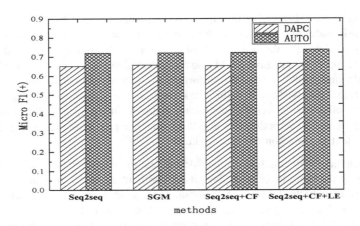

Fig. 5. Comparison of Micro-F1

label distribution vector is added to the decoder layer, it is improved both in two datasets. Comparing with the SGM model, the experimental results show that the proposed method is superior to the SGM model in two datasets, because the our methods adds defect label features suitable for vehicle complaint data, and uses the pre-trained domain word vector model at the same time.

Table 6 shows some instances of a multi-label classification that uses the different sequence models to identify only the "Engine Abnormal Noise" label in the defect description. Our proposed VDIF-M model can not only recognize the "engine-abnormal noise" label, but also generate the "Body Vibration" label according to the words "vehicle" and "jitter". This is because the extended fault description synonymous label library contains synonymous relationships between "vehicle resonance" and "vehicle jitter", which verify the model proposed in this paper can solve the multi-label classification problem of some instances by adding defect label features.

Table 6. Multi-label classification instances

defect description	VDIF-M	seq2seq	correct label
发动机有明显异响，我不懂车都能听出来，而且车辆抖动，去店里检查，说什么都正常，抖动也正常。	发动机-异响 车身附件及电器-车身共振	发动机-异响	发动机-异响 车身附件及电器-车身共振
The engine is obviously abnormal, don't understand the car can hear, and the car jitter, go to the store to check, say what is normal, jitter is normal.	Abnormal engine noise Body Vibration	Abnormal engine noise	Abnormal engine noise Body Vibration
挂d挡速度上升到40时发动机转速达到4000，但车速不上升；挂r挡后退无力踩住刹车时，车身抖动严重。去4s店检测，说是变速箱的3-5模块损坏，要大修变速箱。	发动机-无法提速 变速器-电脑板故障	发动机-无法提速 变速器-异响	发动机-无法提速 变速器-电脑板故障
When the speed of the gearbox increases to 40, the speed of the engine reaches 4000, but the speed of the car does not rise; when the gearbox is unable to step on the brake, the body shakes seriously. Go to 4S shop to check that the 3-5 module of the gearbox is damaged, it is necessary to overhaul the gearbox.	Engine Unable to Speed up Transmission-Computer Board Failure	Engine Unable to Speed up Transmission Abnormal engine noise	Engine Unable to Speed up Transmission Computer Board Failure

5 Conclusion and Future Work

The multi-classification task of vehicle complaint data is of great significance in the process of vehicle defect recall. In this paper, we propose a multi-label classification method based on seq2seq model named VMIF-M to generate the defect label of vehicle complaint data. Firstly, the synonymous extension of defect description is made based on the existing defect classification system and the corpus related to vehicle complaint is collected to train a word vector model of vehicle domain. Then the word vector and defect label feature splicing are used as the input of the encoder, and then the encoder and decoder are connected through attention mechanism to focus on the words closely related to the defect label. Finally, the label distribution vector is added to the decoder, and the final classification prediction result is obtained through the softmax layer. This method avoids a lot of manual data processing. Experimental results show that the proposed methods outperform the baselines. The Macro-F1 reached 73% and 66% on the AUTO corpus and DPAC corpus, respectively. Through the analysis of the experimental data, we notice that the quality and size of the defect label library have a great influence on the prediction results. In the future work, the standardization of the vehicle defect in the process of vehicle recall will be used to improve the identification results of the complaint data.

Acknowledgments. This work is supported by National Natural Science Foundation of China under Grants No. 61671070, National Science Key Lab Fund project 6142006190301, National Language Committee of China under Grants ZDI135-53, and Project of Three Dimension Energy Consumption Saving Strategies in Cloud Storage System in Promoting the Developing University Intension–Disciplinary Cluster No. 5211910940.

References

1. Defective Product Administrative Center Homepage. http://www.dpac.gov.cn. Accessed 24 Jan 2019
2. Boutell, M.R., Luo, J., Shen, X.: Learning multi-label scene classification. Pattern Recogn. **37**(9), 1757–1771 (2004)
3. Zhang, M.L., Wu, L.: Lift: multi-label learning with label-specific features. In: International Joint Conference on Artificial Intelligence, pp. 1609–1614. AAAI Press (2017)
4. Tsoumakas, G., Katakis, I.: Multi-label classification: an overview. Int. J. Data Warehous. Min. **3**(3), 1–13 (2006)
5. Read, J., Pfahringer, B., Holmes, G.: Classifier chains for multi-label classification. Mach. Learn. **85**(3), 333 (2011)
6. Clare, A., King, R.D.: Knowledge discovery in multi-label phenotype data. In: De Raedt, L., Siebes, A. (eds.) PKDD 2001. LNCS (LNAI), vol. 2168, pp. 42–53. Springer, Heidelberg (2001). https://doi.org/10.1007/3-540-44794-6_4
7. Elisseeff, A., Weston, J.: A kernel method for multi-labelled classification (2002)
8. Zhang, M.L., Zhou, Z.H.: ML-KNN: a lazy learning approach to multi-label learning. Pattern Recogn. **40**(7), 2038–2048 (2007)
9. Li, L., Wang, H., Sun, X., et al.: Multi-label text categorization with joint learning predictions-as-features method. In: Conference on Empirical Methods in Natural Language Processing, pp. 835–839 (2015)
10. Zhang, M.L., Zhou, Z.H.: Multi-label neural networks with applications to functional genomics and text categorization. IEEE Trans. Knowl. Data Eng. **18**(10), 1338–1351 (2006)
11. Chen, G., Ye, D., Xing, Z., et al.: Ensemble application of convolutional and recurrent neural networks for multi-label text categorization. In: International Joint Conference on Neural Networks, pp. 2377–2383. IEEE (2017)
12. Baker, S., Korhonen, A.: Initializing neural networks for hierarchical multi-label text classification. In: BioNLP, pp. 307–315 (2017)
13. Yang, P., Sun, X., Li, W., et al.: SGM: sequence generation model for multi-label classification (2018)
14. Chinese synonyms Toolkit. https://github.com/huyingxi/Synonyms. Accessed 24 Jan 2019
15. Chinese Word Segmentation Tool. https://pypi.org/project/jieba/. Accessed 24 Jan 2019
16. Zhang, Y., Li, B., Lv, X.: Research on domain term dictionary construction based on Chinese Wikipedia. Image Processing, Computing and Big Data (2018)
17. Mikolov, T., Chen, K., Corrado, G., et al.: Efficient estimation of word representations in vectorspace. arXiv preprint arXiv:1301.3781 (2013)
18. Graves, A.: 2005 Special Issue: Framewise phoneme classification with bidirectional LSTM and other neural network architectures. Elsevier Science Ltd. (2005)
19. Schapire, R.E., Singer, Y.: Improved boosting algorithms using confidence-rated predictions. Mach. Learn. **37**(3), 297–336 (1999)

20. Manning, C.D., Raghavan, P., Schütze, H., et al.: Introduction to Information Retrieval, vol. 1. Cambridge University Press, Cambridge (2008)
21. Wiseman, S., Rush, A.M.: Sequence-to-sequence learning as beam search optimization. CoRR, abs/1606.02960 (2016)
22. Szymański, P.: A scikit-based python environment for performing multi-label classification. arXiv preprint arXiv:1702.01460 (2017)

Self-similarity Analysis and Application of Network Traffic

Yan Xu[1], Qianmu Li[1,2(✉)], and Shunmei Meng[1]

[1] School of Computer Science and Engineering,
Nanjing University of Science and Technology, Nanjing, China
{xuyan, qianmu, mengshuanmei}@njust.edu.cn
[2] Intelligent Manufacturing Department, Wuyi University, Wuyi, China

Abstract. Network traffic prediction is not only an academic problem, but also a concern of industry and network performance department. Efficient prediction of network traffic is helpful for protocol design, traffic scheduling, detection of network attacks, etc. In this paper, we propose a network traffic prediction method based on the Echo State Network. In the first place we prove that the network traffic data are self-similar by means of the calculation of Hurst exponent of each traffic time series, which indicates that we can predict network traffic utilizing nonlinear time series models. Then Echo State Network is applied for network traffic forecasting. Furthermore, to avoid the weak-conditioned problem, grid search algorithm is used to optimize the reservoir parameters and coefficients. The dataset we perform experiments on are large-scale network traffic data at different time scale. They come from three provinces and are provided by ZTE Corporation. The result shows that our approach can predict network traffic efficiently, which is also a verification of the self-similarity analysis.

Keywords: Network traffic · Self-similarity · Echo State Network

1 Introduction

Traffic prediction is the foundation of network performance analysis. It provides essential evidence for network design and planning. Designing an efficient and accurate model for network traffic prediction can reduce network congestion frequency and improve network communication quality. Either short-term or long-term prediction is beneficial to network control and resource adjustment. By analyzing and forecasting historical traffic data and adjusting the allocation of network resources accordingly, operators can be aware of the future situation of the network in advance. It has a profound impact on the development of key technologies such as network planning, resource allocation and network security.

There are a great number of prediction models for network traffic data and they can be classified into statistical analysis models and machine learning methods [1]. Autoregressive integrated moving average (ARIMA) is a typical statistical analysis model [2, 3], which is the combination of autoregressive and moving average models. Since ARIMA is a linear time series model, some improvements are made to capture

Y. Yin et al. (Eds.): MobiCASE 2019, LNICST 290, pp. 112–125, 2019.
https://doi.org/10.1007/978-3-030-28468-8_9

the non-linearity of network traffic. Zhou et al. [2] combined ARIMA model with GARCH, non-linear model. Shu et al. [3] proposed a seasonal ARIMA model to explore the cyclical patterns of traffic data. With the rapid growth of network and complexity of traffic data, more and more researchers have placed emphasis on machine learning models, especially neural networks [1]. A hybrid ARIMA-ANN model was proposed in [4] to forecast time series data. Three methods: ARIMA, Holt-Winters and a novel neural network ensemble (NNE) approach, were performed on multi-scale internet traffic forecasting and the results showed the advantage of NNE [5]. Multi-layer Perception (MLP) is widely used for network traffic prediction [6–8]. [9] performed SVR, the regression variant of SVM, on heterogeneous Internet traffic collected at the POP of an ISP network. Nie et al. [10] decomposed the network traffic into low-pass and high-pass component, where the low-pass component describe the long-range dependence and the high-pass component gusty and irregular fluctuations of network traffic. As for prediction, a deep belief network and a Gaussian model were utilized for respectively. Poupart et al. [11] aimed at predicting the size of flow in order to detect elephant flow (very large flows). Three machine learning techniques: neural networks, Gaussian Process Regression and Online Bayesian Moment Matching (oBMM), were combined with routing, where GPR achieved the best improvements for elephant flow detection.

However, the most of the models focus on the non-linearity of traffic data to improve the accuracy but ignore the importance of self-similarity. Based on the large-scale network traffic dataset provided by ZTE Corporation, this paper analyzes the characteristics of the dataset, and performs pre-processing on the dataset to obtain suitable traffic data of each node at different time scales. Then by plotting the trend of traffic over time and calculating the Hurst exponent value, it proved that the traffic data of the three provinces provided by ZTE has self-similarity, suddenness and periodicity. Finally we can predict the data using a nonlinear time series. Because of the nonlinear characteristic of network traffic prediction, we utilize Echo State Network (ESN) to learn the output connection weight matrix. The ridge regression learning algorithm is applied instead of traditional linear regression algorithm so that weak-condition can be avoided. Meanwhile the gird search algorithm is used to optimize the reservoir parameters and regularization coefficients.

The reminding portion of the paper is organized as follows. Section 2 clarifies the definition of self-similarity and the estimation of Hurst exponent. Section 3 introduces the structure of Echo State Network, along with parameters to be estimated and the training process. Section 4 focuses on the experiments based on network traffic data from three provinces. Section 5 is the conclusion.

2   Self-similarity

Self-similarity [12–15] means that local structure is partly consistent with the overall structure. A self-similar process is a stochastic process which is statistically constant. In this regard, the concept of fractal to the random process is introduced. Network traffic has long-range dependence (LRD) as opposed to processes with short-range dependence like Poisson process. From a physical point of view, LRD [16, 17] is a phenomenon, i.e. the sustainability and suddenness of a self-similar process exist on all time scales, also known as multi-scale behavioral features [18, 19].

Definition 2.1: $\forall \lambda > 0$, we say that a stochastic process $\{X(t), t \geq 0\}$ is self-similar if $X(t) \overset{d}{=} \lambda^{-H} X(\lambda t)$, where $H \in (0.5, 1)$ refers to Hurst exponent or self-similarity parameter. $\overset{d}{=}$ means that the equation is correct in finite dimensions.

According to Definition 2.1, $\{X(t), t \geq 0\}$ with self-similarity has following properties:

Property 2.1: Time series $\{X(t), t \geq 0\}$ has time-scale invariance, or when $\{X(\lambda t), t \geq 0\}$ is normalized by λ^{-H}, they have the same structure.

Property 2.2: $E\{X(t)\} = 0$

Property 2.3: $E\{|X(t)^q|\} = E\{|X(1)^q|\} t^{qH}$

Table 1. Comparison of commonly used estimation methods for Hurst parameters

	Self-similarity judgement	Graphical	Online	Complexity	Others
Variance-time plot	Yes	Yes	No	$O(n)$	Lots of data required in advance
R/S plot	Yes	Yes	No	$O(n^2)$	Independent of edge distribution
Periodogram	Yes	Yes	No	$O(n\log n)$	Set suitable cutoff frequency at first
Whittle estimator	Yes	No	No	$O(n^2)$	A quantitative method with high complexity
Wavelet analysis	Yes	No	No	$O(n\log n)$	Accurate estimation

The Hurst exponent [20, 21], denoted by H, is an important parameter to characterize self-similarity. A self-similar process will degenerate towards a Poisson process if $H = 0.5$. A value of H in the interval (0.5, 1) refers to positive autocorrelation, i.e. the random variety series is self-similar and the degree grows with the increase of H. A value of H in the interval (0, 0.5) indicates negative autocorrelation, i.e. the series is not self-similar. There are five commonly used and robust estimation methods and we compare them in detail as shown in Table 1. The first three methods are graphical. The estimation of Hurst exponent is the slope of the line, which is plotted by fitting statistical sample points. Among the three methods, the variance-time plot method is less robust and the periodogram method requires determination of the appropriate cutoff frequency. The whittle estimator can only estimate short-range dependent data, rather than the long-range dependent data and it has high complexity. Wavelet analysis can estimate the Hurst parameter more accurately while the confidence interval of the parameter cannot be obtained and the calculation is more complicated. In summary, we select R/S plot to estimate Hurst exponent.

R/S plot is widely used to estimate Hurst exponent. At the beginning, we need to divide a time series of length N into series of length N, N/2, N/4, etc. Then for a time series $\{X_1, X_2, \ldots, X_n\}$, calculate its rescaled range R/S:

1. Calculate the mean: $m = \frac{1}{n} \sum_{i=1}^{n} X_i$, where n is the length of the time series, which is the network traffic;

2. Generate a deviation series $\{Y_1, Y_2, \ldots, Y_n\}$: $Y_t = X_t - m, t = 1, 2, \ldots, n$

3. Calculate the range R: $R = max(Y_1, Y_2, \ldots, Y_n) - min(Y_1, Y_2, \ldots, Y_n)$

4. Calculate the standard deviation S: $S = \sqrt{\frac{1}{n} \sum_{i=1}^{n} (X_i - m)^2}$

5. Get the rescaled range R/S.

3   Echo State Network

Echo State Network (ESN) [22–24] is a new type of recursive neural network. An ESN is made up of an input layer, a hidden layer (dynamic reservoir) and an output layer. It can also remember data by adjusting weights inside the network. The dynamic reservoir contains a large number of sparsely connected neurons, which keep the state of the system and has a capacity of short-term memory.

3.1   Structure of ESN

Echo State Network is a new type of three-layer recurrent neural network. As shown in Fig. 1, an ESN consists of three parts: input layer, hidden layer (reservoir) and output layer. The number of neurons is K, N and L respectively. $W^{in} \in \mathbb{R}^{N \times M}$ and $W^{out} \in \mathbb{R}^{L \times (K+N+L)}$ are the input and output weight matrices respectively as shown in Fig. 1. $W \in \mathbb{R}^{N \times N}$ represents concatenation of neurons inside the reservoir. $W^{back} \in \mathbb{R}^{N \times L}$ is a feedback matrix from the output layer at one moment to the reservoir at the next.

The hidden layer is also known as a dynamic reservoir since it is made up of many dynamic neurons which are connected. The reservoir is the core structure of ESN. Like a human brain, it consists of many neurons. These neurons are connected to constitute a large-scale and complex network so that they can transfer information inside. It can constantly learn and deal with stimuli from the outside world. Considering the condition that information cannot be transferred from one neuron to another, we have weights among neurons in the range [−1, 1]. The weight will be 0 if there is no connection between the two neurons, otherwise it will be a non-zero value in the interval [−1, 1]. A positive weight results in promotion while a negative weight causes neutralization.

Reservoir connection matrix is sparse. To guarantee the reservoir's echo effects, the spectral radius of W should be less than 1. Echo effects refer to the reservoir neuron's short-memory of the states of input traffic data.

3.2   Key Parameters of Reservoir

The reservoir, a recursive structure of randomly generated, large-scale and sparse connections, is the core structure of ESN. It is necessary to set appropriate values for reservoir's key parameters to achieve good performance. Reservoir's key parameters include: spectral radius (SR), size of reservoir (N), input scale (IS) and sparse degree (SD).

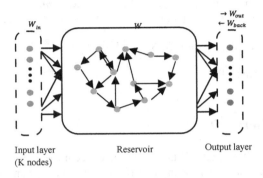

Input layer   Reservoir   Output layer
(K nodes)

Fig. 1. Structure of Echo State Network

- Spectral radius (SR). The feature value, with the largest absolute value, of the connection weight matrix, denoted by λ_{max}. The state of reservoir neurons can stay decaying to keep the network stable if $\lambda_{max} < 1$.
- Size of reservoir (N). The number of neurons in the reservoir. The size of reservoir is closely related to the number of samples to be predicted, which has a great impact on the prediction. There are two ways to set the value of N. The first method is based on the complexity of the problem, which is gradually increasing the value of N; the second method is to select a value in the range $[T/10, T/2]$, where T refers to the size of the training set.
- Input scale (IS). A scale factor that needs to be multiplied by the input signal before it connects neurons inside reservoir, i.e. a certain scaling of the input signal. With a nonlinear time series, the IS is larger.
- Sparse degree (SD). The connection among neurons inside reservoir. Not all neurons have connections between them. SD represents the number of connected neurons out of N, i.e. $SD = \frac{n}{N}$, where n is the number of connected neurons. With a value $SD \in [5\%, 10\%]$, the reservoir can maintain its dynamic characteristics.

3.3   Training

W^{in}, W and W^{back} are randomly initialized at the beginning and they are unchanged during the training and predicting process, which means that we only need to train the weight matrix W^{out}. Linear regression algorithm is applied to calculate W^{out}. State sequences of input, output and reservoir at moment n are defined as follows:

Definition 3.1: Suppose that the ESN has K input nodes and L output nodes, then the input and output vectors are $u(n) = (u_1(n), \ldots, u_k(n))^T$ and $y(n) = (y_1(n), \ldots, y_L(n))^T$ respectively. $W^{in} = (w_{ij}^{in})_{N \times K}$ is the input connection weight matrix, $W = (w_{ij})_{N \times N}$ is reservoir weight matrix and $W^{out} = (w_{ij}^{out})_{L \times (K+N+L)}$ represents the output connection weight matrix.

The training process of ESN can be divided into two stages:

Step1. Data Sampling. Initiate the network state at the very beginning. Generally we set the initial state as 0, i.e. $x(0) = 0$.

- Training samples $\{u(t), t = 1, 2, \ldots, P\}$ are added to reservoir by the means of input connection weight matrix W^{in}.
- According to Eqs. 1 and 2, calculate states of reservoir and corresponding output $y(n)$. Equation 1 is known as an update equation of reservoir neurons. Equation 2 is an output state function, where n is the number of samples of input network. f and f_{out} are the neuron stimulation functions of the dynamic reservoir and output layer respectively. In general, $f = tanh$, $f_{out} = Sigmoig$. You can choose other functions according to specific situation.

$$x(n+1) = f\left(W^{in}u(n+1) + Wx(n) + W^{back}y(n)\right) \qquad (1)$$

$$y(n+1) = f_{out}(W^{out}(u(n+1), x(n+1))) \qquad (2)$$

Step 2. Computing Output Weights. Compute output weights W^{out} based on reservoir state matrix M and corresponding output matrix T collected at step 1, where $M \in \mathbb{R}^{m \times N}$, $T \in \mathbb{R}^{m \times 1}$. In general, the state of reservoir is not stable at the initial phase of step 1. In order to eliminate the influence of the initial transient of the network, data sampling will be simplified, which is removing some steps of sampling, and the value of m is the final number of sampling. Using linear regression method, weights are calculated according to $W^{out} = (M^{-1} \times T)^T$, where M^{-1} is the generalized inverse matrix of M.

4 Experiments and Analysis

4.1 Dataset

ZTE provided us with network traffic data of three provinces: A, B, and C. Traffic data of different time scales: second, hour, day, week, month, are stored in their own csv files. Taking the minute-scale traffic data from March 1st to March 31st for example, bytes of traffic data at several nodes at 100 fixed time points everyday are recorded and stored into 31 files respectively in a common format. Due to the space limitation, we will talk about minute-scale in detail.

After sampling, the size of traffic data in province A is 9.22 GB, along with 19.5 GB in province B and 50.7 GB in province C, which are apparently too large for the self-similarity analysis. It is necessary to find out the rules and apply corresponding pre-processing method to get suitable data.As described above, all the files have a common format with multiple fields, some of which are unnecessary. We need three fields: *noid* for Node number, *time* and *kb* for Bytes count and we can extract these data from the whole dataset. In this way we get a dataset that is much smaller.

There are abnormal values in the dataset after filtering. The abnormal values of field *kb* are −99999999 and 450000, which can also be considered as missing values. If the ratio of abnormal values at one node exceeds 15%, then delete the node. Otherwise, replace the abnormal values with the mean. Actually the ratio is either 0 or 100%.

Besides, the value of field *kb* is relatively large, so that normalization is required for speed. The deviation standard method is applied to scale data into the range [−1.0, 1.0].

4.2 Self-similarity Experiments

We shall observe the flow of traffic data by time in the first place. Considering the minute-scale traffic data, Fig. 2 demonstrates the traffic series of three provinces intuitively. It is easy to tell that all of them have periodicity. The periods all approximate to 96. Besides all of them has a big gap between the maximum value and the minimum value, which means that they are all unstable time series that have strong bursts. Since the local trends are some kind consistent to the overall trend, we can roughly tell that the minute-scale traffic data of each province have self-similarity.

In order to more rigorously judge whether the traffic sequence has self-similarity, the Hurst exponent estimation is applied. We adopt R/S plot to estimate Hurst exponent. Hurst values at different time scales of province A, B and C are shown in Tables 2, 3 and 4 respectively. We omit time scales week and month since the number of traffic data is smaller than 100, which is not persuasive. As what we said above, a time series is self-similar if its Hurst exponent is a value in range 0.5–1. It is proved that network traffic data of three provinces at different time scales is self-similar.

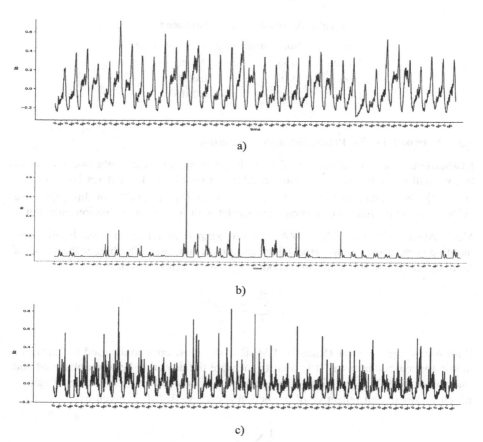

Fig. 2. Minute-scale traffic series: (a), (b), and (c) correspond to Province A, B and C respectively.

Table 2. Hurst values in Province A

Time scale	No. of traffic data	Value of Hurst
Minute	3456	0.8274
Hour	840	0.8335
Day	142	0.8430

Table 3. Hurst values in Province B

Time scale	No. of traffic data	Value of Hurst
Minute	3456	0.7189
Hour	840	0.737
Day	632	0.7511

Table 4. Hurst values in Province C

Time scale	No. of traffic data	Value of Hurst
Minute	3456	0.5755
Hour	816	0.6090
Day	784	0.7016

4.3 Network Traffic Prediction and Evaluation

Evaluation. Ahead of displaying the results of prediction, the evaluation indicators that we will use in this paper are introduced first. Considering test dataset $\{(x_1, y_1), \ldots, (x_m, y_m)\}$, the prediction for vector $(x_1, \ldots, x_m)^T$ is $(\hat{y}_1, \ldots, \hat{y}_m)^T$. In this paper, we evaluate the performance of a prediction model with following evaluation indicators.

Mean Absolute Error (MAE). MAE is also known as L1-norm loss. It offers an intuitive comparison among real values and prediction ones. The bigger the value of MAE is, the worse this prediction model perform. It can be given by:

$$\frac{1}{m} \sum_{i=1}^{m} |(y_i - \hat{y}_i)|$$

Root Mean Square Error (RMSE). RMSE is the most commonly used performance metric for regression tasks. It is used to measure the deviation between observed and true values. RMSE is sensitive to abnormally large or small errors in predicted values, which makes it well reflective of prediction accuracy. RMSE is given by:

$$\sqrt{\frac{1}{m} \sum_{i=1}^{m} (y_i - \hat{y}_i)^2}$$

R-square. R-square is used to describe how well the regression line fits the observations. It reflects the proportion of predictable dependent variables from the unpredictable ones. R-square can be used to describe how well the regression line fit the observations. A larger value of R^2 indicates a better performance of the prediction model. It is given by:

$$R^2(y, \hat{y}) = 1 - \frac{\sum_{i=1}^{m}(y_i - \hat{y}_i)^2}{\sum_{i=1}^{m}(y_i, \bar{y})^2} = 1 - \frac{\sum_{i=1}^{m}(y_i - \hat{y}_i)^2/m}{\sum_{i=1}^{m}(y_i, \bar{y})^2/m} = 1 - \frac{MSE(\hat{y}, y)}{Var(y)}$$

Experiment Result. We predict network traffic data of three provinces with GRID-ESN: finding parameters of ESN using the grid search algorithm, and make comparisons with Elman, SVR and ESN. The key parameters to be set includes: SD, N, SR and regularization factor χ. We set N = 1000. SR, SD and χ are determined by grid search algorithm. Their searching ranges are [0.01, 1], [0.01, 0.1] and [10^{-6}, 10^{-2}] respectively.

Prediction of Network Traffic in Province A. Parameter estimation of GRID-ESN: SR = 0.948, SD = 0.014 and χ = 0.01. The prediction comparison is shown in Fig. 3 and Table 5. From Fig. 3, we can find that ESN can fit the traffic data better than SVR and Elman, especially at the bursts. Besides, the average evaluation values of 30 experiments are shown in Table 5, where GRID-ESN get the smallest RMSE and MAE, and the biggest value of R-square.

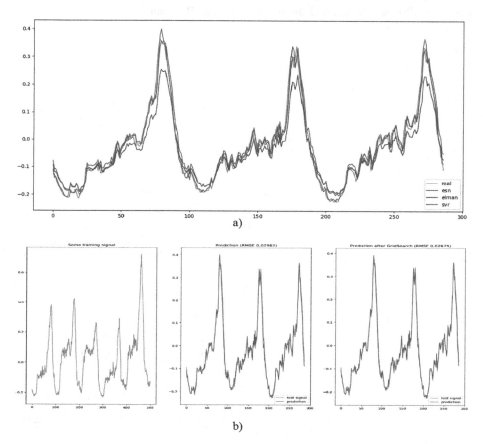

Fig. 3. Prediction comparison for traffic data in Province A: (a) is the prediction comparison among SVR, Elman and ESN; (b) is the prediction comparison between ESN and GRID-ESN

Table 5. Province A: RMSE/MAE/R-square value for ESN, Elman, SVR and GRID-ESN

	RMSE	MAE	R-square
ESN	0.03095	0.02181	0.95747
Elman	0.04237	0.03426	0.92041
SVR	0.03224	0.02643	0.95385
GRID-ESN	0.02673	0.02027	0.96827

Prediction of Network Traffic in Province B. Parameter estimation of GRID-ESN: SR = 0.864, SD = 0.045 and χ = 0.01. It is not sufficient to make a decision based on the regular traffic data, so that we select traffic data on holidays, which contain many bursts. The prediction comparison is shown in Fig. 4 and Table 6. As shown in Fig. 4, ESN is still better than SVR and Elman. Compare GRID-ESN with ESN in Fig. 4(b), GRID-ESN performs better, especially at the error at burst nodes. The average evaluation values of 30 experiments are shown in Table 6, where GRID-ESN get the smallest RMSE and MAE, and the biggest value of R-square.

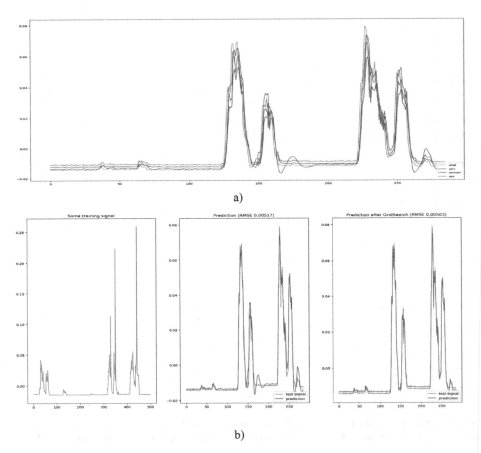

Fig. 4. Prediction comparison for traffic data in Province B: (a) is the prediction comparison among SVR, Elman and ESN; (b) is the prediction comparison between ESN and GRID-ESN

Prediction of Network Traffic in Province C. Parameter estimation of GRID-ESN: SR = 0.948, SD = 0.043 and χ = 0.01. We select a piece of data that is more unstable.

Table 6. Province B: RMSE/MAE/R-square value for ESN, Elman, SVR and GRID-ESN

	RMSE	MAE	R-square
ESN	0.00513	0.00267	0.90525
Elman	0.00676	0.00546	0.84214
SVR	0.00573	0.00425	0.88679
GRID-ESN	0.00503	0.00255	0.91251

The prediction comparison is shown in Fig. 5 and Table 7. From Fig. 5, we can find that ESN can fit the traffic data better than SVR and Elman. The evaluation of the four models including GRID-ESN is shown in Table 7, where GRID-ESN get the smallest RMSE and MAE, and the biggest value of R-square.

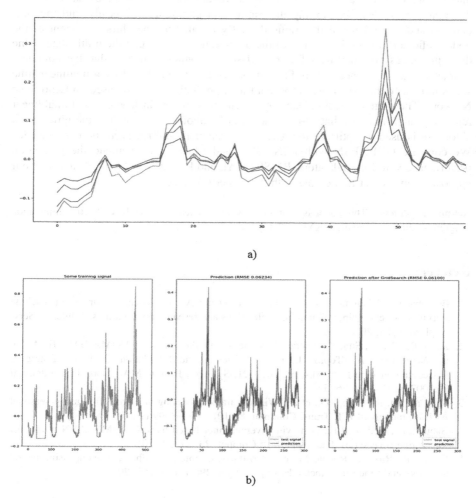

a)

b)

Fig. 5. Prediction comparison for traffic data in Province C: (a) is the prediction comparison among SVR, Elman and ESN; (b) is the prediction comparison between ESN and GRID-ESN

Table 7. Province C: RMSE/MAE/R-square value for ESN, Elman, SVR and GRID-ESN

	RMSE	MAE	R-square
ESN	0.06242	0.03933	0.63412
Elman	0.07233	0.05233	0.50864
SVR	0.06501	0.04610	0.60311
GRID-ESN	0.061	0.03866	0.65056

5   Conclusion

We observe and analyze the characteristics of network traffic dataset, find the law of data storage, and then perform a series of processing on data set, such as specification, integration, transformation and cleaning to obtain the traffic data of each node at different time scales. By plotting the traffic data graph, we can easily find the suddenness and periodicity of the traffic data. By calculating the Hurst exponent of the node traffic at different time scales of the dataset, it is proved that the traffic data of the three provinces provided by ZTE are self-similar, which indicated that the nonlinear characteristics of the network traffic time series can be predicted by a nonlinear time series model. In this paper we propose a traffic prediction method based on Echo State Network. The ridge regression learning algorithm is applied instead of traditional linear regression algorithm so that ill-condition can be avoided. Meanwhile the gird search algorithm is used to optimize the reservoir parameters and regularization coefficients. We compare GRID-ESN with ESN, SVR and Elman, and evaluate the prediction performance with four indicators: RMSE, MAE and R-Square, which indicates that our approach can predict traffic data with better performance.

Acknowledgement. This paper is supported by Postgraduate Research & Practice Innovation Program of Jiangsu Province (KYCX18_0439).

References

1. Boutaba, R., Salahuddin, M.A., Limam, N., et al.: A comprehensive survey on machine learning for networking: evolution, applications and research opportunities. J. Internet Serv. Appl. **9**(1), 16 (2018)
2. Zhou, B., He, D., Sun, Z.: Traffic Modeling and Prediction using ARIMA/GARCH Model. In: Nejat Ince, A., Topuz, E. (eds.) Modeling and Simulation Tools for Emerging Telecommunication Networks, pp. 101–121. Springer, Boston, MA (2006). https://doi.org/10.1007/0-387-34167-6_5
3. Shu, Y., Yu, M., Yang, O., et al.: Wireless traffic modeling and prediction using seasonal ARIMA models. IEICE Trans. Commun. **88**(10), 3992–3999 (2005)
4. Babu, C.N., Reddy, B.E.: A moving-average filter based hybrid ARIMA–ANN model for forecasting time series data. Appl. Soft Comput. **23**, 27–38 (2014)
5. Cortez, P., Rio, M., Rocha, M., et al.: Multi-scale Internet traffic forecasting using neural networks and time series methods. Expert. Syst. **29**(2), 143–155 (2012)

6. Eswaradass, A., Sun, X.H., Wu, M.: Network bandwidth predictor (NBP): a system for online network performance forecasting. In: Proceedings of 6th IEEE International Symposium on Cluster Computing and the Grid (CCGRID), p. 4–pp. IEEE (2006)
7. Chabaa, S., Zeroual, A., Antari, J.: Identification and prediction of internet traffic using artificial neural networks. J. Int. Learn. Syst. Appl. 2(03), 147 (2010)
8. Li, Y., Liu, H., Yang, W., Hu, D., Xu, W.: Inter-data-center network traffic prediction with elephant flows. In: NOMS 2016-2016 IEEE/IFIP Network Operations and Management Symposium, pp. 206–213. IEEE (2016)
9. Bermolen, P., Rossi, D.: Support vector regression for link load prediction. Comput. Netw. 53(2), 191–201 (2009)
10. Nie, L., Jiang, D., Yu, S., et al.: Network traffic prediction based on deep belief network in wireless mesh backbone networks. In: 2017 IEEE Wireless Communications and Networking Conference (WCNC), pp. 1–5. IEEE (2017)
11. Poupart, P., Chen, Z., Jaini, P., et al.: Online flow size prediction for improved network routing. In: 2016 IEEE 24th International Conference on Network Protocols (ICNP), pp. 1–6. IEEE (2016)
12. Song, C., Havlin, S., Makse, H.A.: Self-similarity of complex networks. Nature 433(7024), 392 (2005)
13. Angeles Serrano, M., Krioukov, D., Boguná, M.: Self-similarity of complex networks and hidden metric spaces. Phys. Rev. Lett. 100(7), 078701 (2008)
14. Crovella, M.E., Bestavros, A.: Self-similarity in World Wide Web traffic: evidence and possible causes. IEEE/ACM Trans. Networking 5(6), 835–846 (1997)
15. Park, K., Willinger, W.: Self-Similar Network Traffic and Performance Evaluation. Wiley, New York (2000)
16. Brockwell, A.E.: Likelihood-based analysis of a class of generalized long-memory time series models. J. Time Ser. Anal. 28, 386–407 (2006). https://doi.org/10.1111/j.1467-9892.2006.00515.x
17. Witt, A., Malamud, B.D.: Quantification of long-range persistence in geophysical time series: conventional and benchmark-based improvement techniques. Surv. Geophys. 34, 541–651 (2013). https://doi.org/10.1007/s10712-012-9217-8
18. Crovella, M., Krishnamurthy, B.: Internet measurement: infrastructure, traffic & applications. DBLP (2006)
19. Khayari, R.E.A., Sadre, R., Haverkort, B.R.: A validation of the pseudo self-similar traffic model. In: International Conference on Dependable Systems & Networks. IEEE (2002)
20. Barunik, J., Kristoufek, L.: On Hurst exponent estimation under heavy-tailed distributions. Phys. A Stat. Mech. Appl. 389, 3844–3855 (2010)
21. Alvarez-Ramirez, J., Echeverria, J.C., Rodriguez, E.: Performance of a high-dimensional R/S method for Hurst exponent estimation. Phys. A Stat. Mech. Appl. 387, 6452–6462 (2008)
22. Bianchi, F.M., et al.: Prediction of telephone calls load using Echo State Network with exogenous variables. Neural Netw. 71, 204–213 (2015)
23. Jaeger, H., Haas, H.: Harnessing nonlinearity: predicting chaotic systems and saving energy in wireless communication. Science 304(5667), 78–80 (2004). https://doi.org/10.1126/science.1091277
24. Chatzis, S.P., Demiris, Y.: Echo State Gaussian process. IEEE Trans. Neural Netw. 22(9), 1435–1445 (2011)

Distributed Learning Automata Based Data Dissemination in Networked Robotic Systems

Gerald Henderson and Qi Han$^{(\boxtimes)}$

Department of Computer Science, Colorado School of Mines, Golden, USA
gxhenderson@alumni.mines.edu, qhan@mines.edu

Abstract. Networked robotics systems often work in collaboration to accomplish tasks. The random environments the robots work in render any previous contact data between robots useless as the contact patterns are different for each deployment. In the case of military and disaster scenarios, delivering data items quickly is imperative to the success of a mission. However, robots have limited battery and need a lightweight protocol that maximizes data delivery ratio and minimizes data delivery latency while consuming minimal energy. We present two learning automata based data dissemination protocols, LADD and sc-LADD. LADD uses learning automata with direct connections to all neighboring nodes to make efficient and accurate forwarding decisions while sc-LADD uses learning automata and exploits the clustering nature of the robotic systems to abstract clusters/groups and reduce the number of decisions available to the learning automata, which also reduces overhead.

Keywords: Data dissemination · Networked robotic systems · Learning automata

1 Introduction

In many applications of collaborative networked multi-robot systems, robots need to communicate with each other or a remote server. Data dissemination can be used to send tasks to robots. If this process is not efficient, tasks may expire before the robot can perform them. This becomes increasingly important for critical tasks. Consider a disaster scenario where robots are searching for surviving civilians. Critical updates received by an emergency response personnel coordinating the search mission may need to be disseminated to the robots quickly to save civilians in the most dangerous areas of the disaster zone. Without efficient data dissemination, an area of the disaster zone could potentially go unexplored. Furthermore, multiple robots may need to receive the data based on their capabilities.

This work is supported in part by NASA grant 80NSSC18M0048.

Y. Yin et al. (Eds.): MobiCASE 2019, LNICST 290, pp. 126–140, 2019.
https://doi.org/10.1007/978-3-030-28468-8_10

We specifically consider the scenarios where multiple robots work in groups/swarms. A swarm of robots is a collective group of robots working together to complete a task. In this paper, we use group, swarm, cluster interchangeably. Each robot in the swarm may perform the same task or may perform different parts of a singular, collaborative task. Because robots in a swarm may perform different tasks within the same mission, it is possible that only a certain percentage of the total swarms need to receive data; each of the swarms may also have a different number of nodes that need the data. These types of networks have varying or intermittent network connectivity, resulting in unreliable message transmission.

This work presents Learning Automata based Data Dissemination (LADD) and Swarm Centric Learning Automata based Data Dissemination (sc-LADD), two protocols for data dissemination that use learning automata (LA) to make decisions that are adaptive to the environment; consider residual energy, mobility, link quality, hop count, and local delivery ratio; and works in a scenario which *a-priori* data about cumulative node contacts and centrality is unavailable. Each protocol uses LA to determine the next best hop based on the current network parameters. Detection and tracking of the swarms/groups is outside the scope of this work and has been well studied [21].

2   Related Work

Our work is related to several areas of research in the literature. While this work focuses on data dissemination, it is similar to data forwarding. Data forwarding refers to sending data to one single destination, while data dissemination aims to deliver data to multiple receivers. As we consider the scenarios where multiple robots communicate wirelessly in an ac-hoc manner, essentially forming a a Delay Tolerant Network (DTN), we will focus on techniques developed for DTNs, instead of traditional wired networks. Machine Learning based approaches have been used in a Delay Tolerant Network (DTN) for data forwarding [2,5,10,13, 17,19].

Data dissemination in DTNs has been addressed using graph theory approaches [3,18], community based approaches [6–8,12,15,22–24], or machine learning based approaches. Reinforcement learning techniques have been used for data dissemination to adapt to the dynamic nature of DTNs. For instance, QL has been used to dynamically adjust the broadcast rate of a node [20]. In LAFTRA [14], LA share a goodness table between nodes that helps choose the next hop node. FROMS [4] treats an action of its Q-Learning model as a set of sub-actions to determine goodness of a path. Other work use RL techniques to select best forwarding nodes by considering energy consumption [9,17].

On-Demand Multicast Routing Protocol (ODMRP) [11] is a popular routing protocol designed for wireless ad-hoc networks. It uses a mesh network to create routes on demand instead of proactively. ODMRP determines sets of forwarding nodes used to send data to multicast groups. The mesh network makes the network more stable under intermittent connectivity and helps improve delivery ratio. To avoid the delay the route acquisition incurs, the protocol sends a route discovery packet with the initial data packet. ODMRP listens to multicast addresses. This means the network must know which nodes are registered to which multicast addresses prior to being deployed. In reality, our target scenarios assume that we do not know when nodes may need to receive data or what groups nodes may be a part of during deployment. This means ODMRP will fail as a data dissemination protocol in our targeted scenarios.

3   Swarms and Learning Automata

A swarm consists of multiple robots performing some mission. While the swarm at the high level can have randomly distributed movements, each robot within the swarm moves within a maximum distance from the center of the swarm, making the movements much more predictable and reliable. This allows local data dissemination to occur more easily.

The existence of swarms can be exploited for more efficient data dissemination. At any time instant, a robot belongs to a given swarm. This allows for an abstraction when forwarding data. Once a node in the swarm receives a message, it can forward the message to the other destinations in the swarm and control local data dissemination. Instead of needing to forward to any of the respective nodes in the swarm, this work generalizes the swarm to be considered as a *supernode*.

Swarms also make it simpler to handle nodes that leave or join a swarm. Because the nodes are abstracting the swarm, a message need not be broadcast to all nodes in other swarms about the changing structure of the swarm. Finally, the swarm abstraction saves memory. Nodes do not have to consider the contacts of all nodes in a swarm, but only those in its immediate swarm as it is needed for local dissemination. This work assumes that swarms are formed as a prerequisite to the mission.

Since the swarms formed are transient (i.e. they may never meet again after the mission), there is no data about previous contacts that can be utilized for forwarding nodes. Therefore, nodes in the network must make intelligent dissemination decisions with limited network data in a random environment where data needs to be disseminated to multiple nodes. In order to extend network lifetime, the energy of nodes needs to be considered in a way that does not significantly affect latency in the network. These factors give the foundation to consider learning automata for data dissemination.

LA greatly reduces memory, overhead, and energy consumption. LA have also been shown to be effective in finding near-optimal routes. However, LA can be further improved by having an adaptive action-set where the actions available change based on the nodes that come in contact with the swarm. Furthermore, the reinforcement scheme will be able to account for energy, mobility, and proximity of nodes which will all assist in minimizing the total resources for the network. This work uses an $S - model$ LA with a variable structure. This means the goodness of an action will lie in an interval of $[0, 1]$ and the actions available will be dynamic as nodes come into contact with other swarms.

To illustrate the potential benefits from using LA combined with swarms to assist with data dissemination, consider the example network in Fig. 1. Figure 1a shows a simple topology in which a source is attempting to deliver a data item to a set of destination nodes. To reach the destination, the source has several available forwarding options as it is connected to nodes 1, 3, 5, and 6. Figure 1b shows the same topology, but includes the use of swarms to abstract forwarding to neighboring swarms. This gives the source fewer available actions to choose from and forces swarms to handle local routing. Instead of potentially taking four different actions, each of which needing to take multiple actions to converge, the number of paths that need to be explored is reduced by half. By reducing the number of routes to explore, the LA should be able to converge more quickly and decrease delay times while maintaining a similar level of dissemination quality. Also, in this example, all three destinations are located in one swarm, one delivery to the swarm would be sufficient, thereby further reducing overhead. With the swarm abstraction, the LA will be able to adapt to the changes and re-converge more quickly when changes in optimal routes occur.

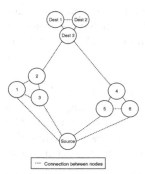

(a) An example of possible dissemination scenarios.

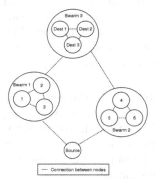

(b) An example of using swarms for dissemination.

Fig. 1. Benefits of using swarms in LADD

4   LADD: Distributed Learning Automata-Based Data Dissemination

We consider a network of robots as a graph $G = (V, E)$ where each robot is a vertex v_i. When two robots v_i and v_j are within communication range of each other, there is a bidirectional edge e_{ij}. We consider a single source node $s \in V$ and a set of destination nodes $D \subseteq V$. Robots are also grouped into swarms $S \subset V$, that together try to accomplish a designated mission. All the nodes inside the same swarm are within one hop of each other. Each swarm S is disjoint from all other swarms in the network such that $\forall S_i, S_j \in S$ $S_i \cap S_j = \emptyset$. Each node belongs to one or no swarm at any given time such that $\forall v \in V$ $v \in S_i | v \in \{\}$. A node can belong to no swarm if it is disconnected from other nodes for various reasons such as in the middle of switching its swarm or has low battery and needs to recharge. Destination nodes may be unevenly distributed among the swarms. As a mission unfolds, robots will move and destination nodes may not stay in the swarms. When data needs to be sent from source s to all nodes in D, our objective is to maximize data delivery ratio, minimize data delivery latency, and minimize overhead incurred (which includes energy consumed by the robots in message transmission and bandwidth used).

This section proposes two Learning Automata-based data dissemination schemes for solving the data dissemination problem in swarm robotic systems: LADD does not exploit swarms, sc-LADD does.

4.1 Swarm-less LADD

Nodes in LADD use the network conditions with its neighbors to adapt to the continuously changing environment instantly. Each node maintains a goodness matrix and uses the goodness values to decide where to forward its messages for the destination(s). The nodes available for forwarding will have a different goodness for each destination. The matrix allows the node's LA to make the differentiation.

Goodness Values. The goodness matrix for node i is denoted as GV_i, which is an $n \times n$ matrix where $gv[j][k]$ describes the goodness of choosing node k as i's next hop in the path to destination j. Each row of the matrix pertains to the respective node in the network if it were the destination of a message, while the column pertains to the goodness value of selecting that node on the path to the destination.

A goodness value is calculated between a node, i, and its predecessor in the path, h, based on its residual energy, current mobility, link quality with the receiver, hop count, and local delivery ratio. These networking factors give information about the goodness of paths throughout the network. It is calculated as

$$gv_{ih} = rf_i * lqf_{ih} * hcf_p * dr_i, \tag{1}$$

where rf_i is the routing factor of the current node, i, sending a response; lqf_{ih} is the link qualify factor between the current node, i, and its predecessor in the path, h; hcf_p is the hop count factor of the path, p; and dr_i is the delivery ratio of the current node, i.

- The routing factor, rf, is a node's general ability to forward. It is calculated as

$$rf_i = \frac{\text{residualEnergy}}{\text{initialEnergy}} * (1 - \frac{\text{velocity}}{\text{maxAllowedVelocity}}).$$

  The first term prefers a high residual energy while the second prefers a low velocity.

– The link quality factor, lqf, is calculated as

$$lqf_{ih} = \frac{rss}{minAllowedRss}$$

where rss is the last received signal strength (RSS) between the current node and its predecessor in the path. An RSS around 0 dBm indicates a strong link quality between two nodes, while 90 dBm (the minAllowedRss) is the lowest usable signal in ad hoc networks.

– The hop count factor, hcf, is calculated as

$$hcf_p = 1 - \frac{hopCount}{numberOfNodes}.$$

Hop count is the path length from the source to the destination and can be at most the number of nodes in the network. This term will prefer paths with shorter hops.

– The local effective delivery ratio, dr, is calculated as

$$dr_i = \frac{number\ of\ delivered\ packets}{number\ of\ sent\ packets}.$$

The local effective delivery ratio is the ratio of packets sent by the node and actually delivered to its destination. Nodes that are consistently able to disseminate data to their destinations should be considered more heavily for forwarding data.

LADD Overview. Each node is equipped with an LA, goodness matrix, and enabled forwarding node set for making forwarding decisions. At the start of LADD, each element of the goodness value matrix is initialized to .5 in order to allow all paths to have a chance to be explored at some point.

Since not all nodes are in communication range of each other all the time, we use an enabled forwarding node set (i.e., enabled actions vector used in LA) which shows the list of forwarding nodes that are available to a node. As a node identifies its neighbors, the enabled forwarding node set will change. If that node then leaves the communication range of the robot, it should no longer be considered for forwarding and is removed from the enabled forwarding node set.

To select forwarding nodes, a node calculates the number of paths using local effective delivery ratio (LEDR) as follows:

$$numPath = \frac{numNeighbors}{2} * (1 - LEDR) \tag{2}$$

The local effective delivery ratio is initialized as zero, so a source node selects a max of half of its neighbors. Multiplying by this factor enables more exploration of paths when fewer packets are being delivered.

Only the first node in a path makes this calculation. Predecessors select one node for further forwarding. Once the number of forwarding nodes is decided, a node will add its *routing factor* to the cumulative routing factor of the message and its id to the path. This cumulative routing factor will tell a destination node how good of a path was chosen. The other elements of Eq. 1 cannot be utilized for this metric as they cannot be calculated until a destination is reached. When a node receives a forward message, the node must determine if it is one of the destinations. If it is, it can then calculate average routing factor of the path by dividing the cumulative routing factor by the hop count. If the average routing factor of the path is greater than the average routing factor of all data items received by the destination, it will send back a response with the calculated goodness relative to the node that sent the data item as in Eq. 1. If more destinations exist, the node forwards the data to the next hop. When a node receives a response message, it will store the received goodness value in its goodness matrix for taking that forward node as the next hop to the destination (i.e., updating gv[destination id][sender of the response's id]). It will then calculate its goodness relative to the predecessor in the path before sending the response to its predecessor.

When a node forwards a message, it decreases the goodness value of the chosen forwarding node by half in the goodness matrix (i.e., gv[destination][forward node] = gv[destination][forward node]/2).

LADD's Learning Automata. Nodes send and receive several different types of messages: *Forward*, *Response*, *Mobility*, and *Hello* messages. When receiving a *Forward* message, a node in LADD will send a *Response* down the path if it is a destination. If the average cumulative routing factor of the message is greater than or equal to its local cumulative routing factor, it will send a reward response. Otherwise, it will send a penalty response. Then, if there are more destinations, it will add its routing factor to the cumulative routing factor of the message and select a forwarding candidate for each destination (which may be a shared hop) from its neighboring nodes.

When receiving a reward *Response* message, the node will update the goodness value from the sending node in its goodness matrix. For either a penalty or reward, the node will send the response down to its predecessor in the path.

Mobility messages let neighboring nodes know when a node has begun moving more quickly. In this event, the node should be removed as an enabled action. These messages are added to a *Hello* message. When receiving a *Hello* message, a node updates or adds the neighboring node to the enabled actions vector.

Figure 2 gives a high-level overview of the data dissemination process in LADD.

4.2   Swarm-Centric LADD (sc-LADD)

Swarms create an abstraction layer for nodes in the network. In order to reduce the memory space needed by the goodness value matrix, a node only maintains its neighbors in its current swarm along with a single connection to the *supernode* of the other swarms. However, having a connection to a single node

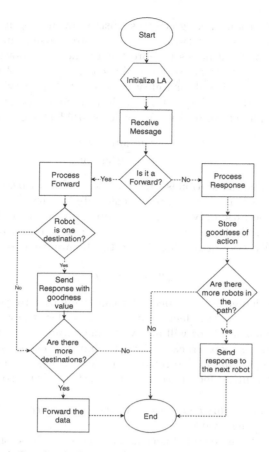

Fig. 2. A flowchart of the data dissemination process in LADD.

in the swarm may not be the most beneficial, as another node may have better routing capabilities. Therefore, sc-LADD also maintains a small table, the
swarm_supernode table, which contains the node most suitable for forwarding in
the swarm. This table maintains swarm ID, supernode reference id, and routing
factor. The supernode reference id is the ID of the node currently being utilized
within a swarm as the *supernode* and the routing factor is its current goodness
value as a routing node. However, the routing factor is not dependent on routing
to specific destinations as goodness values are, but instead its ability to route in
general. Both supernode reference id and routing factor are updated as nodes in
the swarm come into the communication range of a node.

As sc-LADD still applies similar concept of LA, we next discuss how this
algorithm works by only describing the difference from the original LADD.

- The routing factor utilized between swarms does not consider mobility and
  only considers the residual energy of the node. When utilizing swarms, the

granularity of decision making changes. Instead of making fine-grained decisions to each node in the network, there is more coarse-grained abstraction.
Mobility of neighboring nodes is more fine-grained information, while average residual energy of the network remains coarse-grained. When considering
swarms, the individual node mobility is abstracted. Removing the mobility
information from the routing factor matches the more coarse-grained nature
of the swarms. Therefore, routing factor for sc-LADD is calculated as:

$$rf = \frac{residualEnergy}{initialEnergy}$$

The goodness value calculation is also changed to reflect this. In addition, RSS
and local effective delivery ratio are not calculated in the goodness value when
using swarms. Because only energy and hop count are considered, goodness
values begin to reflect the goodness of a path as opposed to an individual
node. Specifically, goodness values for sc-LADD are calculated as:

$$gv = rf * hcf \tag{3}$$

- One additional change needs to occur for the cumulative routing factor stored
  on a node. Because routing factor now only considers the residual energy of
  the node, the routing factor will always be decreasing for a node. To resolve
  this issue, the node keeps track of the rate that it is using battery and occa-
  sionally reduces its cumulative routing factor at this same rate. This allows
  the cumulative routing factor to still be reflective of the good paths in the
  network.
- sc-LADD only maintains connections to its local swarm and the supernode
  from the neighboring swarms.
- sc-LADD only sets the enabled actions for a node to those of its neighboring
  supernodes. When a node receives a forward message, it checks if it is a
  destination as per the original algorithm. However, before forwarding the data
  items, the node will then check if any of the destinations lie in its swarm. If
  this is true, it will broadcast the forward message throughout the swarm.
  Next, it will forward the message to the neighboring swarm with the best
  goodness value. Before sending the message to the neighbors it has selected
  for forwarding, it will add all of the nodes in its swarm to the disabled actions
  list to ensure the swarm will not receive the message again.
- When a node has determined it is a destination, it will build the response
  as per the original algorithm. However, the response will only need to travel
  between the swarms via the supernodes that forwarded the data item. When
  a supernode receives a response, it will broadcast that response to the rest of
  the swarm before sending it back down the path to the next supernode. This
  ensures that all nodes have the updated goodness for routing to the swarm
  in the event that the supernode changes and one of the other nodes is chosen
  for forwarding data.

5   Performance Evaluation

Our simulation studies are conducted using NS-3 [16], a widely used network simulator. Robots communicate with each other using Wi-Fi ad hoc mode. NS-3 provides realistic simulation of Wi-Fi network conditions based on network topology and robot mobility. Using NS3 [16] and node traces generated by Bonnmotion [1], realistic scenarios were created that mimic networked robotic systems being used for disaster relief applications. Each scenario includes several parameters: number of nodes, number of swarms, node mobility, and swarm change rate. By default, we have 10 swarms, a total of 50 robots, each robot's max pause time is 60 s and max allowed velocity is 51 mph and swarms do not change. We chose 51 mph based on the specs of the DJI Phantom 4. One of these parameters is changed to determine how that parameter affects either protocol. These experiments will help evaluate the scalability and adaptability of the algorithms.

We consider several performance metrics: data delivery ratio, data delivery latency, average cost, and average energy consumption.

- Data delivery ratio is the percentage of destinations that actually received a data item.
- Data delivery latency is the average delay for all delivered destinations to receive the data items being disseminated. A low delivery latency is desired as all data should be disseminated as quickly as possible.
- Average cost is the amount of overhead produced by the data dissemination. Overhead is considered as the number of forward and response messages being sent. Reducing the amount of overhead means less energy is spent on transmitting data into the network.

Impact of Number of Nodes. Studying the impact of the number of nodes in the network gives a better indication of how having more or less nodes in the same geographical area affects the performance of our data dissemination algorithms, which provides a sense of the scalability of the algorithms.

Results shown in Fig. 3 are from what we consider the worst case scenario, where nodes constantly move up to the maximum speed of 51 mph and rarely pause, meaning that nodes and their swarms never stop in any single location for more than 60 s. The constant mobility makes it difficult for the LA to converge as it constantly needs to switch paths it just discovered. Despite these conditions, LADD is able to provide high delivery radio ranging between 96% and 98% as shown in Fig. 3a. However, sc-LADD falls about 6–10% below LADD in delivery ratio. Changes in the network propagate more quickly in LADD because of the fine-grained decision making. When considering the delivery latency shown in Fig. 3b, sc-LADD outperforms LADD in all cases but the 20-node case. However, delivery latency for both protocols decreases as more nodes are added to the network.

Finally, the overhead for sc-LADD, shown in Fig. 3c, is significantly lower than the overhead of LADD. Interestingly, after 30 nodes, sc-LADD begins to

decrease in overhead while LADD's overhead only increases on a linear scale
as more nodes are added. This is because the number of decisions for a node
in LADD only increases, while the number of decisions for sc-LADD actually
remains unchanged, causing the overhead gap to continuously grow between the
two protocols.

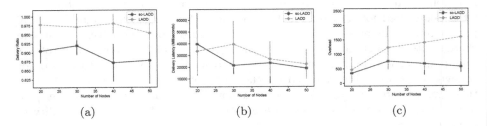

(a)   (b)   (c)

Fig. 3. Impact of number of nodes

Impact of Number of Swarms. Considering the number of swarms shows
how the protocols will work with different sized swarms. Having fewer swarms
indicates that there are more nodes in each swarm while having more swarms
indicates there are less nodes in each swarm.

Figure 4 shows the comparison of LADD and sc-LADD with different number of swarms. As shown in Fig. 4a, delivery ratios of the two protocols are
similar with LADD slightly outperforming sc-LADD; there is an exception of
the 10 swarm, which is given the more extreme parameters of the number of
nodes comparison. In the 20 swarm case, sc-LADD slightly outperforms LADD.
Delivery latency, shown in Fig. 4b is nearly identical between the two protocols.

Finally, sc-LADD again outperforms LADD in overhead as shown in Fig. 4c.
However, the overhead becomes much more similar from 15 to 25 swarms. This is
most likely due to the changing sizes of the swarms. As swarms become smaller,
the protocol gets closer to becoming the same as LADD and removes fewer
actions for the LA to take.

Impact of Node Mobility. The max pause time simulations measure performance when nodes are able to pause from 0 to 60 min in increments of 15 min.
Figure 5a shows the delivery ratio for sc-LADD and LADD are comparable with
LADD outperforming sc-LADD by less than 2% in every setting. This shows
how the mobility in Fig. 3 affected the results of sc-LADD. When there is more
stability in the network, both protocols are able to perform well. It is important
to note the slight performance decrease in the 45 and 60 min scenarios. This may
be due to the methods used by Bonnmotion to create the mobility traces. While
more stop time is allowed for a node, it does not guarantee that all nodes will

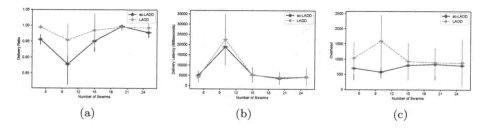

Fig. 4. Impact of number of swarms

stop for that time frame; in fact, nodes can still move continuously even when allowed a pause time, although this is unlikely.

Similar to other results, Fig. 5b shows that the delivery latencies of both protocols perform similarly with LADD slightly outperforming sc-LADD by at most a little over one second. Figure 5c also follows a similar pattern with sc-LADD outperforming LADD in overhead. However, the overhead is more significant in most cases than in Sect. 4 These results show that even with a similar delivery ratio, sc-LADD makes around 100–250 less transmissions per node than LADD in most cases.

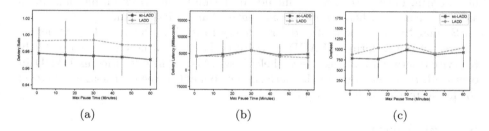

Fig. 5. Impact of node mobility

Impact of Swarm Change Probability. We use swarm change probability to indicate the chances of nodes switching to different swarms. With a probability of 0%, 10%, 20%, 30%, or 40%, a node will move to a different swarm in our simulation. Nodes are not leaving and then returning to the same swarm, which is a less extreme case. The 0% probability change relates to the 15 min max pause time simulation.

Figure 6a shows that while LADD still performs well, sc-LADD has a decreasing delivery ratio. This might be due to the abstraction mechanism used for sc-LADD for swarms. While it would handle a node leaving and returning to the same swarm, the mechanism is not yet suitable to handle nodes permanently changing swarms.

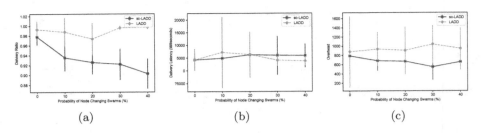

(a)   (b)   (c)

Fig. 6. Impact of swarm change probability

When a node leaves a swarm, it allows its immediate neighbors to know it is leaving and cannot receive messages. In the case of LADD, this immediate change is easily reflected as it has an immediate connection to that node and it does not matter what swarm it belongs to. Furthermore, LADD uses a fine-grained delivery mechanism to send data items directly to nodes. Any change in a node's swarm does not change another node's ability to forward data to the node changing swarms. In the case of sc-LADD, there is no direct contact with every node in a swarm. A node changing its swarm alters the path to that node. Because sc-LADD makes decisions based on paths, this is not immediately reflected in all nodes in said path. This makes it harder to forward to a node's new swarm. Future work would include updating the abstraction mechanism to alert other nodes when a node permanently changes its swarm.

Similar to the reasons stated for delivery ratio, Fig. 6b shows LADD begins to greatly outperform sc-LADD in delivery latency as nodes are more likely to switch between swarms. Nevertheless, sc-LADD still outperforms LADD in overhead. However, some of the performance benefit in the overhead can be tied to the decreasing delivery ratio.

6   Conclusion

In this work, we have created two versions of a data dissemination protocol for networked multi-robot systems that adapt to the rapidly changing topology of the mobile robotic network without the knowledge of a-priori node contact data. A learning automata based approach was taken to keep the algorithm lightweight. The simulation results indicate that the non-swarm based protocol, LADD, slightly outperforms the swarm based protocol, sc-LADD, in terms of delivery ratio in all cases. However, sc-LADD incurs significantly less overhead than LADD, while delivery latency remains similar in all scenarios. In many cases, LADD does not provide significantly higher delivery ratio than sc-LADD. This is especially true in the case of nodes pausing. In these scenarios, sc-LADD can be used to achieve a reasonable delivery ratio with much lower overhead. However, in the scenarios where LADD does provide higher delivery ratio than sc-LADD, sc-LADD could be paired with LADD as an energy conserving mode. When a node goes below a certain energy threshold, it can switch from LADD mode to sc-LADD to conserve energy. This will extend the network lifetime at the price of a lower delivery ratio.

References

1. Aschenbruck, N., Ernst, R., Gerhards-Padilla, E., Schwamborn, M.: BonnMotion: a mobility scenario generation and analysis tool. In: Proceedings of the 3rd International ICST Conference on Simulation Tools and Techniques (SIMUTools), pp. 51:1–51:10 (2010)
2. Dhurandher, S.K., Sharma, D., Woungang, I., Gupta, R., Garg, S.: GAER: genetic algorithm-based energy-efficient routing protocol for infrastructure-less opportunistic networks. J. Supercomput. **69**(3), 1183–1214 (2014)
3. Frey, H., Ingelrest, F., Simplot-Ryl, D.: Localized minimum spanning tree based multicast routing with energy-efficient guaranteed delivery in ad hoc and sensor networks. In: 2008 International Symposium on a World of Wireless, Mobile and Multimedia Networks (WoWMoM), pp. 1–8 (2008)
4. Förster, A., Murphy, A.L.: FROMS: a failure tolerant and mobility enabled multicast routing paradigm with reinforcement learning for wsns. Ad Hoc Netw. **9**(5), 940–965 (2011)
5. Gao, W., Cao, G.: User-centric data dissemination in disruption tolerant networks. In: Proceedings of the IEEE International Conference on Computer Communications (INFOCOM), pp. 3119–3127 (2011)
6. Gao, W., Cao, G., Porta, T.L., Han, J.: On exploiting transient social contact patterns for data forwarding in delay-tolerant networks. IEEE Trans. Mob. Comput. **12**(1), 151–165 (2013)
7. Gao, W., Li, Q., Zhao, B., Cao, G.: Multicasting in delay tolerant networks: a social network perspective. In: Proceedings of the Tenth ACM International Symposium on Mobile Ad Hoc Networking and Computing (MobiHoc), New York, NY, USA, pp. 299–308 (2009)
8. Gao, W., Li, Q., Zhao, B., Cao, G.: Social-aware multicast in disruption-tolerant networks. IEEE/ACM Trans. Netw. **20**(5), 1553–1566 (2012)
9. Hu, T., Fei, Y.: QELAR: a machine-learning-based adaptive routing protocol for energy-efficient and lifetime-extended underwater sensor networks. IEEE Trans. Mob. Comput. **9**(6), 796–809 (2010)
10. Hui, P., Crowcroft, J., Yoneki, E.: BUBBLE Rap: social-based forwarding in delay-tolerant networks. IEEE Trans. Mob. Comput. **10**(11), 1576–1589 (2011)
11. Lee, S., Gerla, M., Toh, C.: On-demand multicast routing protocol (ODMRP) for ad-hoc networks. Mob. Netw. Appl. **7** (2003)
12. Li, F., Zhao, L., Zhang, C., Gao, Z., Wang, Y.: Routing with multi-level cross-community social groups in mobile opportunistic networks. Pers. Ubiquitous Comput. **18**(2), 385–396 (2014)
13. Lindgren, A., Doria, A., Schelén, O.: Probabilistic routing in intermittently connected networks. SIGMOBILE Mob. Comput. Commun. Rev. **7**(3), 19–20 (2003)
14. Misra, S., Krishna, P.V., Bhiwal, A., Chawla, A., Wolfinger, B.E., Lee, C.: A learning automata-based fault-tolerant routing algorithm for mobile ad hoc networks. J. Supercomput. **62**(1), 4–23 (2012)
15. Nguyen, N., Dinh, T., Tokala, S., Thai, M.: Overlapping communities in dynamic networks: their detection and mobile applications. In: Proceedings of the 17th Annual International ACM Conference on Mobile Computing and Networking (MobiCom), New York, NY, USA, pp. 85–96 (2011)
16. Riley, G.F., Henderson, T.R.: The *ns-3* network simulator. In: Wehrle, K., Günes, M., Gross, J. (eds.) Modeling and Tools for Network Simulation, Chap. 2. Springer, Heidelberg (2010). https://doi.org/10.1007/978-3-642-12331-3_2

17. Torkestani, J., Meybodi, M.: Mobility-based multicast routing algorithm for wireless mobile ad-hoc networks: a learning automata approach. Comput. Commun. **33**(6), 721–735 (2010)
18. Torkestani, J., Meybodi, M.: A learning automata-based heuristic algorithm for solving the minimum spanning tree problem in stochastic graphs. J. Supercomput. **59**(2), 1035–1054 (2012)
19. Wu, C., Ohzahata, S., Kato, T.: Flexible, portable, and practicable solution for routing in vanets: a fuzzy constraint q-learning approach. IEEE Trans. Veh. Technol. **62**(9), 4251–4263 (2013)
20. Wu, D., et al.: ADDSEN: adaptive data processing and dissemination for drone swarms in urban sensing. IEEE Trans. Comput. **66**(2), 183–198 (2017)
21. Yu, J., Chong, P.: A survey of clustering schemes for mobile ad hoc networks. IEEE Commun. Surv. Tutor. **7**(1), 32–48 (2005)
22. Zhang, X., Cao, G.: Efficient data forwarding in mobile social networks with diverse connectivity characteristics. In: Proceedings of IEEE 34th International Conference on Distributed Computing Systems (ICDCS), pp. 31–40 (2014)
23. Zhang, X., Cao, G.: Transient community detection and its application to data forwarding in delay tolerant networks. IEEE/ACM Trans. Netw. **25**(5), 2829–2843 (2017)
24. Zhao, W., Ammar, M., Zegura, E.: Multicasting in delay tolerant networks: semantic models and routing algorithms. In: Proceedings of the ACM Special Interest Group on Data Communication (SIGCOMM) Workshop on Delay-Tolerant Networking (WDTN), New York, NY, USA, pp. 268–275 (2005)

Comparison of User Trajectories with the Needleman-Wunsch Algorithm

Maroš Čavojský$^{(\boxtimes)}$ and Martin Drozda

Faculty of Electrical Engineering and Information Technology,
Slovak University of Technology, Bratislava, Slovakia
{maros.cavojsky,martin.drozda}@stuba.sk

Abstract. We show that the Needleman-Wunsch algorithm for sequence alignment can be efficiently applied to comparing user trajectories, where user locations are provided by Global positioning system (GPS). We compare our approach based on this algorithm with other approaches such as the pairwise method and the proximity method. We describe all steps necessary to apply the Needleman-Wunsch algorithm when comparing user trajectories. In our experiments we use two different data sets: a data set that we collected with 455 mobile devices distributed among our students and the Geolife data set (Microsoft Research Asia). We conclude that our approach based on the Needleman-Wunsch algorithm performs better than other approaches, especially, in terms of true negatives, false positives and false negatives, while still offering improvement in terms of true positives.

Keywords: GPS · Needleman-Wunsch algorithm ·
Sequence alignment · User movement patterns ·
Experimental evaluation

1 Introduction

We investigate whether the Needleman-Wunsch algorithm for sequence alignment can perform well for comparison of user trajectories. Comparing user trajectories is relevant when there is a need to group users by visited locations with sequential dependence. Such a grouping has a wide range of applications such as navigation, location recommendation, friend recommendation etc.

The Needleman-Wunsch algorithm was published in 1970 [11]. It is one of the first applications of dynamic programming, where a large problem is divided into a series of smaller problems to reconstruct a solution to the larger problem. The Needleman–Wunsch algorithm is still widely used for optimal global alignment, particularly when the quality of the global alignment is of the utmost importance.

The algorithm takes as input two sequences, score matrix and gap penalty. The objective is to align these two sequences by matching letters and introducing gaps, where score with respect to matched letters and penalty for introducing gaps are computed. Matching only identical letters can be desirable, however,

© ICST Institute for Computer Sciences, Social Informatics and Telecommunications Engineering 2019
Published by Springer Nature Switzerland AG 2019. All Rights Reserved
Y. Yin et al. (Eds.): MobiCASE 2019, LNICST 290, pp. 141–154, 2019.
https://doi.org/10.1007/978-3-030-28468-8_11

(a) Gap - missing location data   (b) Nest - false movement

Fig. 1. Gap and nest.

in bio-informatics score is often set according to mutation probabilities, where matching certain letters can have a higher score than matching other letters. It is also often desirable that alignment has few small gaps, therefore penalty for starting a gap can also be introduced. Let us consider the following sequences:

Sequence 1: G A T T A C A
Sequence 2: G T C G A C G

An alignment for these two sequences, when only identical letters are allowed to match, can be as follows:

Sequence 1: G - T - - C G A C G
Sequence 2: G A T T A C - A - -

We argue that the Needleman-Wunsch algorithm can be efficiently applied for aligning user trajectories defined by coordinates received with GPS (Global Positioning System). When comparing user trajectories, one has to cope with the following phenomena:

- Gaps arise when acquisition of GPS coordinates is interrupted; such gaps naturally map to gaps in the sequence alignment problem.
- Nests arise when signal reflection and multi-path propagation negatively impact GPS signal reception. This phenomenon can be perceived as a random walk around the user's real location.

Examples of these two phenomena are shown in Figs. 1(a) and (b). Our ambition is to show that gaps and nests can be efficiently addressed with algorithms for sequence alignment, in our case with the Needleman-Wunsch algorithm.

The rest of this document is organized as follow. In Sect. 2 we introduce the Needleman-Wunsch algorithm, Sect. 3 has relevant definitions necessary for discussing and introducing our approach and results, in Sect. 4 we review the related work, in Sect. 5 we introduce our approach to user trajectory comparison, in Sect. 6 we present the applied experimental setup, Sect. 7 contains the obtained results, and finally, in Sect. 8 we conclude and give suggestions for possible future work.

2   Needleman-Wunsch Algorithm (NWA)

NWA is a variant of string-editing algorithm, where the objective is to maximize alignment scores along the entire length of two sequences. Let $x_1, x_2, ..., x_m$ and $y_1, y_2, ..., y_n$ be two sequences, one having m letters and the other n letters. The scoring schema S defines scores when letters match or mismatch, for example, $S(G, G) = 1$ or $S(G, T) = -1$. In its simplest form, S returns score 1 for identical letters and -1 for different letters including letter to gap mismatch (gap penalty). More complex schemes were proposed in order to capture different mutation probabilities; see e.g. BLOSUM scoring [3].

Having a scoring scheme, we can build a matrix M of size $(m + 1) \times (n + 1)$, where each entry $M(i, j)$ represents the score for optimal alignment of partial sequences $x_1, ..., x_i$ and $y_1, ..., y_j$. The matrix M needs to be initialized as follows: $M(0, 0) = 0$, $M(i, 0) = i * gp$ and $M(j, 0) = j * gp$, where gp is gap penalty. The remaining entries of M are filled recursively:

$$M(i, j) = max \begin{cases} M(i - 1, j - 1) + S(i, j), \\ M(i - 1, j) + S(i, \_), \\ M(i, j - 1) + S(\_, j), \end{cases} \tag{1}$$

where $S(i, \_)$ and $S(\_, j)$ is gap penalty and $S(i, j)$ is the score of matching (or mismatching) at i-th and j-th position of sequences. In order to compute optimal alignment, we also need to record which of the three considered cases was applied, i.e. which resulted to maximum value. When computing the optimum alignment we need to backtrack from $M(m, n)$ in the direction of recorded choices, where moving up or left means introducing a gap and moving on diagonal means no gap. NWA complexity is $O(mn)$, therefore this algorithm is also suitable for computing sequence alignments of considerable length.

3   Definitions

To define a movement of device (user) it is necessary to determine its location at any point. Therefore, we define *position* as a location of user using geo-location coordinates as follows.

Definition 1. *Position $\mathcal{P}$ is a couple (lat, lon), where*

- *lat is latitude in decimal degrees (e.g. 48.1518568),*
- *lon is longitude in decimal degrees (e.g. 17.0711559).*

Alongside with device position, we also record other relevant information such as time, accuracy or process of obtaining the position.

Definition 2. *Location $\mathcal{L}$ is a tuple $(\mathcal{P}, \mathcal{T}, \mathcal{A})$, where*

- $\mathcal{P}$ *is position,*
- $\mathcal{T}$ *is time in seconds from 1.1.1970 (UTC),*
- $\mathcal{A}$ *is horizontal accuracy in meters.*

According to the Android documentation [2], we define horizontal accuracy $\mathcal{A}$ as a radius with 68% reliability. In other words, if we draw a circle with radius $\mathcal{A}$ and center $\mathcal{P}$, there is 68% probability (one standard deviation) that the actual position is inside of this circle. The value of 0.0 means that the accuracy of the actual position is not defined.

Definition 3. *Path $\mathcal{S}$ is sequence of locations $(\mathcal{L}_1, \mathcal{L}_2, ..., \mathcal{L}_n)$, where $(\mathcal{T}_1, \mathcal{T}_2, ..., \mathcal{T}_n)$ is a non-decreasing sequence of time values at which location was recorded.*

Next we define two quantitative indicators for paths, in particular *length* and *size*.

Definition 4. *The length of path $\mathcal{S} = (\mathcal{L}_1, \mathcal{L}_2, ..., \mathcal{L}_n)$ is the sum of distances between subsequent pairs of locations:*

$$length(\mathcal{S}) = \sum_{i=1}^{n-1} distance(\mathcal{L}_i, \mathcal{L}_{i+1}),$$

where $distance(\mathcal{L}_i, \mathcal{L}_{i+1})$ is the distance based on either Euclidean distance or Vincenty's formulae [5, 13], where the latter calculates the distance of two points on a spheroid.

Herein we apply Vincenty's formulae as they are available in a number of libraries.

Definition 5. *The size of path $\mathcal{S} = (\mathcal{L}_1, \mathcal{L}_2, ..., \mathcal{L}_n)$ is the number of locations in path:*

$$size(\mathcal{S}) = n.$$

In general, as each path contains temporal $\mathcal{T}$ and spatial element $\mathcal{P}$, one can consider three types of path similarities: spatial, temporal and spatial-temporal [19].

- For *spatial* approach, only sequence of positions $(P_i)_n^{i=1}$, regardless of temporal aspect, gets considered. To compare two or several paths, one can calculate distance between individual path positions or compare them with respect to a fixed position Q.
- For *temporal* approach, only sequence of time $(\mathcal{T}_i)_n^{i=1}$, where locations get obtained regardless of their actual positions, gets considered. To compare paths, one can search for appearance of common time intervals in individual paths or appearance of paths in certain interval.

- For *spatial-temporal* approach, both $(P_i)_n^{i=1}$ and $(T)_n^{i=1}$ get considered, we use path $(S)_n^{i=1}$. To compare paths, one can calculate distance between individual path positions in relation to time of the position or given path in given time.

An appropriate approach for modeling, representation and comparison of paths is chosen based on task requirements. In this work, we are focusing on spatial and spatial-temporal representation of paths.

Next, we define clusters and tracks that we need when applying NWA. The interpolated path is referred to as *track*, which is defined with new interpolated locations called *clusters*.

Definition 6. *Cluster* $\mathcal{K} = (P_0, \delta)$ *includes a set of locations* $\{\mathcal{L}_1, ..., \mathcal{L}_n\}$ *such that:*

$$\forall \mathcal{L}_i, \mathcal{L}_j : distance(\mathcal{L}_i, \mathcal{L}_j) < \delta,$$

where $i = 1...n$, $j = 1...n$, δ *is the cluster diameter and* $\mathcal{P}_0$ *is the cluster center such that it holds* $\forall \mathcal{L}_i : distance(\mathcal{L}_i, \mathcal{P}_0) \leq \frac{\delta}{2}$.

Definition 7. *Size of cluster* $|\mathcal{K}|$ *is the number of locations in cluster.*

Definition 8. *Distance between clusters* $\mathcal{K}_i = (\mathcal{P}_i, \delta)$ *and* $\mathcal{K}_j = (\mathcal{P}_j, \delta)$ *is defined as:*

$$distance(\mathcal{K}_i, \mathcal{K}_j) = distance(\mathcal{P}_i, \mathcal{P}_j),$$

for arbitrary i *and* j, $i \neq j$.

Definition 9. *Track* $\mathcal{C}$ *is a sorted sequence of clusters* $(\mathcal{K}_1, ..., \mathcal{K}_n)$ *such that*

$$\forall \mathcal{K}_i, \mathcal{K}_{i+1} : distance(\mathcal{P}_i, \mathcal{P}_{i+1}) = \delta,$$

where $i = 1...(n - 1)$, $\mathcal{K}_i = (\mathcal{P}_i, \delta)$ *and* $\mathcal{K}_{i+1} = (\mathcal{P}_{i+1}, \delta)$.

Definition 10. *Size of track* $|\mathcal{C}|$ *is the number of clusters it contains.*

4 Related Work

A number of approaches such as those described in [4, 8–10] apply various extraction and prediction approaches based on position information provided by GPS. In other approaches, instead of using locations from a collection of GPS positions, the authors constructed a semantic trajectory. Ying et al. [15] proposed a framework by exploring semantic trajectories of mobile users, in order to model the next location of a mobile user in support of various location-based services.

Mavoa et al. [7] attempted to link GPS positions and a manually inserted travel diary using sequence alignment in study of children's independent mobility. They concluded that sequence alignment is a promising method. This approach provided motivation and a starting point for our research.

Herein we focus on approaches that take advantage of comparing user trajectories. As our literature review revealed, such approaches are common when comparing user trajectory with possible trajectories derived from a map. In the following sub-sections we review the most relevant methods for comparing user trajectories and map trajectories. These approaches constitute a consistent set of options that we took into consideration, when proposing our approaches.

4.1 Locational Proximity

The Locational proximity method for comparison of multiple paths has been described by Yang et. al. [14]. In this method distances are calculated between each pair of positions in recorded path and map segment. Comparison of paths is sequential, where each location $(\mathcal{L})_n^{i=1}$ in the path is compared with the map segment in order to find the closest segment. The approach used for assigning locations $(\mathcal{L})_n^{i=1}$ to map segments is based on map-matching. The method calculates distance d from the closest position in assigned map segment for each assigned location in the recorded path. Subsequently, the total deviation is calculated for all locations from the recorded path as:

$$\overline{d} = \frac{\int_0^{l_M} d(l)dl}{l_M},$$

where l_M is a total size of compared path.

4.2 Shape Similarity

Yang et. al. also presented another approach for comparison of paths called the Shape similarity method [14]. To compare a recorded path with matched map segment, the method uses a shape based similarity in geometrical context. A level of similarity is expressed by the differential deviation:

$$\delta\overline{d} = \frac{\int_0^{l_M} |\delta d(l)|dl}{l_M},$$

where $\delta d = d - \overline{d}$. The derived differential deviation is computed as an average of deviations retrieved by the Location proximity method for a given recorded path. Such differential deviation can be then shown in a graph for an easy and quick comparison of both compared paths. The lower the deviation, the more similar is the shape of the compared paths.

4.3 Directional Consistency

The movement direction is another approach for effective comparison of paths [14]. The directional consistency method enables to determine consistency between direction of recorded path and selected map-matched path. To apply this approach, it is necessary to calculate the difference between selected path α_O and direction of map-matched path α_M, for each pair of locations as $\Delta\overline{\alpha} = \alpha_M - \alpha_O$. The overall similarity of the movement direction is calculated as follows:

$$\Delta\overline{\alpha} = \frac{\int_0^{l_M} |\alpha(l)| dl}{l_M}$$

4.4 Behavioral Consistency

The analysis of user behavior is one of the fields focusing on comparison of paths. The behavioral consistency method requires information about the change of speed (e.g. speeding, slowing down) and change of direction. As shown in [14], the similarity of two paths is directly related to the user behavior. This method allows identification of various habits and patterns of the movement when used for comparison of various spacious paths.

4.5 Grid Sequencing

The Grid sequencing method described by Thiagarajan et. al. in [12] uses Hidden Markov Model containing a set of hidden states and observables. Individual states emit an observable whose probability is defined by an emission score $E(F, G)$. This emission score captures the probability of finding a user location F in a cell G (grid cell). The higher the emission score, the higher the probability of user location being matched with the map segment. The location with highest emission score is considered for the one being truly visited by user. The transition score is calculated as a distance between neighboring cells, and it represents the probability of further transition from one cell to another.

5 Our Approaches

5.1 Pairwise Method

This approach is a naive approach aimed at straightforward interpretation of results. We included it as a useful base case. Let $S_a = (L_{a_1}, ..., L_{a_n})$ and $S_b = (L_{b_1}, ..., L_{b_m})$ be paths. In pairwise method we compare pairs of locations (L_{a_i}, L_{b_i}) as follows:

$$d = distance(L_{a_i}, L_{b_i}),$$

where $i = 1...x$ and $x = min(m, n)$. We say that locations (L_{a_i}, L_{b_i}) are similar, if $distance(L_{a_i}, L_{b_i}) < \delta$. In order to compute similarity score for path S_a and S_b, we count the number of similar location pairs. This approach requires that paths get manually synchronized, i.e. it must be decided which initial pair of positions from either path will be used in computation.

5.2   Proximity Method

This approach is derived from the locational proximity approach introduced in the previous section. In proximity method we compare paths by computing:

$$d = distance(L_{a_i}, L_{b_x}), \text{ and}$$
$$\forall L_{a_i} \exists L_{b_x} : distance(L_{a_i}, L_{b_x}) = min(distance(L_{a_i}, L_{b_j}),$$

where $i = 1...n$ and $j = 1...m$. As for pairwise method, we count the number of similar (L_{a_i}, L_{b_j}) with respect to δ. The proximity method applies pairs of positions with least distance, therefore unlike the pairwise method, this method can be applied without any initial synchronization.

5.3   Upward Proximity Method

Upward proximity method is similar to proximity method with the difference that subsequent pairs for comparison are chosen in increasing order. In upward proximity method we compare paths by computing:

$$d = distance(L_{a_i}, L_{b_x}),$$
$$\forall L_{a_i} \exists L_{b_x} : distance(L_{a_i}, L_{b_x}) = min(distance(L_{a_i}, L_{b_j})),$$
$$b_j > k,$$

where $i = 1...n$, $j = 1...m$ and L_k is the location used in previous iteration. As for previous methods, we count the number of similar (L_{a_i}, L_{b_j}) with respect to δ. We have proposed Upward proximity method as an iterative improvement over Proximity method. The rationale is that when comparing pairs of locations, back-tracking should not be possible.

5.4   NWA Approach

Our proposed approach is based on NWA alignment. In order to apply NWA, it is necessary to convert paths S_a and S_b to tracks $\mathcal{C}_a = (\mathcal{K}_{a_1}, ..., \mathcal{K}_{a_r})$ and $\mathcal{C}_b = (\mathcal{K}_{a_1}, ..., \mathcal{K}_{a_s})$. Then we compute alignment of $\mathcal{C}_a$ and $\mathcal{C}_b$ with NWA. As for previous methods, we count the number of aligned clusters with respect to fixed distance δ:

$$d = distance(\mathcal{K}_{a_i}, \mathcal{K}_{b_i}),$$

where the pair $(\mathcal{K}_{a_i}, \mathcal{K}_{b_i})$ is aligned applying NWA.

6   Experimental Setup

6.1   Data Sets

The evaluation of our approach to sequence alignment is based on data sets that record people movement. We considered two data sets:

- A data set that we collected using 455 mobile devices distributed among our students. The results presented herein were collected by our students during a 10-month period starting from September 2016 to July 2017. Over 20 million location records provide insights into our students' behavior patterns (bars, restaurants, clubs etc.). Recording of locations was done using our implemented mobile application for energy efficient trajectory recording of mobile devices using WiFi scanning, described in more details in [1, 6].
- The Geolife data set (Microsoft Research Asia) was collected by 182 users in a period of over three years (from April 2007 to August 2012). This data set contains 17,621 trajectories with a total distance of about 1.2 million kilometers and a total duration of 48,000+ hours. These trajectories were recorded by different GPS loggers and GPS capable phones, and have a variety of sampling rates. This data set recorded a broad range of users' outdoor movements, including not only life routines like go home and go to work but also some entertainments and sports activities, such as shopping, sightseeing, dining, hiking, and cycling [16–18].

6.2   Pre-processing

In pre-processing phase it is necessary to identify errors or incomplete paths, which were excluded from evaluation. Therefore, in the first step we eliminated paths shorter than $size_{min}$; we have set this parameter to 500 m.

During the recording of paths we encountered situations where for some reason devices stopped collecting information about the location. In those cases the location data includes gaps; see Fig. 1(a). Identified gaps can have a length of up to few kilometers, therefore it is crucial to exclude them by dividing the path into separate sub-paths.

In a situation when mobile device does not move, for example it lies on a table, a nest can arise; see Fig. 1(b). Nests are often formed by a large number of positions. For this reason we implemented the process of clustering individual positions that are close to each other.

Initially, we implemented a clustering method based on a fixed-size square with side a, where the center of a square represented the starting location. However, as this approach did not result in an effective clustering of locations, we proposed and implemented a clustering method, where square center gets moved in order to include a new location. In other words, location belongs to the existing square if a center of that square can be adjusted to contain this location with all locations that belonged to this square before.

The proposed clustering with dynamic center can lead to the situation where individual squares overlap each other while each location belongs to only one square. An advantage of the proposed clustering is its ability to minimize the number of required squares.

An example of recorded locations is shown in Fig. 2(a), where locations are marked by circles with diameter representing location accuracy $\mathcal{A}$. The figure represents a usual nature of recorded path with a large number of gaps. The interpolated movement of user is represented by line.

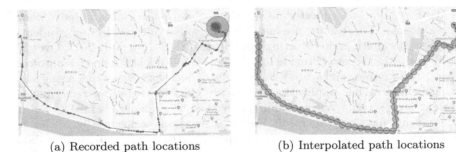

(a) Recorded path locations   (b) Interpolated path locations

Fig. 2. Recorded and interpolated path.

Comparison of paths with many gaps can lead to inaccurate results. In order to overcome this problem, any recorded path needs to be interpolated with evenly distributed locations along the entire path. Therefore we implemented backward interpolation of path. With this process we ensure constant distribution of locations along the path as shown in Fig. 2(b).

The final step was to remove all short paths, that can also be a result of previous steps. As in the first step, we removed all paths shorter than $size_{min}$.

6.3   NWA Parameters

NWA requires scoring schema that defines score for match, score for mismatch and gap penalty. In our case, we set these parameters to 1, −1 and 0, respectively. The given scoring schema was chosen by multiple tests, to ensure the highest accuracy for aligning clusters of given tracks. Arguably, choosing parameters for a scoring schema deserves a separate study with more detail and experimentation. We remind that scoring schemes such as BLOSUM were also derived experimentally with expert knowledge about a specific problem.

7   Experimental Results

7.1   Evaluation Details

When applying NWA, tracks need to get computed; see Definition 9. Figure 3(a) shows an example for computed tracks, more specifically, it shows two tracks that need to get compared.

The comparison of tracks has been based on two criteria: the number of subsequent mismatches and the total number of matches. As accuracy of user movement tracking based on GPS data captured by mobile device varies, we consider for evaluation the maximum number of subsequent mismatches instead of the total number of mismatches. This means, a path can contain any number of mismatches as far as the maximum number of subsequent mismatches does not exceed a certain threshold, in our case we set this threshold to 3.

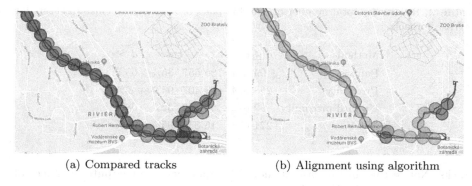

(a) Compared tracks   (b) Alignment using algorithm

Fig. 3. Comparison and alignment applying NWA

When a mismatch in one path is directly followed by a mismatch in other path, this is counted as a single mismatch due to the fact that both mismatches happened in two different clusters. Mismatches are counted as two only if they follow each other. For this reason it is necessary to check also an overall similarity of tracks based on a total number of matches.

Definition 11. *Tracks C_a and C_b are similar if these tracks have at least α matches and no more than β subsequent mismatches.*

Table 1. Alignment computed by NWA

3, 3, 3, 3, 3, 3, 3, 3, 3, 3, 3, 3, 3, 3, 3, 3, 2, 1, 3, 3, 3, 3, 3, 3, 2, 2, 1
(1)=mismatch of Track 1, (2)=mismatch of Track 2, (3)=match

The parameters α and β have been experimentally set to $\alpha = 75\%$ a $\beta = 3$. An example of track alignment is shown in Table 1, representing the same result as depicted in Fig. 3(b).

In this particular case, Table 1 shows 23 matches in interpolated locations and 3 mismatches. In this example, one of the tracks is longer, consisting of 26 clusters, thus having 1 cluster more than the other track. As Track 1 contains 23 matches from 26 and the maximum occurrence of subsequent mismatches is 2, the compared tracks are considered similar.

Table 2 shows the distances of locations for similar or dissimilar pairs of tracks with respect to some threshold ϵ, which was set to $\sqrt{a^2 + a^2} = 70,71$ m, i.e. to the diagonal length of a square with sides equal to 50 m. We remind that such a fixed-size square was used for clustering in the pre-processing phase.

Table 2 shows that shortest distances between pairs of locations can be expected for the proximity approach and the NWA approach. This indicates that these two approaches might be the best candidates for comparing user

Table 2. Results for total number of 286, 431 pairs of locations or cluster centers for NWA approach.

Method	$d \leq \epsilon$	$d > \epsilon$	$d \leq \epsilon$	$d > \epsilon$
Pairwise	99 874	186 557	35%	65%
Proximity	268 024	18 407	94%	6%
Upward proximity	92 672	193 759	32%	68%
NWA	271 078	15 353	95%	5%

tracks. Notice that in the case of the NWA approach, we compute distances of cluster centers, not individual locations.

With respect to Definition 11 we filtered the two considered data sets so that we have 1, 500 pairs of similar tracks and 500 pairs of tracks of dissimilar tracks.

7.2   Results

When evaluating the two data sets, we compared the performance of following approaches:

– NWA approach,
– Pairwise method,
– Proximity method,
– Upward proximity method.

We consider the pairwise method and proximity method to be useful base cases, i.e. approaches with straightforward implementation and arguably leading to results that are simpler to interpret.

Table 3 shows the results for the four considered approaches, where true positive is when a pair of tracks that was correctly identified as similar, true negative is when a pair of tracks that was correctly identified as dissimilar, false positive when a pair of tracks was dissimilar but identified to be similar, and finally, true negative is when a pair of tracks was similar but identified to be dissimilar.

Table 3. Performance of different methods.

Method	True positive	False positive	False negative	True negative
Pairwise	87	159	913	341
Proximity	862	465	138	35
Upward proximity	284	307	716	193
NWA	918	74	82	426

Table 3 thus shows that NWA approach is the winning approach in all four categories, especially, this approach offers very low false positive and false negative rates.

8   Conclusion and Future Work

Our goal was to apply NWA, better known from biology and bio-informatics rather than other research areas, to user trajectory comparison. We proposed several adjustments to this algorithm, so that it can be applied to data sets with different properties than data sets arising in the above mentioned areas.

NWA requires a scoring scheme as an input, and arguably, more research effort might need to be invested in finding optimal scheme. Our results show that NWA can be successfully applied to user trajectory comparison. When comparing NWA to the proximity method, we show that NWA offers 5.6% improvement for true positives. When comparing NWA to the pairwise method, we show that NWA offers 19% improvement for true negatives. NWA dominates other considered approaches in terms of false positives and false negatives. Given the high false positives and high negatives rates of other methods, these can be considered useless, at least in the context of the applied data sets.

We plan to do further tests with other existing data sets, which could lead to improved knowledge about the performance of our NWA approach in situations insufficiently covered by the data sets considered herein.

Acknowledgment. The authors were supported by the project "STU ako líder Digitálnej koalície", project no. 002STU-2-1/2018, financed by Ministry of Education, Science, Research and Sport of the Slovak Republic. Maroš Čavojský also thankfully acknowledges a conference grant received from MAIND, s.r.o.

References

1. Čavojský, M., Drozda, M.: Energy efficient trajectory recording of mobile devices using wifi scanning. In: Ubiquitous Intelligence & Computing, Advanced and Trusted Computing, Scalable Computing and Communications, Cloud and Big Data Computing, Internet of People, and Smart World Congress (UIC/ATC/ScalCom/CBDCom/IoP/SmartWorld), 2016 International IEEE Conferences, pp. 1079–1085 (2016)
2. Google: Location—Android Developers. https://developer.android.com/reference/android/location/package-summary.html
3. Henikoff, S., Henikoff, J.G.: Amino acid substitution matrices from protein blocks. Proc. Natl. Acad. Sci. **89**(22), 10915–10919 (1992)
4. Hung, C.C., Chang, C.W., Peng, W.C.: Mining trajectory profiles for discovering user communities. In: Proceedings of the 2009 International Workshop on Location Based Social Networks - LBSN 2009. pp. 1–8. ACM (2009). https://doi.org/10.1145/1629890.1629892
5. Karney, C., Deakin, R.E.: FW bessel (1825): The calculation of longitude and latitude from geodesic measurements. Astron. Nachr. **331**(8), 852–861 (2010)
6. Čavojský, M., Uhlar, M., Ivanis, M., Molnar, M., Drozda, M.: User trajectory extraction based on wifi scanning. In: FiCloud 2018, The IEEE 6th International Conference on Future Internet of Things and Cloud, pp. 115–120 (2018)
7. Mavoa, S., Oliver, M., Witten, K., Badland, H.M.: Linking GPS and travel diary data using sequence alignment in a study of children's independent mobility. Int. J. Health Geogr. **10**(1), 64 (2011)

8. Michael, K., McNamee, A., Michael, M., Tootell, H.: Location-based intelligence – modeling behavior in humans using GPS location-based intelligence – modeling behavior in humans using GPS location-based intelligence – modeling behavior in humans using GPS. In: 2006 IEEE International Symposium on Technology and Society (ISTAS 2006), pp. 1–8 (2006)

9. Monreale, A., Pinelli, F., Trasarti, R., Giannotti, F.: WhereNext: a location predictor on trajectory pattern mining. In: Proceedings of the 15th ACM SIGKDD International Conference on Knowledge Discovery and Data Mining, pp. 637–646. ACM (2009)

10. Montoliu, R., Blom, J., Gatica-Perez, D.: Discovering places of interest in everyday life from smartphone data. Multimed. Tools Appl. **62**(1), 179–207 (2013)

11. Needleman, S.B., Wunsch, C.D.: A general method applicable to the search for similarities in the amino acid sequence of two proteins. J. Mol. Biol. **48**(3), 443–453 (1970)

12. Thiagarajan, A., Ravindranath, L., Balakrishnan, H., Madden, S., Girod, L.: Accurate, low-energy trajectory mapping for mobile devices. In: Proceedings of USENIX Association (2011)

13. Van Brummelen, G.: Heavenly Mathematics: The Forgotten Art of Spherical Trigonometry. Princeton University Press, Princeton (2012)

14. Yang, D., Zhang, T., Li, J., Lian, X.: Synthetic fuzzy evaluation method of trajectory similarity in map-matching. J. Intell. Transp. Syst. **15**(4), 193–204 (2011)

15. Ying, J.J.C., Lee, W.C., Weng, T.C., Tseng, V.S.: Semantic trajectory mining for location prediction. In: Proceedings of the 19th ACM SIGSPATIAL International Conference on Advances in Geographic Information Systems, pp. 34–43. ACM (2011). https://doi.org/10.1145/2093973.2093980

16. Zheng, Y., Li, Q., Chen, Y., Xie, X., Ma, W.Y.: Understanding mobility based on GPS data. In: Proceedings of the 10th International Conference on Ubiquitous Computing, pp. 312–321. ACM (2008)

17. Zheng, Y., Xie, X., Ma, W.Y.: Geolife: a collaborative social networking service among user, location and trajectory. IEEE Data Eng. Bull. **33**(2), 32–39 (2010)

18. Zheng, Y., Zhang, L., Xie, X., Ma, W.Y.: Mining interesting locations and travel sequences from GPS trajectories. In: Proceedings of the 18th International Conference on World Wide Web, pp. 791–800. ACM (2009)

19. Zheng, Y., Zhou, X.: Computing with Spatial Trajectories. Springer, New York (2011). https://doi.org/10.1007/978-1-4614-1629-6

Progress in Interpretability Research of Convolutional Neural Networks

Wei Zhang[1,2], Lizhi Cai[1,2], Mingang Chen[2(✉)], and Naiqi Wang[1,2]

[1] School of Information Science and Engineer,
East China University of Science and Technology, Shanghai, China
zweing1995@163.com, slytherinwnq@163.com,
clz@ssc.stn.sh.cn
[2] Laboratory of Computer Software Testing & Evaluating, Shanghai
Development Center of Computer Software Technology, Shanghai, China
{clz, cmg}@ssc.stn.sh.cn

Abstract. Convolutional neural networks have made unprecedented breakthroughs in various tasks of computer vision. Due to its complex nonlinear model structure and the high latitude and complexity of data distribution, it has been criticized as an unexplained "black box". Therefore, explaining the neural network model and uncovering the veil of the neural network have become the focus of attention. This paper starts with the term "interpretability", summarizes the results of the interpretability of convolutional neural networks in the past three years (2016–2018), and analyses them with interpretable methods. Firstly, the concept of "interpretability" is introduced. Then the existing research achievements are classified and compared from four aspects, data characteristics and rule processing, model internal spatial analysis, interpretation and prediction, and model interpretation. Finally pointed out the possible research directions.

Keywords: Convolutional neural networks · "black box" · Interpretability

1 Introduction

The concept of artificial neuron was first proposed in the 1940s. After decades of research, Yann LeCun designed and trained LeNet-5 model — classic CNN structure, in 1998, giving the basic component and framework structure of Convolutional Neural Network. Later, neural networks such as AlexNet, VGGNet, GoogLeNet, ResNet, DenseNet appeared, and they became deep and complex. These convolutional neural networks have achieved unprecedented breakthroughs in various tasks of computer vision, such as image classification, semantic segmentation, target detection and visual problem answering.

Although these neural networks have been successful in various scenarios, the entire network lacks intuitive and understandable components, making the results of the network model difficult to interpret. In particular, the application of neural network in the fields of medicine, financial markets, criminal justice, etc., interpretability is an extremely important standard for model evaluation, and has become the most worrying "black box".

© ICST Institute for Computer Sciences, Social Informatics and Telecommunications Engineering 2019
Published by Springer Nature Switzerland AG 2019. All Rights Reserved
Y. Yin et al. (Eds.): MobiCASE 2019, LNICST 290, pp. 155–168, 2019.
https://doi.org/10.1007/978-3-030-28468-8_12

Therefore, how to understand the interpretability of neural networks better is a common concern of academia and industry.

2 An Overview of "Interpretability"

As for interpretability, there is no strict mathematical symbol definition and no general (non-formula) literal definition. However, with the development of artificial intelligence, it is particularly important to study the interpretability of models. In general, it is far from enough to obtain simple prediction results for models from low-cost general fields (such as commodity recommendation) to high-cost key fields (such as finance and medical treatment). People began to pay attention to how the model made predictions.

The PhD student Leilani Gilpin from MIT's Computer Science and Artificial Intelligence Lab (CSAIL) has published a paper [1] that analyzes "interpretability" and several related semantic approximate terms, classifies the current machine learning model interpretability methods, and puts forward the evaluation of interpretability methods. Gilpin informally defines "interpretability" as understanding what the model does or has done. This paper discusses the difference between "explanation" and "interpretability". In a word, the model with interpretability can be interpreted by default, but not vice versa. The proposed interpretative understanding is divided into three types: (i) was proposed some explanation, while the key to this explanation does not represent a model will make the decision making process, but can provide a certain degree of reason to make a choice; (ii) was the representation of data in the network; (iii) was the establishment of a network model that generates interpretation.

In the 2nd ICML 2017 Workshop on Human Interpretability in Machine Learning (WHI), Google brain senior research scientist, Been Kim [2] reported on the interpretability study of machine learning and provided a preliminary understanding of the "interpretability" study of the AI model. This is a tutorial report that shows what is interpretability, why interpretability, and what we can do on interpretability. She said, Interpretation is the process of giving explanations To Humans. Comparing the AI model with traditional software shows that the AI model also needs security, debugging, principle support, iterative optimization and fairness and legality. Been Kim divided the third question into three aspects: pre-modeling, modeling time, and post-modeling. For example, consider data distribution before modeling, consider feature functions in modeling process, and consider hidden layer information in model completion.

Dr. Zachary C. Lipton, of the University of California, San Diego, and assistant professor of computer science at Carnegie Mellon University, shared a report on "The Mythos of Model Interpretability" [3] on the ACM Queue and discussed the interpretability of the supervised machine learning model. Lipton said that people have realized the importance of interpretability for a model, especially in key areas such as medicine, criminal justice systems, and financial markets. He believes that the results of the interpretable analysis of the deep model from the current academia can be seen that people generally agree with the term "interpretability", but there is absence of a definition. In other words, the meaning of "interpretability" is unclear, so that there are various papers that claim to be interpretable after optimizing a model or building a model. Such an article may interpret the model based on different starting points, leading to such a vague situation. Lipton divided the work of "interpretability" into two categories by analyzing the need for interpretability research. The first relates to transparency, i.e., how does the model work? The second consists of post-hoc explanations, i.e., what else can the model tell me? Finally, in order to standardize the "interpretability" study, he proposed that the interpretability study of the model should achieve one of the above two as a specific goal.

3   Convolutional Neural Networks "Interpretability" Research

Combining the above researches, in this paper, the "interpretability" of the convolutional neural network model (hereinafter referred to as the model) is summarized into four aspects (As shown in Fig. 1):

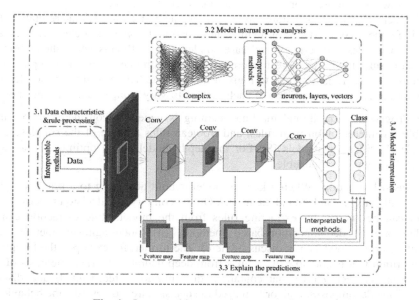

Fig. 1. Interpretable research structure diagram

- Data characteristics and rule processing. Initial exploration of model data or adding some known rules to the model (see Sect. 3.1 for details).
- Model internal space analysis. By analyzing the internal components of the model, such as unit level, hierarchical analysis (see Sect. 3.2 for details).
- Explain the predictions. Focus on the analysis of the results of the model, that is, post-hoc explanations (see Sect. 3.3 for details).
- Model interpretation. Based on the entire model, such as model simulation, construction of interpretable systems (see Sect. 3.4 for details).

3.1 Data Characteristics and Rule Processing

Data Characteristic. [4] has proposed feature selection can help to build better models with finer data. Removing the unrelated and redundant attributes can reduce the complexity of the model, so that the model can be understood and explained. When understanding a model, the first starting point is the characteristics of the original data. [5, 6] analyzed the influence of the original data features on the model interpretability from medical image data and material microstructure image data. [5] compared the results of the original image scaling $\times$ 1/2, $\times$ 1/4 and $\times$ 1/8 post-resolution pairs, indicating that the difference in the details of the two images provides an explanation for the prediction. However, the experimental comparison can only confirm that the detail features in the image can increase the prediction accuracy, but it is difficult to explain the influence of the details on the model decision. [6] used CNN to extract micro-texture features on Titanium, Steel, and Powder dataset images, and discussed the generalization and classification features between datasets when convolutional neural networks are used for microscopic image classification.

The selection of data features as a specific method of Model interpretation [7]. Based on the maximization of mutual information between selected features and response variables, a function model based on learning method is established to extract the feature subset with the largest amount of information in each given example. Then, an importance score is assigned to a given instance prediction result for each feature, allowing the relative importance of each feature to vary from instance to instance.

Rule Processing. Traditional machine learning is generally considered to be more suitable for interpretation with rules, and Boolean rules are one of the simplest interpretable classification models [8]. For the depth model, some optimized rule-based methods are equally applicable.

Rule-Based Extraction. When a known model is built according to a priori rule, it is theoretically easy to understand the model. On the contrary, the decision process of the model can be studied by extracting rules from the model. Rule extraction can be divided into (i) decomposition-based methods; (ii) model-agnostic methods (for machine learning models, not discussed here). The former, for example, the DeepRED [9] algorithm that is able to extract rules from deep neural networks. The basis of this method is the CRED [10] that contain both continuous (real-valued) and discrete literals. This decomposition algorithm used the decision tree to describe the behavior of the hidden layer elements of the NN. DeepRED extracted intermediate rules for each layer of the DNN through the CRED algorithm, then merged the previously generated rules and generated behaviors(rules) describing the DNN through input data.

Embedding of Prior Rules. A priori rules is embedded in the NN to explaining the model. [11] proposed a rule embedded neural network (ReNN) to cope with the shortcomings of neural network. ReNN breaks down the "black box" of ANN into two parts: local-based reasoning (local patterns learned from data sets) and global-based reasoning (a priori knowledge of human long-term accumulation) (As shown in Fig. 2). Through the local inference mode and rule analysis of the ReNN, the entire network is better interpretable.

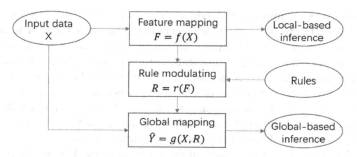

Fig. 2. Computational graph of ReNN(adapted from [7]).

3.2 Model Internal Space Analysis

The classical CNN structure given by Yann LeCun usually consists of input layer, hidden layer and output layer. Understanding the neural network from such a model structure requires an analysis of the roles of its components. It is divided into neural unit, neural network layer, hierarchical neuron combinations and perturbation-based models interpret four aspects of analysis.

Component Analysis Based on Neural Unit. On the analysis of neural network neurons, on the one hand, under what conditions a single neuron is activated, on the other hand, when a neuron is activated, it expresses information. The method displays the sensing area of the activated neuron by maximizing the activated input image and highlights a particular portion of the neuron image used to activate the convolutional layer through the deconvolution network.

[12, 13] both adopted the activation maximization method to analyze the information contained in the neuron, that is, to find the optimal stimulus of each unit by performing gradient descent to maximize the activation of the unit, mainly calculating the input sample when the activation of the ith neuron in the jth hidden layer is maximized. The downside is that the complex input distribution will fail. The latter optimized it and proposed that a single neuron can detect multiple characteristics (color, size and direction) on the original basis, while the existing maximum activation method only considers one of them. Therefore, the algorithm is proposed to synthesize the multi-aspect information that each neuron can express into the sample activation image through the activation method, which can more fully understand the function of each neuron.

The other [14], which adds a deconvolution operation (convolution operation is carried out on the filter with both horizontal and vertical directions reversed) on each convolutional layer of the classification CNN to visualize the image region activated by each neuron. In this paper, 9 images with the highest activation value are shown after convolution of each feature image. It can be seen that each feature map is "interested" in different images.

[15] evaluated the consistency between individual neural units and the quantified interpretability of visual semantic concepts (color, material, structure, parts, objects and scenes). And indicated that neural units is assigned different identifiable labels.

Hierarchical-Based Component Analysis. The formula $y = h(\omega \cdot x + b)$ for each layer of the neural network is the transformation of the input vector x to the output vector y. Where, $\omega \cdot x$ represents lifting dimension, scaling and rotation, b represents translation, and the function $h(x)$ represents distortion, namely the transformation of linear and non-linear matrix space is completed. The graphical explanation can be seen here [16, 17]. From the perspective of classification neural network, a hyperplane is found in the space after the linear transformation of the original space through the nodes in each layer and the nonlinear transformation of the activation function. This is explained by a operation from each layer of the neural network.

As for the expression of each layer of the neural network, [18] proposed that each layer of the classification neural network recognized the distribution of each category in the two data sets of ImageNet-CNN and Places-CNN, as well as the detection of an object by a single neuron. [19] illustrated the transferability of neural networks, quantifies the comparison between the universality and specificity of each layer of deep convolutional networks, and two factors affecting its portability are found: fragile coadaptation of middle layers and specialization of higher layers.

Component Analysis Based on Hierarchical Unit Combination. Instead of studying individual neurons or the concept of layers in a neural network, exploring linear combinations of hierarchical units brings new perspectives.

On the basis of theory, [20, 21] proposed different concepts. The former mapped semantic concepts to vectors based on the corresponding filter response. Analysis model internal filter proof: (i) In most cases, need more than one filter to code a concept; (ii) Not a single filter specific to a concept; (iii) For single filter activation, filter embedding can better represent the meaning of the representation and its relationship with other concepts. The latter proposed two counter-intuitive properties of deep neural network. [21] found that it is the space, rather than the individual units, that contains the semantic information in the high layers of neural networks. This provides a new point of view with the general understanding of neural networks. At the same time, this paper also proposed the existence of adversarial example in neural networks.

Subsequently, [22] introduced the concept activation vector(CAV), and represented that the model interpretation is formally expressed as a set of model state space vector *Em* and a set of unknown human understandable concepts *Eh*. The model interpretation can be expressed as a mapping relationship g:*Em* → *Eh*. As a way of conversion between *Em* and *Eh*, a set of human understandable input data examples are defined as concepts. The relative importance of concepts to classification is quantitatively analyzed to explain the neural network. [23] proposed each neuron in DNN is interpreted as an activation vector whose value is the scalar output generated by it on the input data. By collecting two groups of neurons and then outputting the alignment feature, it can be seen that the potential representations acquired by the two networks have similar characteristics. The advantages of this method are: one is to compare the representations learned by the two neural networks, and the other is to explain the representations of DNN hidden layer learning.

Internal Space Analysis Based on Perturbation. The perturbation in the neural network is not to delete or modify the model structure, but to input the processed test samples and then observe the prediction results of the neural network. The specific processing methods include occlusion experiment, noise study and adversarial sample study. [14] studied which region of the image has the largest effect, the experiment used a gray square to cover different positions of objects and then monitored the output of the classifier. The results are consistent with the results of human cognitive knowledge, that is, the key position in line with human knowledge will have a greater impact. [24] studied the effects of noises on the interpretation of neural networks. The deep Taylor decomposition is used to show the interpretation results of different interpretation rules in response to noise. [25] found out which part of the image has the greatest influence on its output score when disturbed, so as to understand the search position of the algorithm. [26] proposed a new scoring formula on the basis of antagonistic samples and characteristic scores. Based on the adversarial example, seeking the minimum data perturbation of model input can identify the important input characteristics and the minimum allowable data perturbation by looking for the maximum data perturbation that does not change the output. Among them, occlusion experiment is the most consistent with human cognition, but it has a strong artificial purpose. Some noise studies have achieved good results. Although the results of adversarial sample experiment are eye-catching, there are some deficiencies for human understanding.

[27] proposed LIME(Local Interpretable Model-agnostic Explanation), a novel explanation technique that explains the predictions of any classifier in an interpretable and faithful manner, by learning an interpretable model locally around the prediction. Observing the predictive behavior of the model by perturbing the input samples (actually a sampling method), and then assigning weights based on the distances of the perturbed data points from the original data, based on which they learn an interpretable model and prediction results. The essence of perturbation is that these around disturbances must be understandable by humans.

3.3   Explain to Predict

This part focus on the results of the model, such as analyzing the reason why an image is classified into a certain category from a CNN, which is explained by the two aspects of feature and visualization. And, feature interpretation is divided into feature importance and feature text interpretation.

Feature Importance. The interpretation of feature importance is to evaluate the features concerned by the model, and then measure the importance of the features with scores. Compared with the perturbation-based method above, it is easier because each perturbation requires a forward propagation of the network, which is computationally inefficient.

DeepLIFT (Deep Learning Important FeaTures) [28], an algorithm for recursive predictive interpretation of depth models that assigns importance scores to inputs for a given output. The difference is that DeepLIFT uses backpropagation to calculate the scores, so they can be efficiently obtained by a single reverse network propagation. LRP (Layer-Wise Relevance Propagation) [29] achieved pixel-level decomposition, using a single pixel to evaluate the impact of sample images in a kernel classifier and neural network, and visualize it. This method is equivalent to performing a DeepLIF operation, activating all input reference values (DeepLIFT will set a reference value for each input) to zero. [30] proposed the use of Shapley value to quantify the importance of characteristics of a given input, and proposed a sample-based method and "kernel SHAP" to approximate Shapley value. The commonality of the above methods is to use a local additional model to approximate the local model, and its inadequacy is also localized.

The difficulty with the importance of features is that it is difficult to evaluate them with experience. To compensate for this shortcoming, [31] proposed an integrated gradient approach. And two basic axioms that the attribution method should satisfy— sensitivity and implementation invariance. Integrated gradient is a new attribute method guided by these axioms. This method does not require any network tools, and can be easily calculated by a few calls to gradient operations.

For the deficiency of localization, [7] proposed the L2X (Learning to Explain) method, which learns the feature selection function different from the local approximation method of the previous function in the global scope, and takes the instantiated feature selection as the method of model interpretation. In particular, the importance score of each feature of an instance is given to indicate which features are the key for the model to predict on this instance.

Feature Text Interpretation. [32] focused on the description and interpretation of the recognition features, for example, when the neural network identifies a bird, it will give "this is a bird, because its beak is recognized" instead of "filter ith is activated at the highest level in the model". Such an explanation would be more useful to non-professionals with no knowledge of modern computer vision. The paper proposes that such interpretations must meet two criteria: they must be class sensitive and accurately describe specific image instances (Table 1).

Table 1. Feature importance methods comparison

Method	Train	Efficiency	Locality	Model-agnostic
LIME [27]	No	Low	Yes	Yes
DeepLIFT [28]	No	High	Yes	No
LRP [29]	No	High	Yes	No
SHAP [30]	No	Low	Yes	Yes
Integrated gradient [31]	No	High	No	Yes
L2X [7]	Yes	High	No	Yes

Summary of the properties of different methods. "Training" indicates whether a method requires training on an unlabeled data set. "Efficiency" qualitatively evaluates the computational time during single interpretation. "Locality" indicates whether a method is locally additive. "Model-agnostic" indicates whether a method is generic to black-box models (adapted from [7]).

[33] interpreted the output results of the model by generating counterfactual explanations of text types afterwards. The counterfactual interpretation here refers to a description of a characteristic fact that distinguishes Category A from Category B, for example, "This is not a scarlet tanager because it has no black wings."

Visualization. Further research into the interpretability of neural networks has shown that Deep Visualization is a good way to understand neural networks, and leads to the direction of Deep Visualization. These methods are mainly composite images, which can be divided into two directions: gradient-based method and network-based activation method.

Gradient-Based Approach. The Gradient Explanation of the input x is $E_{grad}(x) = \frac{\partial S}{\partial x}$. The gradient quantifies the extent to which a change in each input will change the predicted value $S(x)$ in its neighborhood. By iterating the gradient of the objective function and updating the random input x, the original image can be reconstructed in reverse [34] or the image that maximizes the score for a certain category can be realized [35].

[36, 37] proposed DeConvNet and [38] proposed Guided Backpropagation(GBP) based on the gradient method where negative gradient entries are set to zero while back-propagating through a ReLU unit to generate a clearer visualization.

[31] combined the axioms of previous research to guide a new approach, called Integrated Gradients (IG). With summing over scaled versions of the input solves gradient saturation. IG for an input x is defined as $E_{IG}(x) = (x - \bar{x}) \times \int_0^1 \frac{\partial S(\bar{x} + \alpha(x - \bar{x}))}{\partial x} d\alpha$, where   is a "baseline input" that represents the absence of a feature in the original input x.

[35, 38] demonstrated that the gradient could be used for extracting a saliency map of an image. However, they also tend to be noisy, covering many irrelevant pixels and missing many relevant ones. SmoothGrad [39] achieved the denoising effect by adding noise to the image, then sampling the similar image, and average the sensitivity map of the sampled image. Take an input x and average the resulting sensitivity maps E, $E_{SG}(x) = \frac{1}{N}\sum_{i=1}^{N} E(x + N(0, \sigma2))$, where $N(0, \sigma2)$ represents Gaussian noise with standard deviation σ.

Above classifier-dependent saliency maps can be utilized to analyze the inner workings of a specific network. [40] proposed a saliency map extraction method that does not rely on a classifier, which can find the portion of the image that any classifier can use.

Methods Based on Network Activation. Activation maximization is the search for an image that maximizes the activation of a specific neuron (also known as a "unit," "feature," or "feature detector") to reveal the neural response what it has learned (the features it has detected) in DNN. This technique can be performed for output neurons, such as neurons that classify image types [35], or for each hidden neuron in DNN [12, 41, 42], to explain the representation of neuron activation during prediction [34, 43].

Another set of visual activation methods not only focus on single neuron activation, but also take into account the global information of the image.

[31, 39, 44, 45] Integrated Gradient, SmoothGrad, CAM, GradCAM, each method show that the correlation between highly activated region (the area where neurons are highly activated) and highly sensitive region (the area where changes have the greatest influence on the output).

These methods provide useful insights into deep neural networks, but they also have some shortcomings. Based on gradient method, artifacts caused by discontinuity of gradient in the process of back propagation; Based on the network activation method, when the filter response is displayed in the deeper sensory field, the enlarged activation diagram may lose the details obviously. [28, 46] proposed methods to alleviate the problem of introducing artifacts. There is no good solution to the problem of missing details in the enlargement of the activation diagram.

Semantic-Based Feature Representation. [47] proposed the Network Dissection framework, a method for accurately calculating the receptive field regions of neural activation in feature maps. The Network Dissection effectively partitions the input image into multiple parts with various semantic definitions (accurate estimates of receptive fields) that match six semantic concepts (such as scenes, targets, parts, materials, textures, and colors). The semantics directly represent the meaning of the features to improve the interpretability of neurons. [20] proposed the Net2Vec framework, in which semantic concepts are mapped to vector embeddings based on corresponding filter responses. Through this method, the article can better describe the semantics of the filter and its relationship with other semantics. However, the common shortcoming of both is that the interpretation of network components (neurons, filters) is limited by semantic concept annotations, and the annotation of new concepts is costly.

For the deficiencies of the above methods, [48, 49] proposed an unsupervised method, that is, without the annotation concept part. [48] presented a graphical explanatory diagram that reveals the hidden semantic features in pre-trained CNNs. In the explanatory graph, each node represents a part pattern, and each edge encodes co-activation relationships and spatial relationships between patterns. [49] proposed a decision tree for coding potential decision patterns stored in a fully connected layer. The decision tree quantitatively interprets the logic of each CNN prediction, that is, given an input image, the decision tree tells people which object parts activate which filters for the prediction and how much they contribute to the prediction score. The decision tree can be used to explain the basic principles of each CNN prediction at the semantic level, which object parts are used by CNN for prediction.

3.4   Model Interpretation

Explain the model from the perspective of the entire model. The main methods are: simulation model and establishment of an interpretable model system.

Model processing. One is to simulate the model by constructing a simple human-understandable model to simulate the decision function of the depth model, so that the results of the simple model are close to the original model results to achieve the purpose of interpretation. [50] proposed Model Compression method to simulate a shallow network training shallow network, and obtain a single-layer neural network model. This new shallow model can achieve the same effect as the depth model. [51] also uses the method of compressing the model, but it is trimmed according to the filter importance index in the CNN model to achieve the effect of compression. The filter importance index is defined as the classification accuracy reduction (CAR) of the network after pruning that filter.

The other is through model decomposition, which is usually using decision trees that are well interpretable in machine learning as a tool. Both the DeepRED [9] and CRED [10] algorithms in the Rule Processing Section decompose the DNN model into decision tree models to obtain interpretable rules.

Interpretable model system. Building an interpretable model, [52] proposed a method to modify traditional CNN into an interpretable CNN to clarify the knowledge representation in high conv-layers of CNNs. In an interpretable CNN, each filter in a high conv-layer represents a particular object portion. And it automatically assigns each filter in a high conv-layer to the object portion during the learning process. The explicit knowledge representations in CNN can help people understand the logic within CNN.

[53] proposed the learning of qualitatively interpretable models for object detection based on the R-CNN. This method utilize a top-down hierarchical and compositional grammar model embedded in a directed acyclic AND-OR Graph (AOG) to explore and unfold the space of latent part configurations of RoIs. Then proposed an AOG Parsing operator to substitute the RoI Pooling operator widely used in R-CNN. In detection, a bounding box is interpreted by the best parse tree derived from the AOG on-the-fly, which is treated as the extractive rationale generated for interpreting detection.

4   Summary

Being able to understand a "black box" model is the most important issue related to model security, model optimization, and model generalization, especially in medical, financial and other engineering applications. Therefore, model interpretability has been the focus of research in recent years. This paper summarizes the related work based on the interpretability of the CNN, such as the meaning of "interpretability", and the classification of interpretable methods. Then, we find that the current model interpretability research is divergent, and there is no unified main line. They are basically based on their own previous studies and turned to interpret the results of these studies. Therefore, future studies on interpretability can focus on the following points:

(1) *Conceptual definition of "interpretability"*

At present, there is no unified definition of "interpretability" in the academia. This is not appropriate for the development of follow-up research. It is necessary to formulate a brief explanation for "interpretability".

(2) *Visual interpretation is the focus of interpretable studies*

Of the 53 references cited in this paper, 21 involved "observing" and understanding models from the perspective of visual interpretation. This is not a denial of other work, but it seems to be a trend, because the graphical interpretation gives the most direct understanding.

(3) *Establishing an interpretable system is the goal*

At present, there are not many achievements in the research on the construction of an interpretable system, but with the emphasis on the concept of "interpretability", people need a complete interpretative system to meet the needs of interpretation. Such a system does not merely provide a local interpretation, but an integrated end-to-end interpretation system.

Acknowledgment. This work was funded by Science and Technology Commission of Shanghai Municipality Program (No. 17411952800, No. 18441904500, 18DZ1113400) and Science and Technology Department of Hainan Province (No. ZDYF2018022).

References

1. Gilpin, L.H., et al.: Explaining Explanations: An Overview of Interpretability of Machine Learning (2018)
2. WHI: 2017 Homepage. https://sites.google.com/view/whi2017/home
3. Lipton, Z.C.: The Mythos of Model Interpretability. Communications of the ACM (2016)
4. Guyon, I., Elisseeff, A.: An introduction to variable and feature selection. J. Mach. Learn. Res. **3**(6), 1157–1182 (2003)
5. Geras, K.J., et al.: High-Resolution Breast Cancer Screening with Multi-View Deep Convolutional Neural Networks (2017)
6. Ling, J., et al.: Building data-driven models with microstructural images: generalization and interpretability. Mat. Discov. **10**, 19–28 (2018). S235292451730042X
7. Chen, J., et al.: Learning to Explain: An Information-Theoretic Perspective on Model Interpretation (2018)
8. Freitas, Alex A.: Comprehensible classification models: a position paper. ACM Sigkdd Explor. Newsl. **15**(1), 1–10 (2014)
9. Zilke, J.R.: DeepRED – Rule Extraction from Deep Neural Networks (2016)
10. Sato, M., Tsukimoto, H.: Rule extraction from neural networks via decision tree induction. In: International Joint Conference on Neural Networks (2001)
11. Wang, H.: ReNN: Rule-embedded Neural Networks (2018)
12. Erhan, D., et al.: Visualizing higher-layer features of a deep network. University of Montreal, 1341.3(1) (2009)
13. Nguyen, A., Jason Y., Jeff C.: Multifaceted feature visualization: Uncovering the different types of features learned by each neuron in deep neural networks (2016). arXiv preprint arXiv:1602.03616
14. Zeiler, M.D., Fergus, R.: Visualizing and Understanding Convolutional Networks (2013)
15. Bolei, Z., et al.: Interpreting Deep Visual Representations via Network Dissection. In: IEEE Transactions on Pattern Analysis and Machine Intelligence, p. 1 (2018)
16. http://colah.github.io/posts/2014-03-NN-Manifolds-Topology/
17. https://cs.stanford.edu/people/karpathy/convnetjs//demo/classify2d.html
18. Zhou, B., et al.: Object detectors emerge in deep scene CNNS (2014). arXiv preprint arXiv: 1412.6856
19. Yosinski, J., et al.: How transferable are features in deep neural networks?. Eprint Arxiv 27, 3320–3328 (2014)
20. Fong, R., Vedaldi, A.: Net2Vec: Quantifying and Explaining how Concepts are Encoded by Filters in Deep Neural Networks (2018)
21. Szegedy, C., et al.: Intriguing properties of neural networks. Computer Science (2013)
22. Kim, B., et al.: Interpretability Beyond Feature Attribution: Quantitative Testing with Concept Activation Vectors (TCAV) (2017)
23. Raghu, M., et al.: SVCCA: Singular Vector Canonical Correlation Analysis for Deep Learning Dynamics and Interpretability (2017)

24. Kindermans, P.J., et al.: Investigating the influence of noise and distractors on the interpretation of neural networks (2016)
25. Fong, R.C., Vedaldi, A.: Interpretable explanations of black boxes by meaningful perturbation. In: 2017 IEEE International Conference on Computer Vision (ICCV) IEEE Computer Society (2017)
26. Hara, S., et al.: Maximally Invariant Data Perturbation as Explanation (2018). arXiv preprint arXiv:1806.07004
27. Ribeiro, M.T., Singh, S., Guestrin, C.: Why should i trust you?: Explaining the predictions of any classifier. In: 22nd ACM SIGKDD International Conference ACM (2016)
28. Shrikumar, A., Greenside, P., Kundaje, A.: Learning Important Features Through Propagating Activation Differences (2017)
29. Sebastian, B., et al.: On pixel-wise explanations for non-linear classifier decisions by layer-wise relevance propagation. PLoS ONE 10(7), e0130140 (2015)
30. Lundberg, S., Lee, S.I.: A Unified Approach to Interpreting Model Predictions (2017)
31. Sundararajan, M., Taly, A., Yan, Q.: Axiomatic Attribution for Deep Networks (2017)
32. Hendricks, L.A., et al.: Generating Visual Explanations. In: European Conference on Computer Vision (2016)
33. Hendricks, L.A., et al.: Generating Counterfactual Explanations with Natural Language (2018)
34. Mahendran, A., Vedaldi, A.: Understanding Deep Image Representations by Inverting Them (2014)
35. Simonyan, K., Vedaldi, A., Zisserman, A.: Deep inside convolutional networks: visualising image classification models and saliency maps. Computer Science (2013)
36. Zeiler, M.D., et al.: Deconvolutional networks. Computer Vision & Pattern Recognition (2010)
37. Mahendran, A., Vedaldi, A.: Salient deconvolutional networks. In: European Conference on Computer Vision (2016)
38. Springenberg, J.T., et al.: Striving for simplicity: the all convolutional net (2014). arXiv preprint arXiv:1412.6806
39. Smilkov, D., et al.: Smoothgrad: removing noise by adding noise (2017). arXiv preprint arXiv:1706.03825
40. Zolna, K., Krzysztof, J.G., Kyunghyun, C.: Classifier-agnostic saliency map extraction (2018). arXiv preprint arXiv:1805.08249
41. Le, Q.V., et al.: Building high-level features using large scale unsupervised learning (2011). arXiv preprint arXiv:1112.6209
42. Yosinski, J., et al.: Understanding neural networks through deep visualization (2015). arXiv preprint arXiv:1506.06579
43. Dosovitskiy, A., Thomas B.: Inverting visual representations with convolutional networks. In: Proceedings of the IEEE Conference on Computer Vision and Pattern Recognition (2016)
44. Zhou, B., et al.: Learning deep features for discriminative localization. In: Proceedings of the IEEE Conference on Computer Vision and Pattern Recognition (2016)
45. Selvaraju, R.R., et al.: Grad-CAM: Visual Explanations from Deep Networks via Gradient-based Localization (2016)
46. Oramas, J., Kaili W., Tinne, T.: Visual explanation by interpretation: improving visual feedback capabilities of deep neural networks (2017). arXiv preprint arXiv:1712.06302
47. Bau, D., et al.: Network dissection: quantifying interpretability of deep visual representations. In: Proceedings of the IEEE Conference on Computer Vision and Pattern Recognition (2017)
48. Zhang, Q., et al.: Interpreting CNN Knowledge via an Explanatory Graph (2017)

49. Zhang, Q., et al.: Interpreting CNNs via Decision Trees (2018)
50. Ba, L.J., Caruana, R.: Do deep nets really need to be deep?. In: International Conference on Neural Information Processing Systems, MIT Press (2014)
51. Abbasi-Asl, R., Yu, B.: Interpreting Convolutional Neural Networks Through Compression (2017)
52. Zhang, Q., Wu, Y.N., Zhu, S.-C.: Interpretable Convolutional Neural Networks (2018)
53. Wu, T., et al.: Towards Interpretable R-CNN by Unfolding Latent Structures (2017). arXiv preprint arXiv:1711.05226

Edge Computing

Load-Aware Computation Offloading with Privacy Preservation for 5G Networks in Edge Computing

Xiaolong Xu[1,2], Xihua Liu[1,2], Xuyun Zhang[3], Lianyong Qi[4], and Yuan Yuan[5(✉)]

[1] School of Computer and Software,
Nanjing University of Information Science and Technology, Nanjing, China
njuxlxu@gmail.com, liuxihua710@gmail.com
[2] Jiangsu Collaborative Innovation Center of Atmospheric Environment and Equipment Technology (CICAEET),
Nanjing University of Information Science and Technology, Nanjing, China
[3] Department of Electrical and Computer Engineering,
University of Auckland, Auckland, New Zealand
xuyun.zhang@auckland.ac.nz
[4] School of Information Science and Engineering,
Qufu Normal University, Qufu, China
lianyongqi@gmail.com
[5] Department of Computer Science and Engineering,
Michigan State University, East Lansing, MI, USA
yyuan@msu.edu

Abstract. Nowadays, with the advances in wireless communication, the mobile devices are becoming important due to various applications which provide mobile users with plentiful services in the devices. The mobile devices can hardly complete all the computing tasks as they have limitations on the battery capacity, physical size, etc. In order to release these limitations, in the fifth generation (5G), the computing tasks can be offloaded from the mobile devices to the central units (CUs) which are enhanced into edge nodes (ENs) for processing. However, it is still a problem to select the appropriate offloading destination, aiming to improve the load balance for all the ENs. In this paper, we first formulate an optimization problem to improve the load balance of all the ENs for 5G networks in edge computing, considering the time consumption and the privacy conflicts. Then, a load-aware computation offloading method with privacy preservation, named LCOP, is designed. Finally, experimental results and evaluations validate our proposed method is both effective and feasible.

Keywords: Mobile devices · 5G · Edge nodes · Load balance · Privacy conflicts

© ICST Institute for Computer Sciences, Social Informatics and Telecommunications Engineering 2019
Published by Springer Nature Switzerland AG 2019. All Rights Reserved
Y. Yin et al. (Eds.): MobiCASE 2019, LNICST 290, pp. 171–183, 2019.
https://doi.org/10.1007/978-3-030-28468-8_13

1   Introduction

In recent years, along with the advances in the mobile communication technologies, a increasing number of mobile users are attracted to enjoy the services supported by the mobile devices, which leads to an unprecedented growth in the mobile data traffic. Based on the analysis of Cisco's networking visual index report, it is expected that the data traffic will grow at the rate of 57%, a tenfold increase over 2014, by 2019 [1]. In order to cope with this condition, fifth generation (5G) is developed [2]. In 5G networks, the theoretical peak transmission speed can reach more than 10 Gb/s, which is hundreds of times faster than that of 4G networks [3].

Generally, the computing resources of mobile devices are limited due to the restrictions like physical size, battery capacity, etc. Therefore, the computing tasks from the mobile devices need to be offloaded to the cloud via the distributed units (DUs) and central units (CUs) in 5G networks [4]. However, on condition that the tasks are executed on the remote cloud, the efficiency of processing the computing tasks will be affected. However, driven by the edge computing technology, the CUs can be enhanced into edge nodes (ENs) to provide storage and process ability [5]. The computing tasks which do not need to be dealt with immediately are offloaded to the remote cloud for processing, and the other tasks which have high priority are executed in the ENs. In this way, the experience of the mobile users is greatly improved.

However, the offloading process among ENs in 5G networks is imposed with several weaknesses, especially the security and privacy issues [6,7]. Some important security information, including current location, remote video, voice chat, etc., may also need to be offloaded from the mobile devices for processing [8]. On condition that the privacy information is offloaded from the mobile devices, the networks can obtain the contents of these information, which may lead to the risk of privacy leakage. The disclosure of private information will bring out many terrible problems. Therefore, it is of utmost significance to avoid privacy leakage during the computation offloading in 5G networks [9].

On the other hand, while the CUs have been enhanced into ENs which have data-processing ability in 5G networks, some computing tasks offloaded from the DUs need to be migrated to the other ENs for resource response due to the limited ENs computing power, which may lead to the number of the tasks hosted on ENs are not nearly equal. Hence, from the perspective of ENs, the load balance should be taken into consideration. The load balance makes differences in the throughput, data-processing capability, flexibility and availability of the networks in 5G. Hence, it is important and necessary to make an appropriate strategy for the computing tasks to find a better route to be offloaded across ENs [10].

To improve the response time and efficiency for executing the computing tasks in 5G networks, the ability of CUs has been expanded into ENs to provide storage and computation power for the tasks. However, due to the privacy conflicts of the datasets for running the tasks, some tasks cannot be offloaded to the same EN for execution to avoid the privacy leakage. Furthermore, the resource limitations of ENs need to be taken into consideration when the ENs are employed to execute the computing tasks. On condition that the computing task hosted on the first EN need to be offloaded to the other ENs, the load balance of all the ENs in 5G networks is also a significant problem waiting to be solved.

The main contributions of this paper are as follows:

(1) Analyze the load balance during the offloading of all the CUs, and the computation offloading problem with privacy preservation for 5G in edge computing is defined as a standard simple objective optimization problem.
(2) A load-aware computation offloading method with privacy preservation (LCOP) is adopted to realize the optimization to improve the load balance of all the CUs while guarding against privacy conflicts of the mobile applications.
(3) Conduct comprehensive experiments and evaluations to demonstrate the effectiveness and efficiency of our proposed method.

The reminder of this paper is organized as follows. Section 2 describes the mathematical modeling and the formulation. Section 3 develops a load-aware computation offloading with privacy preservation method for 5G networks in edge computing. In Sect. 4, simulation experiments and comparison analysis are presented. In Sect. 5, the related work is summarized. Finally, conclusions and future work are outlined in Sect. 6.

2 System Model and Problem Formulation

In this section, we establish the offloading task in 5G infrastructure. Besides, the resource usage and the load balance of EN are also analyzed.

Table 1. Key notations and descriptions.

Terms	Descriptions
MD	The set of mobile devices, $MD = \{md_1, md_2, md_3, \ldots, md_k\}$
K	The number of data-processing tasks and mobile devices
DA	The set of data-processing tasks, $DA = \{da_1, da_2, da_3, \ldots, da_k\}$
Q	The number of DUs
SD	The set of DUs, $SD = \{sd_1, sd_2, sd_3, \ldots, sd_q\}$
N	The number of ENs
SC	The set of ENs, $SC = \{sc_1, sc_2, sc_3, \ldots, sc_n\}$
RV	The set of running VM, $RV = \{rv_1, rv_2, rv_3, \ldots, rv_m\}$
RU_n	The resource utilization of n-th computing nodes
ALB	The overall load balance variance
UT	The urgency of the task in mobile devices
AT	The time consumed by the task migration

2.1   Resouce Model

We assume that there are k mobile devices, k data-processing tasks, Q DUs and N ENs in 5G, denoted as $MD = \{md_1, md_2, \ldots, md_k\}$, $DA = \{da_1, da_2, \ldots, da_k\}$, $SD = \{sd_1, sd_2, sd_3, \ldots, sd_q\}$ and $SC = \{sc_1, sc_2, \ldots, sc_n\}$, respectively. Consider a scenario, only one server is deployed in each EN. Besides, we assume that there are M VMs running in ENs, denoted as $RV = \{rv_1, rv_2, \ldots, rv_m\}$ (Fig. 1).

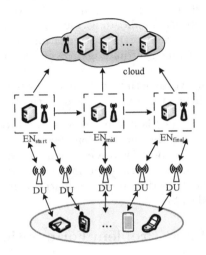

Fig. 1. The framework of migrating tasks in 5G.

2.2   Load Balance Analysis of ENs

VMs are rented for resource allocation in the ENs. The data-processing tasks from mobile devices are hosted by VMs. Note that the resource requirement of datasets and the capacity of servers in this paper are weighed by the number of VMs.

The resource usage is a pivotal index to measure the performance of the ENs. Note O_n as the variable to estimate whether the sc_n $(1 \leq n \leq N)$ is occupied, which is determined by

$$O_n = \begin{cases} 1, \text{if } sc_n \text{ isoccupied,} \\ 0, \text{otherwise.} \end{cases} \tag{1}$$

Then the OS_c^n is a binary variable to judge whether the dataset DA_c $(1 \leq c \leq C)$ is deployed on sc_n, which is defined by

$$OS_c^n = \begin{cases} 1, \text{if } DA_c \text{ is placed on } sc_n, \\ 0, \text{otherwise.} \end{cases} \tag{2}$$

The average resource usage of the EN is calculated according to the number of servers which are occupied. The number of occupied servers, denoted as MS, is determined by

$$MS = \sum_{n=1}^{N} OS_c^n. \tag{3}$$

The resource utilization represents the usage of the VM instances. The resource utilization of sc_n is calculated by

$$RU_n = \frac{1}{\alpha_n} \sum_{c=1}^{C} v_c \cdot O_n, \tag{4}$$

where α_n represents the capacity of the n-th EN and v_c represents the consumed number of VMs for dataset DA_c.

Finally, the average resource usage of the EN is calculated by

$$AU = \frac{1}{MS} \sum_{n=1}^{N} RU_n \tag{5}$$

Then, we consider the load balance of ENs in 5G. Through calculating the variance of resource utilization, the load balance variance of sc_n is calculated by

$$LB = (AU - RU_n)^2. \tag{6}$$

For all ENs, the average load balance variance is calculated by

$$ALB = \frac{1}{MS} \sum_{n=1}^{N} LB \cdot OS_c^n. \tag{7}$$

2.3 Privacy Model of Computing Tasks

In 5G networks, the computing tasks from different mobile devices combine privacy conflicts. These tasks need different datasets to accomplish their targets. However, the datasets may have requirements of different privacy preservation. Therefore, some computing tasks cannot be deployed in the same EN for further process.

A graph $\gamma = (A, R)$, where A represents the set of computing tasks and R represents the set of conflicting relations, is used to model the privacy conflicts of computing tasks. In order to make sure the privacy information of the mobile devices, a pair of conflict relations $(a_k, a_{k'}) \, (a_k, a_{k'} \in A)$ is incapable of the deployment in the same EN. The conflict computing tasks for a_n are obtained based on $ca_k = \{a_{k'} \,|\, (a_k, a_{k'}) \in R, k' = \{1, 2, 3, ..., K\}\}$.

The load-aware computation offloading strategy for the computing tasks is denoted as $OS = \{os_1, os_2, os_3, ..., os_N\} \, (os_n \in N)$, where os_n is the destination EN for hosting a_n.

Based on the acquired conflicting tasks set for hosting a_n, the deployed location a_n has the conflicting EN set, which is acquired by $cc_k = \{os_j \,|\, os_j \in ca_k, j = \{1, 2, 3, ..., |ca_k|\}\}$.

2.4   Time Consumption of Migration

On condition that the server of the first EN is full of tasks, we shall migrate the VMs from hosted EN to other ENs or the cloud. However, the process of migration consumes a quantities of transmission time.

$VF_m^{n,n'}$ is a binary variable that indicates whether the vm_m is migrated from sc_n to $sc_{n'}$ and the cloud, which is calculated by

$$VF_m^{n,n'} = \begin{cases} 1, \text{if } vm_m \text{ is migrated from } sc_n \text{ to } sc_{n'} \text{ and the cloud,} \\ 0, \text{otherwise.} \end{cases} \tag{8}$$

When the EN sc_n needs to be transferred between the EN, the time consumed by the AP and the VM is calculated by

$$TC = \sum_{m=1}^{M} \sum_{n'=1}^{N} OS_c^n \cdot VF_m^{n,n'} \cdot \frac{DS_m}{TE_1}, \tag{9}$$

where DS_m is the data size of the vm_m, and TE_1 is the transmission efficiency between the ENs.

Let $NU_{n,n'}$ be the number of ENs between the EN_{start} and the EN_{final}. The time consumed by migration from EN_{start} and the EN_{final} is calculated by

$$TM = \sum_{m=1}^{M} \sum_{n'=1}^{N} OS_c^n \cdot VF_m^{n,n'} \cdot \frac{DS_m}{TE_2} \cdot (NU_{n,n'} - 1), \tag{10}$$

where TE_2 represents the transmission efficiency between ENs.

If the VMs are migrated from the EN_{start} to the cloud, the time consumed by migration from EN_{start} and the cloud is calculated by

$$UC = \sum_{m=1}^{M} \sum_{n'=1}^{N} OS_c^n \cdot VF_m^{n,n'} \cdot \frac{DS_m}{TE_3}, \tag{11}$$

where TE_3 represents the transmission efficiency between EN and the cloud.

$flag$ is a binary variable that indicates where the vm_m is migrated, which is calculated by

$$flag = \begin{cases} 1, \text{if VMs in the EN}_{\text{final}}, \\ 0, \text{if VMs in the cloud.} \end{cases} \tag{12}$$

During the entire process of migration, the time consumption is calculated by

$$AT = \begin{cases} \sum_{n=1}^{N} 2TC + TM, \text{if } flag = 1, \\ \sum_{n=1}^{N} 2TC + UC, \text{if } flag = 0. \end{cases} \tag{13}$$

2.5   Problem Formulation

From the foregoing, the load balance of ENs is analyzed and quantified. In this paper, we aim to achieve the target of minimizing the load balance variance presented in (7). The formalized problem is formulated by

$$min ALB. \tag{14}$$

$$s.t. AT \leq \varphi(t). \tag{15}$$

$$os_k \notin cc_k. \tag{16}$$

Formula (15) means that the time consumption should meet the time constraint which is defined as $\varphi(t)$ according to the data size, delay and distance. Besides, formula (16) means that the privacy constraints must be satisfied.

3   Load-Aware Computation Offloading Method with Privacy Preservation

In this paper, our goal is to make optimization of the load balance under several constraints. Compared with the traditional algorithms such as weighted coefficient method, GA has been widely used in the optimization problems because of its good robustness, parallel processing mechanism and global optimization.

3.1   Encoding

Firstly, the computing tasks should be encoded in this operation. The computing tasks which are offloaded from the mobile devices should be represented as a gene. All of the genes consist of the chromosome which represents the efficient offloading strategy for the computing tasks. In this paper, the chromosome is encoded in integer. In GA, the fitness functions are used to evaluate the pros and cons of each individual. Then, the inheritance opportunity is determined. In this paper, the fitness functions include one category: the average load balance variance (7). As is shown in (14), this method aims to make optimization of the load balance. The constraints are given by (15) (16), representing the time consumption should meet the time limitation, and some computing tasks cannot be deployed in the same EN for execution to meet the privacy constraint.

3.2   Initialization

In the operation of initialization, the related paraments including the size of population SP, the probability of crossover PC, the probability of mutation PM, the number of iterations NI and the size of archive SA need to be determined at first. For each offloading strategy, $OS^j = \{os_1, os_2, \ldots, os_K\}$, where OS^j represents the j-th chromosome in the population.

3.3   Selection

The selection operation selects those individuals which have better fitness from the current evolutionary group into the mating pool. The crossover operation and the mutation operation can only select individuals from the mating pool to generate a better population.

3.4   Crossover and Mutation

In the traditional single-point crossover operation, two parental chromosomes are combined to generate two new chromosomes. Firstly, one crossover point is selected in the crossover operation. Afterwards, two chromosomes are changed.

On condition that the offspring chromosomes perform no longer better than the parental chromosomes of them but do not reach global optimal solution, the premature convergence will take place. The mutation operation is selected to keep the individual diversity in the population. In the mutation operation, the probability of each gene which will mutate is exactly equal.

3.5   Method Review

In this paper, we aim at optimizing the average load balance for all ENs. GA-based algorithm is selected to solve this problem because of its good performance in the optimization problem. Firstly, all of the computing tasks are encoded. Both the fitness functions and the constraints are given for the load-aware computation offloading problem. Secondly, after the fine-grained fitness assignment strategy, better chromosomes are selected from the population, the environmental selection and mating selection. Besides, the crossover operation and mutation operation are leveraged to avoid the premature convergence and produce new better offspring chromosomes.

4   Experimental Evaluation

In this section, comprehensive experiments and simulations are conducted to evaluate the performance of our proposed load-aware computation offloading with privacy preservation method for 5G networks in edge computing. In this comparison, we denote the running state without migration as benchmark, first fit decreasing-based computation offloading is marked as FFD, and the abbreviation of our proposed method is marked as LCOP.

4.1   Experimental Context

In this experiment, LENOVO TS250 is configured as the server. The basic configurations of this server are Intel Xeon-E3-1225V6, Quad-Processor clocked at 3.4 GHz and 4 GB of RAM. In Table 2, there are five basic parameters and the range of the values in our experiment. For the effectiveness of this experiment, we set five different numbers of the computing tasks to generate five different scale datasets. The numbers of the computing tasks are set as 50, 100, 150, 200 and 250, respectively.

Table 2. Parameter settings.

Parameter description	Value
The number of computing tasks	50,100,150,200,250
The number of VMs on each EN	7
The number of running VMs on each cloudlet	[1,6]
The transmission rate between AP and the ENs	1200 Mb/s
The transmission rate between APs	540 Mb/s

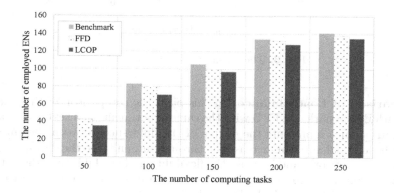

Fig. 2. The number of employed ENs.

Comparison of Employed ENs. In this part, the comparison of the whole employed ENs with Benchmark and FFD with the same experimental context is analyzed in detail. More ENs employed, lower resource utilization it has. Therefore, the number of the employed ENs is an important parameter which needs to be taken into consideration. Based on the outcome of this experiment, if the number of the computing tasks increases, the number of employed ENs will increase too. Besides, with the increase of the computing tasks, the increase of the number of employed ENs will be slow. In our proposed method, the number of computing tasks of 50, 100, 150, 200, 250 corresponds with the employed ENs of 35, 71, 97, 128 and 135, respectively. The number of the employed ENs is shown in Fig. 2.

Comparison of Resource Utilization. In this part, the comparison of the resource utilization with Benchmark and FFD with the same experimental context is analyzed. The resource utilization represents the percentage of the used VMs in ENs. If the resource utilization is low, the number of the employed ENs will increase. On this condition, the energy consumption will increase. Analyzed from our experiment, with the increase of the computing tasks, the resource utilization of LCOP will increase. In our proposed method, the number of computing tasks of 50, 100, 150, 200, 250 corresponds with the resource utilization of 59%, 63%, 67%, 70% and 75%, respectively. The resource utilization of ENs is shown in Fig. 3.

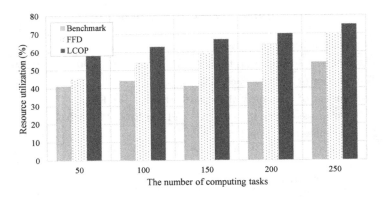

Fig. 3. The resource utilization of ENs.

Comparison of Load Balance. In this part, the comparison of the load balance with Benchmark and FFD with the same experimental context is conducted. The load balance represents the degree of the difference between the employed ENs. The load balance can increase the throughput, enhance the data-processing ability of the network, and increase the flexibility and availability of the network. Analyzed from our experiment, with the increase of the computing tasks, the value of the load balance in FFD and LCOP changes just a bit, and the value of the load balance in Benchmark changed a lot. In LCOP, the number of computing tasks of 50, 100, 150, 200, 250 corresponds with the load balance of 3%, 3%, 1%, 1% and 1%, respectively. The load balance for all the ENs is shown in Fig. 4.

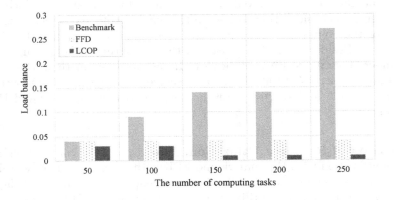

Fig. 4. The load balance for all the ENs

5   Related Work

Recently, due to advancements in wireless and mobile communication technologies, mobile devices such as tablets, laptops and smartphones are gaining great popularity in our daily life. There are various applications in these mobile devices such as remote video and GPS, which leading to quantities of data waiting to be solved [11,12]. Currently, in order to release the above problem, the 5th generation mobile network (5G), which can provide high data rate and low latency, is gaining much attention among the society [13,14]. The mobile applications can be offloaded from the mobile devices to the CUs or the cloud via DUs for execution in 5G networks.

However, some important information, including personal data and current locations, also needs to be offloaded for further processing. The privacy information may be leaked and the privacy leakage will bring a lot of problems with the customers [15–17].

In [18], Eiza et al. proposed a novel system for vehicular network in 5G, aiming to provide customers with a real-time, secure, reliable and privacy-aware video reporting service. In [19], Ni et al. introduced a secure and efficient service-oriented authentication framework. This network supports fog computing and network slicing for 5G-enabled IoT services. In [20], Fang et al. introduced the current features of different technologies and proposed a new 5G wireless security architecture in 5G networks.

If all the mobile applications are offloaded to the CUs without management, the load balance of the CUs will be very low. In this way, the data-processing capabilities, availability and flexibility of the 5G networks will be worse. Therefore, it is highly necessary for us to find the optimal migration strategy.

In [4], by implementing a mobile DBA and a fixed delay function firstly, Keita et al. illustrate the next generation-PON2 (NG-PON2) with low latency and small delay variation for 5G MFH. In [8], Zhang et al. proposed a mechanism for MEC named energy-efficient computation offloading (EECO) in 5G network, aiming to minimizing the energy consumption during the offloading. In [21], in order to release the end-to-end delay in 5G network, Chen et al. introduced a novel network architecture using data engine and a resource cognitive engine. Then, an optimal caching strategy was introduced for the macro-cell cloud and the small-cell cloud. In [22], Ketyko et al. summarized the NP-hard methods and problems related to load balancing, resource sharing, fairness and deployment among multiple users in 5G mobile networks. In [23], a statistical QoS-driven power adaptation scheme is proposed for the distributed caching assisted offloading scheme by Zhang et al. in 5G wireless networks. They also set up the system models for the partial in-network transcoding and the D2D assisted caching.

Based on the above analysis, the previous researches and studies have limitations on computation offloading for 5G networks in edge computing, and few works took the multiple-objective optimization for improving the load balance and protecting the privacy into consideration. In view of this challenge, a load-aware computation offloading with privacy preservation method for 5G networks in edge computing is proposed in this paper.

6   Conclusion and Future Work

In recent years, 5G has emerged as an important technology to release the mobile data traffic. The MEC paradigm, which is an effective paradigm, plays an important role in processing computing tasks in 5G networks. In order to optimize the load balance of all the ENs for 5G networks in edge computing while meet the constraints of the time consumption and the privacy conflicts of the computing tasks, a load-aware computation offloading with privacy preservation method is proposed in this paper. First, where the computing tasks are offloaded to is based on the priority of the computing tasks. Then, GA is leveraged to achieve the goal of optimizing the load balance. Subsequent experimental evaluations are conducted to verify the effectiveness and efficiency of our proposed method.

For future work, we plan to adjust and extend our proposed method to a scenario in the real-world and make investigation for other specific applications.

Acknowledgment. This research is supported by the National Natural Science Foundation of China under grant no. 61702277.

References

1. C. V. N. Index: Global mobile data traffic forecast update, 2014–2019, White Paper, 1 February
2. Dai, L., Wang, B., Yuan, Y., Han, S., Chih-Lin, I., Wang, Z.: Non-orthogonal multiple access for 5G: solutions, challenges, opportunities, and future research trends. IEEE Commun. Mag. **53**(9), 74–81 (2015)
3. Gupta, A., Jha, R.K.: A survey of 5G network: architecture and emerging technologies. IEEE Access **3**, 1206–1232 (2015)
4. Takahashi, K., et al.: NG-PON2 demonstration with small delay variation and low latency for 5G mobile fronthaul. In: 2017 European Conference on Optical Communication (ECOC), pp. 1–3. IEEE (2017)
5. Wang, X., Yang, L.T., Xie, X., Jin, J., Deen, M.J.: A cloud-edge computing framework for cyber-physical-social services. IEEE Commun. Mag. **55**(11), 80–85 (2017)
6. Li, S., Da Xu, L., Zhao, S.: 5G Internet of Things: a survey. J. Ind. Inf. Integr. **10**, 1–9 (2018)
7. Wang, X., Yang, L.T., Kuang, L., Liu, X., Zhang, Q., Deen, M.J.: A tensor-based big-data-driven routing recommendation approach for heterogeneous networks. IEEE Netw. **33**(1), 64–69 (2018)
8. Zhang, K., et al.: Energy-efficient offloading for mobile edge computing in 5G heterogeneous networks. IEEE Access **4**, 5896–5907 (2016)
9. Alliance, N.: 5G white paper, Next generation mobile networks, white paper, pp. 1–125 (2015)
10. Ren, L., Cheng, X., Wang, X., Cui, J., Zhang, L.: Multi-scale dense gate recurrent unit networks for bearing remaining useful life prediction. Future Gen. Comput. Syst. **94**, 601–609 (2019)
11. Beyranvand, H., Lévesque, M., Maier, M., Salehi, J.A., Verikoukis, C., Tipper, D.: Toward 5G: FiWi enhanced LTE-A hetnets with reliable low-latency fiber backhaul sharing and wifi offloading. IEEE/ACM Trans. Network. **25**(2), 690–707 (2017)

12. Mumtaz, S., Huq, K.M.S., Ashraf, M.I., Rodriguez, J., Monteiro, V., Politis, C.: Cognitive vehicular communication for 5G. IEEE Commun. Mag. **53**(7), 109–117 (2015)
13. Wang, S., Zhou, A., Yang, M., et al.: Service composition in cyber-physical-social systems. IEEE Trans. Emerg. Top. Comput. (2017)
14. Wang, S., Zhou, A., Bao, R., et al.: Towards green service composition approach in the cloud. IEEE Trans. Serv. Comput. (2018)
15. Ferrag, M.A., Maglaras, L., Argyriou, A., Kosmanos, D., Janicke, H.: Security for 4G and 5G cellular networks: a survey of existing authentication and privacy-preserving schemes. J. Netw. Comput. Appl. **101**, 55–82 (2018)
16. Xu, X., et al.: An IoT-oriented data placement method with privacy preservation in cloud environment. J. Netw. Comput. Appl. **124**, 148–157 (2018)
17. Xu, X., et al.: An edge computing-enabled computation offloading method with privacy preservation for internet of connected vehicles. Future Gen. Comput. Syst. **96**, 89–100 (2019)
18. Eiza, M.H., Ni, Q., Shi, Q.: Secure and privacy-aware cloud-assisted video reporting service in 5G-enabled vehicular networks. IEEE Trans. Veh. Technol. **65**(10), 7868–7881 (2016)
19. Ni, J., Lin, X., Shen, X.S.: Efficient and secure service-oriented authentication supporting network slicing for 5G-enabled iot. IEEE J. Sel. Areas Commun. **36**(3), 644–657 (2018)
20. Fang, D., Qian, Y., Hu, R.Q.: Security for 5G mobile wireless networks. IEEE Access **6**, 4850–4874 (2018)
21. Chen, M., Qian, Y., Hao, Y., Li, Y., Song, J.: Data-driven computing and caching in 5G networks: architecture and delay analysis. IEEE Wirel. Commun. **25**(1), 70–75 (2018)
22. Ketykó, I., Kecskés, L., Nemes, C., Farkas, L.: Multi-user computation offloading as multiple knapsack problem for 5G mobile edge computing. In: 2016 European Conference on Networks and Communications (EuCNC), pp. 225–229. IEEE (2016)
23. Zhang, X., Wang, J.: Statistical QoS-driven power adaptation for distributed caching based mobile offloading over 5G wireless networks. In: IEEE INFOCOM 2018-IEEE Conference on Computer Communications Workshops (INFOCOM WKSHPS), pp. 486–491. IEEE (2018)

A Pricing Incentive Mechanism for Mobile Crowd Sensing in Edge Computing

Xin Chen[1], Zhuo Li[1,2], Lianyong Qi[3(✉)], Ying Chen[1], Yuzhe Zhao[1], and Shuang Chen[1]

[1] School of Computer Science,
Beijing Information Science and Technology University, Beijing, China
{chenxin,lizhuo,chenying}@bistu.edu.cn,
duyadude@163.com, 1980995580@qq.com
[2] Beijing Key Laboratory of Internet Culture and Digital Dissemination Research,
Beijing, China
[3] School of Information Science and Engineering,
Qufu Normal University, Jining, China
lianyongqi@gmail.com

Abstract. Mobile crowd sensing (MCS) has been recognized as a promising method to acquire massive volume of data. Stimulating the enthusiasm of participants could be challenging at the same time. In this paper, we first propose a three-layer mobile crowd sensing architecture and introduce edge servers into it. The edge servers are used to process raw data and improve response time. Our goal is to maximize social welfare. Specifically, we model the social welfare maximization problem by Markov decision process and study a convex optimization pricing problem in the proposed three-layer architecture. The size of the tasks the edge servers assign is adjustable in this system. Then Lagrange multiplier method is leveraged to solve the problem. We derive the experimental data from real-world dataset and extensive simulations demonstrate the performance of our proposed method.

Keywords: Mobile crowd sensing · Pricing · Social welfare · Incentive mechanism · Convex optimization

Supported by the National Natural Science Foundation of China (Nos. 61872044, 61502040), Beijing Municipal Program for Excellent Teacher Promotion (no. PXM2017_014224.000028), Beijing Municipal Program for Top Talent Cultivation (CIT&TCD201804055), Open Program of Beijing Key Laboratory of Internet Culture and Digital Dissemination Research (ICDDXN001), Qinxin Talent Program of Beijing Information Science and Technology University, Supplementary and Supportive Project for Teachers at Beijing Information Science and Technology University (No. 5111823401) and Key Research and Cultivation Projects at Beijing Information Science and Technology University (No. 5211823411).

Y. Yin et al. (Eds.): MobiCASE 2019, LNICST 290, pp. 184–197, 2019.
https://doi.org/10.1007/978-3-030-28468-8_14

1   Introduction

There are many smart-phones with sensor devices proliferating in our daily life, which promote the prevalence of mobile crowd sensing. Mobile crowd sensing can be considered as a novel method to obtain data, handle and share the data [1]. It can be applied in many scenes, such as location [2,3], environmental monitoring [4] and smart transportation [5,6]. However, the process of obtaining data causes consume of the power, flow. Meanwhile, high quality of sensory data is crucial to the platform. Therefore, we need some incentive mechanisms to stimulate the users [10–16].

The traditional mobile crowd sensing system is two-layer framework [10]. With the rapid development of Internet of Thing (IoT), the platform need response quickly and provide service with high reliability [11]. Considering of the above, we introduce edge servers into traditional mobile crowd sensing system [12]. The flow of a typical three-layer mobile crowd sensing system in edge computing is shown in Fig. 1. It is composed of mobile crowd sensing cloud platform, crowds and edge servers. The edge servers can be deployed with mobile equipments (base stations, wireless routers). The task initiators and crowds could use the system to acquire or provide sensing data. The cloud platform could be regarded as an interface of task initiators and crowds.

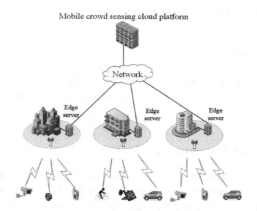

Fig. 1. A mobile crowd sensing system

In the three-layer system, each part of crowds wants to maximize its own utility because of the selfish of users. So we focus on designing an incentive mechanism to stimulate them. Our goal is to maximize the social welfare.

To design an efficient pricing incentive mechanism, there are three challenges we have to address. First, we introduce edge servers in a three-layer structure in mobile crowd sensing system. Second, our goal is to make the social welfare maximization and we must solve the problem in a polynomial time. The third challenge is on how to adjust the demand and supply according to the ability of crowds. Faced with these challenges, we consider a three-layer architecture and tend to boil down the social welfare maximization problem as a Walrasian equilibrium problem. Then convex optimization and Markov decision process(MDP) are used to model and solve the problem. Experiments show that our proposed method is efficient.

The contributions of our paper are listed as follows:

(1) First, we first propose a three-layer mobile crowd sensing platform and introduce edge servers into the platform to make the platform response quickly;
(2) Second, the dynamic of the crowds is considered in this paper. Then we use Walrasian Equilibrium to describe the problem and model by convex optimization and Markov decision process;
(3) Finally, the performance of our proposed algorithms are evaluated through Matlab. The performance of our proposed algorithms is 32.4% better than the existing method SWMA algorithm [17] and 39.3% better than the existing method NWSA [18]. We also compare the overpayment radio and our proposed algorithms is most closest cost than [17, 18].

The organization of this paper is as follows. We review the related work in Sect. 2. In Sect. 3, we present the model and the problem formation. The algorithms of pricing for mobile crowd sensing are presented in Sect. 4. Section 5 conducts simulations to evaluate the performance of our proposed algorithms. We conclude the simulation results in Sect. 6.

2   Related Work

We review the related works from three aspects: incentive of mobile crowd sensing, pricing on mobile crowd sensing and incentive of edge computing in this section.

2.1   Mobile Crowd Sensing Applications

The mobile crowd sensing could be applied in transportation, environmental monitoring, healthcare and social network. Tse et al. [5] analyzed the relationship between traffic jam and weather conditions in Beijing through Sina Weibo using social networks. Kalejaiye et al. [6] developed a mobile application for developing areas to predict bus arrival time. Matarazzo et al. [7] used the moving smartphones to monitor bridge vibrations and evaluated bridge avoiding unexpected rehabilitation. Xu et al. developed a NoiseSense system to house a rel-time urban mapping service [8]. Wang et al. [9] leveraged the influenced propagation on the social network to recruit workers.

2.2   Incentive of Mobile Crowd Sensing

The incentive mechanisms of mobile crowd sensing solve the problem that stimulating the enthusiasm of users' participation. Sun *et al.* [14] designed an online incentive mechanism and solved the social welfare maximization problem. It was based on heterogeneous belief values for joint social states and realtime throughput. However, it doesn't consider the optimality of the proposed auction. Jin *et al.* [13] guaranteed near-optimal social welfare based on reverse auction. But this paper doesn't consider the demand of the platform and can't adjust the supply according to the required. Peng *et al.* [15] considered the effort levels of participants to bridge the gap between sensing data quality and reward. However, the aforementioned incentive mechanisms don't consider the uncertainty of the mobile crowd sensing. Gao *et al.* [16] ensured a high probability of success to perform tasks using reverse-auction-based incentive mechanism.

2.3 Pricing on Mobile Crowd Sensing

A proper price of sensing data makes users willing to submit high quality sensing data [19]. Zheng *et al.* [19] presented the architecture of mobile crowd-sensed data market and introduced in-depth study into online data pricing. The method is leveraged to aggregate raw data and determine the trading pricing of sensing data. Duan *et al.* [17] introduced Walrasian Equilibrium as a comprehensive metric to price and solved social welfare maximization problem by dual decomposition. Like this, He *et al.* [20] solved the same problem but leveraged reverse flow network. The aforementioned works don't consider the data quality while pricing. The data quality is took into consideration in [13,21]. Han *et al.* [21] treated the pricing problem as non-submodular optimization problem and then converted it into submodular problem by Poisson binomial distributions.

2.4 Incentive of Edge Computing

The incentive mechanisms of edge computing are based on game theory mostly. Yang *et al.* [22] designed a distributed manner to solve the multi-user computation offloading problem in a multi-channel environment. Liu *et al.* [23] modeled the edge server owners' interaction and solved simulating computation offloading problem based on stackellberg game. Yu *et al.* [24] proposed Wi-Fi monetization model and used stackellberg game to analyse the factors affecting the venue owners. The above works don't solve the computation offloading problem effectively. Zhou *et al.* [25] combined deep learning and edge computing. They leveraged edge computing to process raw data and used reservation pricing auction to recruit participants.

Unlike the aforementioned studies, we first propose a three-layer mobile crowd sensing architecture and add edge servers into the system in this paper. Then we transfer the social welfare maximization problem as convex optimization and solve it by lagrangian multiplier method.

3 System Model and Problem Formulation

In this section, we first present variables to be used in the article. Each edge server plays a game with the crowds to decide which crowds to perform the task.

The crowds are dynamically moving because they may move to another spot while performing the tasks. So we suppose they can accomplish the tasks with a certain probability. The social welfare maximization problem is conducted in this section. Then we use MDP and convex optimization to model and solve it.

3.1   System Overview

Each task needs to be performed in serval spots called Area of Interest (AoI). We divide all task areas into several interest spots $Z = \{z_1, z_2, ..., z_l\}$. There are many interest spots in the AoI. The task set is $A = \{A_1, A_2, ..., A_m\}$, where A_i is a quintuple $A_i = \{Z_i, t_i^b, t_i^f, t_i, N_i\}$. Each task is interested in several spots. There are n crowds $U = \{u_1, u_2, ..., u_n\}$ to perform tasks. Suppose each edge server can receive and perform several tasks at the same time. The edge servers x can be defined as $G = \{G_1, G_2, ..., G_M\}$ where $G_x = \{l_x, g_x^b, g_x^f, c_x, M_x, M_X\}$. We consider that each user can perform a task at one time. The sensing time to perform the task can be divided into many time slots. p_{ij} is the unit price of task a_i in spot z_j. t_{ij} is the time performing task a_i in z_j. We consider the unit price p_{ij} of completing task a_i in different interest spots is different because of the complexity and cost of performing tasks.

$Z_i = \sum_{a_i \in z_j} z_j$ is the locations of task i requests. t_i^b and t_i^f are the earliest beginning time and the latest finishing time respectively. t_i is the sensing time of the task i required and N_i is the number of crowds the sensing task needs. l_x is the location of edge server x. g_x^b, g_x^f is the beginning time and the finish time of the edge server x correspondingly. c_x is the cost of the edge server x calculating from its crowds. M_x is the number of tasks currently being completed and M_X maximum number of performing tasks at the same time.

In this system, each part of the system wants to maximize their own utility and every member works toward this goal in each layer game. We formulate it as a social welfare maximization problem.

3.2   System Model

In this section, the edge servers and the crowds paly a game and decide which crowds to perform the task. Because the crowds are mobile, we can not accurately know the location of crowd. MDP is a common method to deal with continuous optimization in discrete-time. The basic idea of MDP is to choose the appropriate decision-making behavior to maximize the expected return value in the current state.

The MDP consists of a quintet $M = (D, S, A, P_{sa}, R)$, where

D: is the decision points. $D = \{0, 1, 2, ..., N\}$ where N represents that the time all sensing tasks completed.

S: is the states set, $s \in S$, s_i is the state of step i. $S = G \times L \times T \times V = \{G_1, G_2, ..., G_m, L_1, L_2, ..., L_m, T_1, T_2, ..., T_m, V\}$, where $G = \{G_1, G_2, ..., G_m\}$ is an m-dimensional vector represented currently-executing task. $G_i \in \{0, 1\}, i = 1, 2, ..., m$. $G_i = 1$ indicates that the crowds is performing the task and $G_i = 0$

means that the task isn't performed. $L = \{L_1, L_2, ..., L_m\}$ is an m-dimensional vector represented the location of the tasks. $T = \{T_1, T_2, ..., T_m\}$ is an m-dimensional vector represented the sensing time of the tasks and V is the moving rate of the crowds. In a time, the state of crowd is $s \in S$, the current task is $t \in T$, the movement rate is $v \in V$.

a: is the set of actions, a_i is the action of step i. The crowds can perform many different tasks, so $a = (a_1, a_2, ..., a_m)$, where $a_i \in \{0, 1\}, i = 1, 2, ..., m$, $a_i = 1$ indicates that the crowds is performing the task and $a_i = 0$ means that the task hasn't been performed.

P_{sa}: is the probability of state transition. P_{sa} is the probability distribution of the other states in the current state $a \in S$ after performing action a. For example, when the crowd takes action a at state s, the probability transferring to s' can be expressed as $p(s'|s, a)$. The current state is $s = [a_1, a_2, ..., a_m, l_1, l_2, ..., l_m, t_1, t_2, ..., t_m, v]$. We choose action a then the transition probability of next state $s' = [a_1', a_2', ..., a_m', l_1', l_2', ..., l_m', t_1', t_2', ..., t_m', v']$ is

$$P(s'|s, a) = \begin{cases} P[v'|v] \prod P[l_i', t_i'|l_i, t_i], & \text{if } g' = a \\ 0, & \text{else} \end{cases} \tag{1}$$

where $P[v'|v]$ is the transition probability of moving rate. $P[l_i', t_i'|l_i, t_i]$ is the union transition probability of the sensing time and the location of task i.

The arrival time of crowds follows a random point distribution. We suppose the arrival of crowds obeys the poisson distribution which is shown in Eq. (2). The arrival time is a random sequence of independent exponentially and distribution identically. Because the arrival of crowds is a poisson distribution, the number of crowds in different time is independent. The transition probability of location also obeys the poisson distribution.

$$P_n(k) = \frac{(\lambda t)^n}{n!} e^{-\lambda t} \tag{2}$$

R: $S \times A \rightarrow \mathbb{R}$, R is the reward function. If (s, a) transfers to the next state $s\prime$, the reward function is $r(s'|s, a)$. In each state, the value function of task a_i is $V_i(a_i)$ and it is a convex function. The utility of edge server $U_i(a_i)$ is $V_i(a_i)$ minus the payoff paid to crowds, which is defined in Eq. (3).

$$U_i(a_i) = V_i(a_i) - \sum_{j=1}^{l} p_{ij} t_{ij} \tag{3}$$

For the user u_k, the cost function of performing task a_i is $C_{ki}(t_{ki})$ and it is a convex function increased with sensing time. The utility function $U_k(u_k)$ of user u_k is the payoff getting from the edge server minus the cost $C_{ki}(t_{ki})$ of performing tasks which is defined in Eq. (4).

$$U_k(u_k) = \sum_{i=1}^{m} p_{ij} t_{ij} - \sum_{i=1}^{m} C_{ki}(t_{ki}) \tag{4}$$

For the edge servers and crowds, they all want to maximum their utility while the supply from the crowds and the demand from the edge servers are equal. According to exchange market theory of economics, this state reaches Walrasian equilibrium. Walrasian equilibrium means that the total amount of excess demand and excess supply in the entire market must be equal. Then the overall system reaches a Pareto optimal point. Pareto optimal is a kind of ideal state of resource allocation.

3.3   Problem Formulation

Social welfare of the whole system can be defined as Eq. (5)

$$W = \sum_{i=1}^{m} U_i(a_i) + \sum_{j=1}^{n} U_k(u_k) \tag{5}$$

For the edge servers and the crowds, they want to maximize their utilities. Then the problem can be described as a social welfare maximization problem which is defined as follows.

$$\max \quad W \tag{6}$$
$$\text{s.t.} \quad t_{ij} \leq t_i \tag{7}$$

Each task assigned by edge server is t_i, we divide the task t_i into several subtasks, the size of each subtask is less than or equal to corresponding task, which is described in Eq. (7).

4   Pricing Incentive Mechanism for Mobile Crowd Sensing

4.1   Convex Optimization Problem

The social welfare maximization problem proposed in Eqs. (6)–(7) is a convex optimization problem. We transform constrained optimization problem into unconstrained optimization problem using penalty function. The value of edge server $V(a_i)$ and the cost function of performing task a_i is $C_{ki}(t_{ki})$ are convex functions. We can apply Lagrange multiplier method to solve them. First, we introduce Lagrange multiplier method to obtain the augmented matrix where $\lambda_k > 0$. The Lagrange function is defined as Eq. (8)

$$W = \sum_{i=1}^{m} V(a_i) - \sum_{k=1}^{n} \sum_{i=1}^{m} C_{ki}(t_{ki}) + \sum_{j=1}^{l} \sum_{i=1}^{m} \lambda_{ij}(t_i - t_{ij}) \tag{8}$$

Then we define the value function $V(a_i)$ of task a_i as

$$V(a_i) = \omega log(1 + \omega) \tag{9}$$

Different application scenarios have different selection and measurement indicators of t_{ij}. Yang *et al.* [27] used the sensing time submitted by users to evaluate t_{ij}.

In [28], t_{ij} depends on the locations of users through a coverage function. In this paper, t_{ij} is the sensing time the task a_i requests.

The cost of the crowds performing task a_i is

$$C_{ki}(t_{ki}) = b_{ki}t_{ki}^2 + c_{ki}t_{ki} \tag{10}$$

where $b_{ki} > 0$ and $c_{ki} > 0$.

We bring Eqs. (9) and (10) into Eq. (8) then we have

$$W(\mathbf{t},\boldsymbol{\lambda}) = \sum_{i=1}^{m} \omega log(1+\omega) - \sum_{k=1}^{n}\sum_{i=1}^{m}(b_{ki}t_{ki}^2 + c_{ki}t_{ki}) + \sum_{j=1}^{l}\sum_{i=1}^{m}\lambda_{ij}(t_i - t_{ij}) \tag{11}$$

where $\mathbf{t}$ is the vector of sensing time got from the crowds, $\mathbf{t} = (t_{ij})_{z_j \in Z}$. $\mathbf{p}$ is the price vector, $\mathbf{p} = (p_{ij})_{a_i \in A, z_j \in Z}$.

We are motivated the method of constructing lagrange function by literature [29], we modify the lagrange function and consider the MDP problem into it as follows:

$$\begin{aligned} W(\mathbf{t},\boldsymbol{\lambda}) = &\sum_{i=1}^{m} \omega log(1+\omega) - \sum_{k=1}^{n}\sum_{i=1}^{m}(b_{ki}t_{ki}^2 + c_{ki}t_{ki}) + \sum_{j=1}^{l}\sum_{i=1}^{m}\lambda_{ij}(t_i - t_{ij}) \\ &+ \sum_{s' \in S} \tau p(s'|s,a)v_k(s')) + \frac{1}{2\sigma}||\Delta||_2^2 \end{aligned} \tag{12}$$

We consider the Lagrangian dual problem of problem (6), which is shown as follows:

$$\min_{\boldsymbol{\lambda} \geq \mathbf{0}} \max_{\sum_{i=1}^{m} t_{ki} \leq \chi_k} W(\mathbf{t},\boldsymbol{\lambda}) \tag{13}$$

$$\text{s.t.} \quad t_{ij} \leq t_i \tag{14}$$

4.2 Walrasian Equilibrium Algorithm

The dual decomposition method mainly aims at the convex optimization problems. It introduces the Lagrange multiplier, absorbs the constraint conditions into the objective function. Then we solve the optimal Lagrange multiplier as the main problem and decompose the optimization problem of the given Lagrange multiplier into several subproblems and solve separately.

In our paper, the dual problem (13)–(14) can be decomposed into main problem and sub-problem. The sub-problem is that given the Lagrange multiplier $\boldsymbol{\lambda}$, how to optimize $\mathbf{t}$ and $\mathbf{p}$ to maximize $W(\mathbf{t},\boldsymbol{\lambda})$. The main problem is that how to optimize the Lagrange multiplier $\boldsymbol{\lambda}$ to minimize $W(\mathbf{t}, \mathbf{p}, \boldsymbol{\lambda})$. Then the problem can be solved by two layers of circulation.

Sub Problem Algorithm. The sub problem is how to allocate the task to each crowd in each spot to maximize $W(\mathbf{t}, \mathbf{p}, \boldsymbol{\lambda})$ while given the Lagrange multiplier $\boldsymbol{\lambda}$. We can take the partial derivatives to get the optimal task allocation. We take the derivative of the Eqs. (9) and (10) which is shown in Eq. (15). Then we use the greedy iteration to allocate the task. The algorithm is shown in Algorithm 1.

$$\frac{\partial W(\mathbf{t}, \boldsymbol{\lambda})}{\partial \mathbf{t}} = \omega log(1 + \omega) - 2b_{ki}t_{ki} - c_{ki} - \lambda_k \qquad (15)$$

Algorithm 1. The task allocation algorithm between the edges and the crowds

---

Require: $\boldsymbol{\lambda}$
Ensure: $\boldsymbol{P}, \boldsymbol{T}, \boldsymbol{W}$
1: initialize the task allocation matrix $T_{i,j,k} \leftarrow \overrightarrow{0}$, the price matrix $P_{i,j,k} \leftarrow \overrightarrow{0}$, the social welfare matrix $W_{i,j,k} \leftarrow \overrightarrow{0}$, where $i \in m$, $j \in l$, $k \in n$
2: **for** $i \in m, j \in l, k \in n$ **do**
3:     calculate $T^*_{i,j,k}$ and $P^*_{i,j,k}$ according to Eq.(15)
4: **end for**
5: **repeat**
6:     **for** each task in each spot **do**
7:         calculate $W_{i,j,k}$ according to Eq.(12)
8:     **end for**
9:     $(i^*, j^*, k^*) \leftarrow arg \max\limits_{(i,j,k) \in T} W_{i,j,k}$
10:     allocate the task to user k^*
11:     $T \leftarrow T \setminus \{(i^*, j^*, k^*)\}$
12: **until** $T \in \phi$
13: **return** $\boldsymbol{P}, \boldsymbol{T}, \boldsymbol{W}$

Line 1 initializes the parameters used in this algorithm. We initialize the task allocation matrix $T_{i,j,k} \leftarrow \overrightarrow{0}$, the price matrix $P_{i,j,k} \leftarrow \overrightarrow{0}$ and the the social welfare matrix $W_{i,j,k} \leftarrow \overrightarrow{0}$. For all tasks in all spots, we calculate $T^*_{i,j,k}$ and $P^*_{i,j,k}$ according to the derived function Eq. (15) which is shown in line 2–4. Line 5–12 is the process of allocating tasks to appropriate crowds. Line 6–8 calculates the social welfare of tasks in each spot for each user. Then we select the crowd of maximizing social welfare and allocate the task to him. Finally we get the $\boldsymbol{P}, \boldsymbol{T}, \boldsymbol{W}$.

The time complexity of the Algorithm 1 is $O(lmn + ln^2S)$, where S is the average sensing ability of each crowds.

Main Problem Algorithm. We use the subgradient method to optimize Lagrange multiplier $\boldsymbol{\lambda}$ until it converge to $\boldsymbol{\lambda}^*$. In every iteration, the Lagrange multiplier is updated according to Eq. (16)

$$\lambda_{N+1} = [\lambda_N - \mu_\lambda(N)\frac{\partial W(\mathbf{t}, \boldsymbol{\lambda})}{\partial \lambda^N}]^+ \qquad (16)$$

where $[x]^+ = max\{0, x\}$. In Eq. (16), $\mu_\lambda(N)$ is the iteration steps. When $N \to \infty$, $\mu_\lambda(N) \to 0$ to ensure convergence. If the objective function is derivable, $\frac{\partial W(\mathbf{t}, \boldsymbol{\lambda})}{\partial \lambda^N}$ is the corresponding gradient value of the objective function in λ_N. Else, $\frac{\partial W(\mathbf{t}, \boldsymbol{\lambda})}{\partial \lambda^N}$ is the time gradient value of the objective function in λ_N.

Through the gradual release and transformation of the original optimization problem, the iterative optimization algorithm is finally obtained which is shown in Algorithm 2.

Algorithm 2. The main problem solution algorithm

Require: N^{max}
Ensure: $\boldsymbol{\lambda}, \boldsymbol{\sigma}, \boldsymbol{P}^*, \boldsymbol{T}^*, \boldsymbol{W}^*$
1: set the initialize number of iteration as $N_0 = 0$, set the initialize lagrangian multiplier λ.
2: **while** $N_0 < N^{max}$ **do**
3:     use algorithm 1 to calculate $\boldsymbol{P}^*, \boldsymbol{T}^*$
4:     update $\boldsymbol{\lambda}$ according to the Eq.(16) using the output of algorithm 1
5:     **if** $|\lambda^{N+1} - \lambda^N| > \varepsilon$ **then**
6:         $t_{ij} = t_{ij} + \alpha$
7:     **else**
8:         break
9:     **end if**
10:     $N_0 = N_0 + 1$
11: **end while**
12: $p_{ij}^* = p_{ij}$
13: $t_{ij}^* = t_{ij}$
14: $\lambda_{ij}^* = \lambda_{ij}$
15: $W_{ij}^* = W_{ij}$
16: **return** $\boldsymbol{p}^*, \boldsymbol{t}^*, \boldsymbol{W}^*, \boldsymbol{\lambda}^*$

Line 1 sets the initialize number of iteration as $N_0 = 0$ and the initialize lagrangian multiplier λ. Line 2–11 is the process of getting the finally P^*, T^*, W^*. In line 3 we use Algorithm 1 to calculate $\boldsymbol{P}^*, \boldsymbol{T}^*$. Then we use the output of Algorithm 1 to update λ. If $|\lambda^{N+1} - \lambda^N| > \varepsilon$, we increase the size of task and continue the iterative process. After the iterative process, we get the $\boldsymbol{p}^*, \boldsymbol{t}^*, \boldsymbol{W}^*, \boldsymbol{\lambda}^*$.

In Algorithm 2, line 3 use Algorithm 1, so the time complexity is $O(lmn + ln^2 S)$. The time complexity the Algorithm 2 is $O((n+1)^2(lmn + ln^2 S)(n+1))$, that is $O(n^4 l(m + nS))$.

5   Performance Evaluation

5.1   Simulation Setup

To evaluate the performance of our proposed algorithms, we take simulations on Matlab. We choose the data set from Stanford Large Network Dataset Collection [33]. The dataset contains the user's id, check-in time, latitude, longitude and location. We use the latitude and longitude to simulate the crowds' location. We classify the latitude between 40–41 and longitude between −123–122 of the crowds to edge servers and they can work for the edge servers. Other edge servers are in a similar manner. The size of tasks, the beginning time and ending time are generated randomly.

5.2   Simulation Results

First we generate 10 edge servers and 100 crowds. First we analyse the convergence and optimality, which is shown in Fig. 2. From the figure, we can get that the more iterations, the greater the social welfare. As the number of iterations increases, the social welfare converges when the iteration at around 800. The more accurate of the Lagrange multiplier λ, the greater the social welfare.

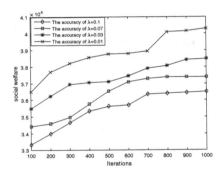

Fig. 2. The convergence of the proposed algorithms

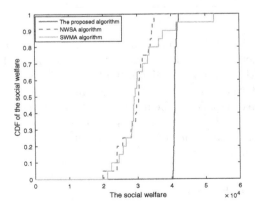

Fig. 3. The CDFs of the social welfare

To evaluate the performance of our proposed method, we take 100 experiments at each scenario. We compare our method with the existing methods Nonoptimal Winner Selection Algorithm(NWSA) [18] and Social Welfare Maximization Algorithm (SWMA) [17]. The cumulative distribution function (CDF) of the social welfare is shown in Fig. 3. The performance of our proposed algorithms are 32.4% better than the existing method SWMA algorithm and 39.3% better than NWSA.

Then we compare the overpayment ratio of our proposed method and the other existing methods. We define the overpayment ratio as $(payoff - cost)/cost$. The payoff is the payment the edge server pays to the crowd and the cost is the crowd performs the task. Figure 4 is the CDFs of the overpayment ratio. The average overpayment ratio of our proposed method is 0.05. The average overpayment ratios of SWMA algorithm and NWSA are 9.65 and 1.83 respectively.

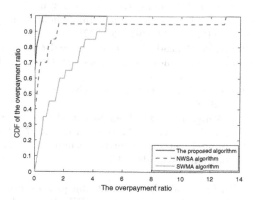

Fig. 4. The CDFs of the overpayment ratio

6   Conclusion

In this work, we first propose a three-layer mobile crowd sensing system structure. The edge servers are introduced to improve the response speed and service with high reliability. Then we conduct a game between the crowds and the edge servers. We build an MDP model and considered the social welfare maximization problem. Then we solve the problem by lagrangian multiplier method. The algorithms are designed to calculate the Lagrange multiplier and the social welfare. We implement them and evaluate the performance by real-world dataset. Our proposed algorithms are better than the existing methods NWSA and SWMA in social welfare and overpayment ratio.

References

1. Ni, J., Zhang, K., Yu, Y., et al.: Providing task allocation and secure deduplication for mobile crowdsensing via fog computing. IEEE Trans. Dependable Secur. Comput. (2018)
2. Jing, Y., Guo, B., Wang, Z., et al.: CrowdTracker: optimized urban moving object tracking using mobile crowd sensing. IEEE Internet Things J. 5(5), 3452–3463 (2018)
3. Zhou, R., Li, Z., Wu, C.: A truthful online mechanism for location-aware tasks in mobile crowd sensing. IEEE Trans. Mob. Comput. 17(8), 1737–1749 (2018)
4. Jezdović, I., Nedeljković, N., Živojinović, L., et al.: Smart city: a system for measuring noise pollution. Smart Cities Reg. Dev. (SCRD) J. 2(1), 79–85 (2018)
5. Tse, R., Zhang, L.F., Lei, P., et al.: Social network based crowd sensing for intelligent transportation and climate applications. Mob. Netw. Appl. 23(1), 1–7 (2017)
6. Kalejaiye, G.B., Orefice, H.R., Bafutto, M., et al.: Frugal crowd sensing for bus arrival time prediction in developing regions: poster abstract. In: International Conference on Internet-Of-Things Design and Implementation, pp. 355–356. ACM (2017). https://doi.org/10.1145/3054977.3057328
7. Matarazzo, T.J., Santi, P., Pakzad, S.N., et al.: Crowdsensing framework for monitoring bridge vibrations using moving smartphones. Proc. IEEE 106(4), 577–593 (2018)
8. Xu, Y., Zhu, Y., Qin, Z.: Urban noise mapping with a crowd sensing system. Wirel. Netw. 2018(3), 1–14 (2018)
9. Wang, J., Wang, F., Wang, Y., et al.: Social-network-assisted worker recruitment in mobile crowd sensing. IEEE Trans. Mob. Comput. 18(7), 1661–1673 (2018)
10. Zhang, Y., Jiang, C., Song, L., et al.: Incentive mechanism for mobile crowdsourcing using an optimized tournament model. IEEE J. Sel. Areas Commun. 35(4), 880–892 (2017)
11. Ni, J., Zhang, K., Xi, Q., et al.: Enabling strong privacy preservation and accurate task allocation for mobile crowdsensing. IEEE Trans. Mob. Comput. (2019). https://doi.org/10.1109/TMC.2019.2908638
12. Li, W., Liao, K., He, Q., Xia, Y.: Performance-aware cost-effective resource provisioning for future grid IoT-cloud system. J. Energy Eng. (2019, to appear). https://doi.org/10.1061/(ASCE)EY.1943-7897.0000611
13. Jin, H., Su, L., Chen, D., et al.: Thanos: incentive mechanism with quality awareness for mobile crowd sensing. IEEE Trans. Mob. Comput. (2018)
14. Sun, J.: An incentive scheme based on heterogeneous belief values for crowd sensing in mobile social networks. In: 2013 Global Communications Conference (GLOBECOM), pp. 1717–1722 (2013). https://doi.org/10.1109/GLOCOM.2013.6831321
15. Peng, D., Wu, F., Chen, G.: Data quality guided incentive mechanism design for crowdsensing. IEEE Trans. Mob. Comput. 17(2), 307–319 (2018)
16. Gao, G., Xiao, M., Wu, J., et al.: Truthful incentive mechanism for nondeterministic crowdsensing with vehicles. IEEE Trans. Mob. Comput. 17(12), 2982–2997 (2018)
17. Duan, X., Zhao, C., He, S., et al.: Distributed algorithms to compute walrasian equilibrium in mobile crowdsensing. IEEE Trans. Ind. Electron. 64(5), 4048–4057 (2017)
18. Li, J., Cai, Z., Wang, J., et al.: Truthful incentive mechanisms for geographical position conflicting mobile crowdsensing systems. IEEE Trans. Comput. Soc. Syst. 5(2), 324–334 (2018)

19. Zheng, Z., Peng, Y., Wu, F., et al.: An online pricing mechanism for mobile crowd-sensing data markets. In: Proceedings of the 18th ACM International Symposium on Mobile Ad Hoc Networking and Computing, pp. 1–10. ACM (2017). https://doi.org/10.1145/3084041.3084044
20. He, S., Shin, D.H., Zhang, J., et al.: An exchange market approach to mobile crowdsensing: pricing, task allocation, and walrasian equilibrium. IEEE J. Sel. Areas Commun. **35**(4), 921–934 (2017)
21. Han, K., Huang, H., Luo, J.: Quality-aware pricing for mobile crowdsensing. IEEE/ACM Trans. Netw. **26**(4), 1728–1741 (2018)
22. Chen, X., Jiao, L., Li, W., et al.: Efficient multi-user computation offloading for mobile-edge cloud computing. IEEE/ACM Trans. Netw. **2016**(5), 2795–2808 (2016)
23. Liu, Y., Xu, C., Zhan, Y., et al.: Incentive mechanism for computation offloading using edge computing: a Stackelberg game approach. Comput. Netw. **129**(201), 399–409 (2017)
24. Yu, H., Cheung, M.H., Gao, L., et al.: Economics of public Wi-Fi monetization and advertising. In: IEEE INFOCOM 2016-The 35th Annual IEEE International Conference on Computer Communications, pp. 1–9 (2016)
25. Zhou, Z., Liao, H., Gu, B., et al.: Robust mobile crowd sensing: when deep learning meets edge computing. IEEE Netw. **32**(4), 54–60 (2018)
26. Hu, T., Yang, T., Hu, B.: A data quality index based incentive mechanism for smartphone crowdsensing. In: 2016 IEEE/CIC International Conference on Communications in China (ICCC), pp. 1–6. IEEE (2016). https://doi.org/10.1109/ICCChina.2016.7636875
27. Yang, D., Xue, G., Fang, X., et al.: Crowdsourcing to smartphones: incentive mechanism design for mobile phone sensing. In: Proceedings of the 18th Annual International Conference on Mobile Computing and Networking, 2012, pp. 173–184. ACM (2012). https://doi.org/10.1145/2348543.2348567
28. Singla, A., Krause, A.: Incentives for privacy tradeoff in community sensing. In: First AAAI Conference on Human Computation and Crowdsourcing (2013)
29. Esser, E., Zhang, X., Chan, T.F.: A general framework for a class of first order primal-dual algorithms for convex optimization in imaging science. SIAM J. Imaging Sci. **3**(4), 1015–1046 (2010)
30. Ota, K., Dong, M., Gui, J., et al.: QUOIN: incentive mechanisms for crowd sensing networks. IEEE Netw. **32**(2), 114–119 (2018)
31. Wang, Z., Tan, R., Hu, J., et al.: Heterogeneous incentive mechanism for time-sensitive and location-dependent crowdsensing networks with random arrivals. Comput. Netw. **131**(2018), 96–109 (2018)
32. Jiang, C., Gao, L., Duan, L., et al.: Data-centric mobile crowdsensing. IEEE Trans. Mob. Comput. **17**(6), 1275–1288 (2018)
33. Snap Datasets: Stanford Large Network Dataset Collection, June 2014. http://snap.stanford.edu/data

An Active Defense Model in Edge Computing Based on Network Topology Mimetic Correlation

Shuo Wang[1], Qianmu Li[1,2(✉)], Shunmei Meng[1], Bo Zhang[1],
and Cangqi Zhou[1]

[1] School of Computer Science and Engineering, Nanjing University of Science
and Technology, P.O. Box 210094, Nanjing, People's Republic of China
qianmu@njust.edu.cn
[2] Intelligent Manufacturing Department, Wuyi University,
P.O. Box 529020, Jiangmen, People's Republic of China

Abstract. A large amount of real-time data, including user privacy information, control commands, and other sensitive data, are transmitted in edge computing networks. Aiming at the high-speed and reliable transmission requirements of data in the uncontrollable environment of edge computing networks, and maximizing the defense revenue, this paper proposes an active defense method for data interaction attacks in edge computing networks based on network topology mimic correlation, by pseudo-randomly constructing a moving communication path alliance and combining the network security state with a reliable prediction of transmission. A network topology mimetic association diagram and a communication path alliance mimetic transformation method based on dynamic threshold are proposed to ensure the data transmission service quality of the active defense technology of edge computing networks. The active defense model of the edge data network interaction process against the new attack and with the optimal defense cost is constructed, which provides a powerful guarantee for the active defense before the attack. The experimental results show that our method outperforms the popular methods in terms of transmission efficiency, reliability, and anti-attack performance.

Keywords: Network attack · Active defense · Edge computing

1 Introduction

One of the primary latent risks in a network is a cyber-attack on the network data interaction layer in the form of edge computing. This is due to the large amount of real-time state acquisition data, user privacy information and control command data present in an edge computing network. These data play a decisive role in user privacy protection and system decision control [3]. Alternatively, an edge computing network can

This paper supported by The Fundamental Research Funds for the Central Universities (No. 30918012204), Jiangsu province key research and development program (BE2017739), 2018 Jiangsu Province Major Technical Research Project "Information Security Simulation System".

Y. Yin et al. (Eds.): MobiCASE 2019, LNICST 290, pp. 198–212, 2019.
https://doi.org/10.1007/978-3-030-28468-8_15

perform real-time monitoring and control services on the edge of the critical infrastructure, with strict requirements on the performance of real-time data transmission [14, 15]. Considering data security interactions in an edge computing network, it is important to suppress attacks and execute evasive responses before a network attack causes damage [2, 3]. Therefore, edge computing networks urgently require active defense during data transmission.

However, the current network attack methods (CNAMs) such as the advanced persistent threat (APT) are concealed, and the attack principle is complex. Attack monitoring and passive blocking technologies based on traditional misuse detection have been unable to cope with such attacks. For this reason, active defense faces challenges. Fortunately, the self-organizing nature of edge computing networks provides a foundation for active defense of data interaction [21, 22]. However, previous technologies do not consider a moving adjustment in the case of reduced network connectivity and link quality caused by an attack [4]. Thus, the defense strategy of a moving adjustment algorithm requires further optimization and improvement.

Therefore, this paper proposes an active defense model for data interaction processes in edge computing based on a network topology mimetic correlation, achieved by pseudo-randomly constructing a moving communication path alliance under the premise of ensuring service quality. Then, this method integrates the network security state and transmission reliability prediction to adaptively mimic change and actively evade network attacks. The model includes an edge-aware node, an edge computing terminal node, and a primary station system and uses a negotiated moving multipath communication alliance to secure data communication. Figure 1 shows the framework of our research.

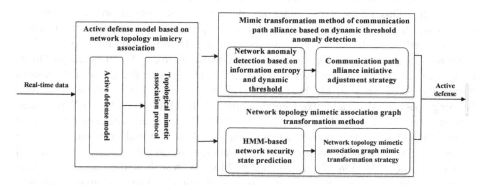

Fig. 1. Framework of active attack defense technology for edge computing network data interactions

The rest of this paper is organized as follows: Sect. 2 discusses relevant studies on moving network technology in mimicry defense. Section 3 gives the overall model framework and design for network topology mimetic association protocols. In Sect. 4, it describes a mimetic transformation method of communication path and a mimetic transformation method utilizing a mimetic topology correlation graph. In Sect. 5, the security of the model and verify the performance through experiments is analyzed. Section 6 summarizes the contents of this paper.

2   Related Works

In recent years, the moving target defense (MTD) proposed by the US Science and Technology Commission has attracted much attention as a new cybersecurity mimicry defense technology [1]. Moving network technology, as one of the most critical technologies for MTD at the network layer, has a promising application prospect in active defense.

A suitable communication path transformation strategy is crucial for implementation in moving networks. The communication path transformation strategy is used to generate a network management configuration of nodes that are used during the subsequent adjustment period. The randomness of the configuration increases the difficulty for the attacker in predicting the network management configuration. Recently, the pseudorandom approach has been extended to address the transformation strategy of moving networks. Atighetchi et al. [5] proposed a virtual port address association scheme for the client association proxy and a network address translation gateway to fill fake random addresses and ports into the corresponding fields of the data packet. Then, the data stream is redirected to defend against the attack. Once an "expired" node network management configuration is used, the possibility of detection will increase. Antonatos et al. [6] established a method for randomizing the network address space based on a transparent address association, which performs a header address translation of data stream packets. This approach maintains the novelty of the address translation table and prevents connection requests outside the service period. Badishi et al. [7] developed a random port association mechanism termed random port hopping (RPH). In this paper, the author designed a robust communication protocol to spread the impact of attackers. This protocol calculates the next association based on the number of successfully transmitted data packets and a shared private key. The port information is synchronized by sending an Acknowledgement (ACK) confirmation message. In 2012, Jafarian et al. proposed an OpenFlow random host mutation (35) [9] based on Open-Flow. The authors used OpenFlow to transparently change the IP address of the host to ensure the consistency of the host configuration. Aimed at the problems of limited hopping space in IPv4 and fixed hopping period, Dunlop et al. [16, 17] proposed moving target defense mechanism based IPv6 (MT6D). In order to enlarge the hopping space, IPv6 address space is adopted. Besides, MT6D uses pseudo-random number to set hopping period so as to improve the randomness. In 2014, Jafarian et al. [8] associated a host IP address with an address block with a short lifetime. The authors proposed a random association method based on the time and space domains to block, spoof and detect attackers. In 2015, MacFarland et al. [18] hide the link, IP, and port numbers of endpoint by setting up DNS hopping controller so as to prevent the leakage of MAC address. In 2016, Skowyra et al. [19] proposed network identity elimination mechanism called PHARE. It prevents MAC address leakage by randomly transforming header when packets flow out of the endpoint. Moreover, Sun et al. [20] proposed Decoy-Enhanced Seamless IP Randomization (DESIR) to increase the unpredictability. When unauthenticated nodes access the platform, DESIR uses honeypots to observe its behavior. When the user is judged as the attacker, DESIR prevents attack by changing endpoint information of node providing service and increasing the number of honeypots deployed. In order to prevent service interruption, DESIR separates the network identifier and transmission identifier of endpoint when it migrates services, thus ensuring the continuity of service provision by reserving the transmission identifier. Pseudorandom functions are exposed to higher security; however, it is possible that the node network management configuration will collide, in which case, scalability is not desirable.

In general, the implementation of the current moving network technology is simple, but there are several shortcomings: (1) The moving network adjustment strategy needs to compress or amplify the state space of the available node network management configuration. However, current methods with a pseudorandom function have a single control factor, and the generated space of the node network management configuration is difficult to accurately control. Thus, the scalability of the algorithm is weak. (2) In the existing literature, moving network adjustment strategies primarily focus on static and fixed methods. These approaches cannot be adaptively adjusted in combination with the current network security status.

Therefore, this paper proposed a moving network active defense technology based on network topology mimicry correlation, with the consideration of high security and real-time requirements of data interaction in an edge computing network.

3   Secure Transmission Model Based on Network Topology Mimic Association

3.1   Framework

The proposed model deploys the network topology mimicking association agent in the primary station system and the sensor node. The structure of the model is shown in Fig. 2.

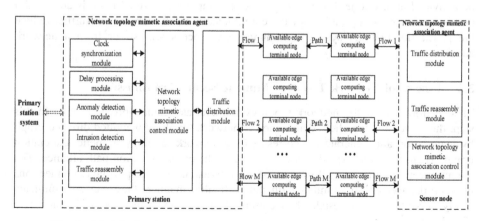

Fig. 2. Model of active defense for edge computing network data interaction

- The network topology mimicking association agent module is essential. This module controls other modules and available associated communication nodes, coordinating the communication path between the sensor node and the primary station service node server. This module generates a moving communication path alliance, and after the sensor node and the primary station server node negotiate the network topology mimetic map, the time synchronization module is used to calibrate the local clock and to enter the network topology mimetic association communication mode.
- The traffic distribution module allocates traffic according to the established communication path. The data legally sent by sensor nodes are transmitted to the proxy control module through the currently active communication path. Then, the data are sent to the primary station service node by the traffic reorganization module. The server is also returned to the client by passing the traffic distribution module and the active path node.
- The delay processing and anomaly detection modules sample the network data stream to evaluate network anomalies and delays. The associated agent control module dynamically changes the mimetic mapping configuration of the network topology and the moving communication path alliance according to the evaluation results by using a self-tuning strategy.
- The intrusion detection module detects intrusion based on the redundancy voting mechanism of the mimicry defense model for the edge computing terminal. By comparing the execution results of the heterogeneous redundant execution body, result deviations and network intrusion behavior can be identified.

The moving communication path alliance and the network topology mimetic association graph in the network topology mimetic association model change by using an adaptive strategy. This action increases the diversity and randomness of transmission throughout the entire edge computing network and increases the defense strength. In addition, only the available edge computing terminal nodes in the active period can be activated at any time. Each available edge computing terminal node is allocated a node association configuration for the communication path, which will further reduce the possibility that the system communication process will suffer from a network attack.

3.2   Process of Network Topology Mimetic Secure Transmission

This section designs the network topology mimetic association protocol flow. In this step, the server and the client determine the network topology weighted directed graph by negotiation and generate the corresponding network topology mimetic association graph. Then, the client pseudo-randomly selects the communication path alliance. The communication parties are allowed to establish independent transport layer connections on multiple dynamic communication paths. In this manner, they can communicate safely according to the established communication path. This process is shown in Fig. 3.

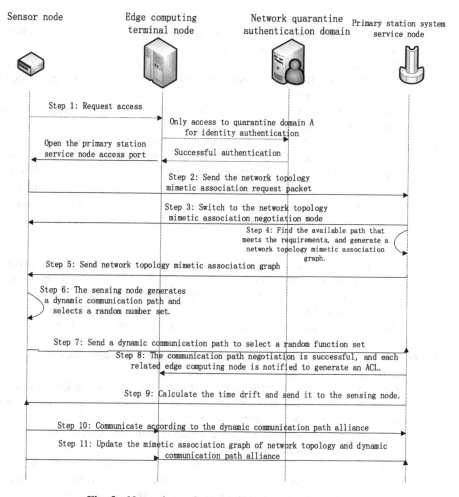

Sensor node   Edge computing   Network quarantine   Primary station system
                   terminal node   authentication domain   service node

Step 1: Request access

Only access to quarantine domain A
for identity authentication

Open the primary station
service node access port   Successful authentication

Step 2: Send the network topology
mimetic association request packet

Step 3: Switch to the network topology
mimetic association negotiation mode

Step 4: Find the available path that
meets the requirements, and generate a
network topology mimetic association
graph.

Step 5: Send network topology mimetic association graph

Step 6: The sensing node generates
a dynamic communication path and
selects a random number set.

Step 7: Send a dynamic communication path to select a random function set

Step 8: The communication path negotiation is successful, and each
related edge computing node is notified to generate an ACL.

Step 9: Calculate the time drift and send it to the sensing node.

Step 10: Communicate according to the dynamic communication path alliance

Step 11: Update the mimetic association graph of network topology and dynamic
communication path alliance

Fig. 3. Network topology mimetic association protocol

Step 1: When a sensor node supporting the network topology mimicking association accesses the edge access network for the first time and prepares to
communicate with the primary station system, direct access will be denied.
Because the edge computing terminal node does not control the related
network access for data transmission, the sensor node can access only
quarantine authentication domain A for identity authentication and trust
evaluation. However, once the node authentication and trust evaluation are
successful, the edge computing terminal node will open the network access
port of the primary station service node.

Step 2: The sensor node sends the regular request message $\text{Req}\{ID_c, Ip_c, ReqID,$
$p_{lower}, mark, T_1\}$ to the primary station node. ID_c is the identity of the sensor
node, Ip_c is the IP address of the sensor node, and $ReqID$ is the

corresponding unique ID of each Req message. p_{lower} is the minimum reliability requirement, *mark* is the support flag of the network topology mimetic association, and T_1 is the time.

Step 3: The primary station service node records the time T_2 at which the message *Req* is received. If the server does not support the network topology mimetic association, the message can be ignored. If the association is supported, the primary station service node switches to the network topology mimetic association negotiation mode.

Step 4: The primary station service node initiates a deep search algorithm to find an available path that satisfies p_{lower} between the sensor nodes. Then, a network topology weighted directed graph is generated. Let us use $p_{i,j}$ to denote the path reliability between the connecting nodes i and j. $p_{s,t}^k$ denotes the path reliability of the kth path between the primary station serving node s and the sensor node t at time t. In this case, $p_{s,t}^k = \prod_{(i,j)\in k} p_{i,j}$, and $p_{s,t}^k$ should be greater than p_{lower}.

Step 5: The primary station service node generates a corresponding network topology mimetic association graph $S_i = \{s_k | 1 \leq k \leq m\}$ based on the network topology weighted directed graph. Next, a response message Rsp$\{ID_s, S_i, T_3\}$ is sent to the sensor node, including the server identity ID_s, the network topology mimicking association graph S_i, and the response packet sending timestamp T_3.

Step 6: The sensor node records the time T_4 at which the message Rsp$\{ID_s, S_i, T_3\}$ is received. At the same time, the sensor node generates $\Phi_{i1}, \Phi_{i2}, \Phi_{GS}$ by a random function to determine the network topology mimicking dynamic communication path alliance $GS_i(t)$ and the communication path node association network configuration space $\Omega_i(t)$.

Step 7: The sensor node sends a response message Rsp$\{ID_c, \Phi_{i1}, \Phi_{i2}, \Phi_{GS}, T_5\}$ to the primary station serving node.

Step 8: The primary station serving node receives the packet Rsp$\{ID_c, \Phi_{i1}, \Phi_{i2}, \Phi_{GS}, T_5\}$ and records the time at which the packet is received as T_6. Then, a corresponding ACL is sent to notify all edge computing terminal nodes on the communication path with Ip_c and $\Omega_i(t)$ together.

Step 9: The primary station service node calculates the time drift $\theta = (T_2 - T_1 + T_3 - T_4 + T_6 - T_5)/2$ according to the timestamps $T_1, T_2, T_3, T_4, T_5, T_6$ and sends θ to the sensor node.

Step 10: The primary station service node adjusts the local time according to the time drift θ by synchronization correction. The sensor node and primary station node implement secure communication according to the established dynamic communication path alliance.

Step 11: When any life cycle of the network topology mimicry, T_S^i or T_{GS}^i, ends normally or abnormally at the end of the network attack, the network topology mimetic association is re-updated.

4 Mimetic Transformation Method

4.1 Communication Path Alliance Mimetic Transformation Method

Cyber-attacks necessitate a process of scanning, lifting, destroying, and so on. Before some of the preliminary steps are completed, the attack does not pose a real threat to the entire system, but it does cause network anomalies to a certain degree [12, 13]. Therefore, in this section, the communication path is adjusted based on a network anomaly metric. When the network anomaly metric exceeds a certain threshold, the moving communication path will be adjusted automatically.

The dynamic adjustment of the life cycle of the moving communication path alliance must meet the principle of "increase slowly and decrease rapidly". That is, when no network abnormality is detected and the probability a network attack is small, the survival time of the moving communication path alliance of the next association cycle slowly increases. Moreover, as the duration of the non-attack state increases, the growth rate of the current moving communication path alliance should also increase to improve the quality of the communication service. When a network abnormality is detected and the probability of a network attack is substantial, the survival time slot of the active communication path alliance in the next period is rapidly reduced. As the abnormal state duration increases, the reduction range of the survival time slot of the active communication path alliance in the next cycle should also increase to ensure communication security [23, 24].

Here, let us assume that $\sigma'_{t,f}$ is the standard deviation at time t and δ' is the threshold for a network outlier. Based on expert experience, this method chooses a function that meets the principle of "increase slowly and decrease rapidly", i.e.,

$$g(\sigma'_{t,f}) = \begin{cases} g_1(\sigma'_{t,f}), & 0 < \sigma'_{t,f} \le \delta' \\ g_2(\sigma'_{t,f}), & \sigma'_{t,f} > \delta' \end{cases} \quad (1)$$

with $g_1(\delta') = g_2(\delta')$, $g'_1\left(\sigma'_{t,f}\right) < 0$, $g'_2\left(\sigma'_{t,f}\right) > 0$, $g'_1\left(2\delta' - \sigma'_{t,f}\right) + g'_2\left(\sigma'_{t,f}\right) > 0$. The active adjustment strategy is

$$T_{GS}^{i+1} = \begin{cases} (1 + g_1(\sigma'_{t,f})) * T_{GS}^i, & 0 < \sigma'_{t,f} \le \delta' \\ (1 - g_2(\sigma'_{t,f})) * T_{GS}^i, & \sigma'_{t,f} > \delta' \end{cases} \quad (2)$$

4.2 Transformation Method for the Network Topology Mimetic Association Graph

When there is a given sequence of observed symbols, the hidden Markov model is suitable to predict the probability of occurrence of a new observed symbol sequence. The hidden Markov model is a stochastic process of the relationship between the observable variable O and the hidden variable S. It is very similar to the abnormal metric (hidden state) and the security state (observable state) of the security situation system [25, 26]. Therefore, using the hidden Markov model can well analyze the network security situation.

Here, this section proposes a hidden Markov based reliability prediction model of network security to realize a network security reliability prediction based on network security anomaly metric data. Based on the security reliability prediction results, the proposed method expands or compresses the network topology mimetic association graph and set a reasonable survival time slot T_S^i for the network topology mimetic association graph.

Network Security State Prediction Based on the HMM

The HMM can be described by a quintuple $\lambda = (N, M, \pi, A, B)$. In this quintuple, N indicates the number of possible hidden state values in the HMM, which can be recorded as $IS = \{IS_i | 1 \leq i \leq N\}$. Each hidden state value IS_i corresponds to M observable states O, which is recorded as $O = \{O_i | 1 \leq i \leq M\}$. Here, π is a $1 \times$ N-order initial probability distribution matrix, indicating the initial probability distribution of the hidden state q_1 for each possible hidden state value for the observable sequence O at time t = 1, $\pi_i = P(q_1 = IS_i), 1 \leq i \leq N$

$A = (a_{ij})_{N \times N}$ is a hidden state probability transfer matrix for Markov chains. For a first-order HMM,

$$a_{ij} = P(q_{t+1} = IS_j | q_t = IS_i), \sum_{j=1}^{N} a_{ij} = 1, 1 \leq i \leq N, 1 \leq j \leq N \tag{3}$$

$B = (b_{im})_{N \times M}$ is a probability matrix of the observed indicators, and the observed probability is $b_{im} = P(O_t = v_m | q_t = IS_i), 1 \leq i \leq N, 1 \leq m \leq M$.

To predict the security reliability of all accessible paths in the network topology mimetic map, the network security reliability hidden state levels are classified into five categories: safe, mild, general, moderate, and high-risk, expressed as $IS_1, IS_2, IS_3, IS_4, IS_5$ and assigned to 1, 2, 3, 4, and 5, respectively. Then, the reliability of each accessible path is transferred at a given probability in these five states. At the same time, the network security reliability of each path is defined by two observable indicators, the network transmission efficiency TE and network threat TH. The reliability is expressed as a random variable $x_i (1 \leq i \leq 2)$. The current security reliability of the entire network is measured from two different dimensions. Then, after time t, the observation sequence $O = \{o_1, o_2, \cdots, o_t\}$ is obtained from observation x_i.

Mimetic Transformation Strategy for the Network Topology Mimetic Association Graph

In the network topology mimetic correlation graph, it is assumed that there are n available nonintersecting paths at time t being assessed as medium-risk or high-risk paths at time $(t + 1)$ in forming the network topology mimetic map $S_n^-(t + 1)$. At the same time, there are m non-usable and nonintersecting paths at time t being assessed as safe, mild or general risk at time $(t + 1)$ for the network topology mimetic association graph $S_m^+(t + 1)$. Thus, the next network topology mimic map is $S_i(t + 1) = S_i(t) - S_n^-(t + 1) + S_m^+(t + 1)$.

At time $(t + 1)$, the new path $S_m^+(t + 1)$ will be added; if this path is selected as the communication path, only the primary station serving node needs to notify the edge computing terminal node on the path with the relevant ACL and other information, according to the network topology mimetic association negotiation algorithm. However, for the communication path $S_n^-(t+1)$ at time t, the primary station service node needs to notify the relevant parties to revoke the ACL and other information.

After the network topology mimetic map is adjusted at the completion time $(t+1)$, there will be a new map $S_i(t+1) = \{s_k(t+1)|1 \leq k \leq m\}$. Then, the overall reliability prediction value corresponding to $S_i(t+1)$ can be obtained as $SA_{S_i(t+1)} = \sum_{i=1}^{m} Sp_{t+1}^i$.

The function is then updated, satisfying the principle of "increase slowly and decrease rapidly".

$$h(SA_{S_i(t+1)}) = \begin{cases} h_1(SA_{S_i(t+1)}), & SA_{S_i(t+1)} = 1 \\ h_2(SA_{S_i(t+1)}), & SA_{S_i(t+1)} \in (2,3) \end{cases} \tag{4}$$

The self-adjusting strategy is as follows:

$$T_S^{i+1} = \begin{cases} (1 + h_1(SA_{S_i(t+1)})) * T_S^i, & SA_{S_i(t+1)} = 1 \\ (1 - h_2(SA_{S_i(t+1)})) * T_S^i, & SA_{S_i(t+1)} \in (2,3) \end{cases} \tag{5}$$

5   Experiments

The experiment performs a system simulation of the network topology mimetic association algorithm based on the NS2 network simulation environment. This model uses C++ to write the synchronization module, association module, communication module, attack module, delay processing module, sampling module, anomaly detection module, and deception processing module, and implements the network topology simulation by writing an OTcl script. The number of available IPv4 addresses in the network is 28, and the number of available ports is 1000. The initial correlation period is 120 s. We suppose that $g_1(x) = -ln(20x + 0.5)$, $g_2(x) = 16x^2 - 0.8x + 0.01$, $h_1(z) = -ln(20x + 0.6)$, $h_2(z) = 16z^2 - 0.64z + 0.064$. To mention that the simulation experiments are conducted in different scenarios with the same resources. The simulation results are shown in Figs. 6 and 7.

5.1   Security Analysis

Security is an important indicator for evaluating the advantages and disadvantages of a defense method. This section analyzes the anti-attack capability of the proposed active defense technology for an edge defense network attack based on network topology mimetic correlation. The active defense principle for edge computing network attacks based on the network topology mimetic association algorithm is shown in Figs. 4 and 5.

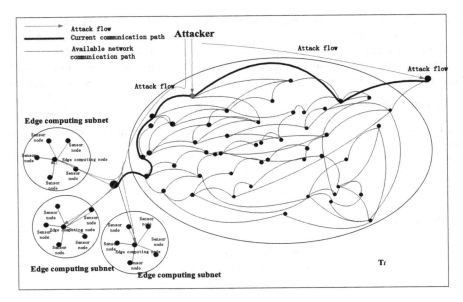

Fig. 4. Defense before network topology mimetic correlation

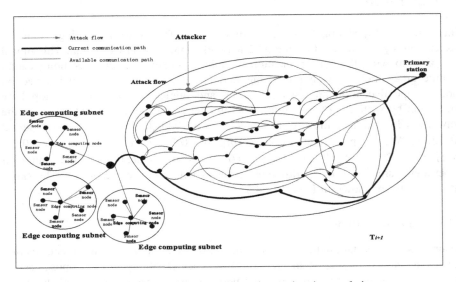

Fig. 5. Defense after network topology mimetic correlation

- DDos attacks

After the network topology mimetic association defense strategy is implemented, the IP address and port of the communication host and the protocol used by the communication parties will be associated after each corresponding time slot. For an attacker who performs a DoS attack, it is necessary to continuously send a large number of service requests to the target host and consume the target host resources. However, the node network configuration of the target host is continuously associated; thus, a DoS attack cannot be initiated [27].

- Anti-semi-blind attacks

A blind attack occurs when an attacker cannot locate the current active node network configuration and attacks all available nodes of the node network configuration state space that are detected. The attack strength is evenly distributed across all available nodes. The network topology mimetic association algorithm further increases the difficulty for an attacker to detect and locate the current active node network configuration of the associated system, and thus, the ability to resist and anti-semi-blind attacks is improved [28].

5.2 Experiment Against DDoS Attacks

In this section, the SYN-Flood mode is used to guide a DoS attack. Experiments test the average service response time of the network topology mimetic association system under different SYN-Flood attack rates to reflect the service availability performance. Figure 6 shows results for the non-topology-association algorithm (No NTAA), the simple topology association algorithm (Simple NTAA), the end-hopping-based topology association algorithm (EH NTAA) proposed in [10, 11], and the network topology mimetic association (PA NTAA) proposed in this paper. The results show that the network topology mimetic association strategy proposed in this paper can better resist DoS attacks. This result occurs because the mimetic correlation technology of the network topology dynamically measures network anomalies according to the strength of cyber attacks. Then, the network topology mimetic maps and communication paths are automatically adjusted. Adjustments increase the difficulty of hitting a path for DDoS attacks. However, the difference between the results for the association strategy in EH NTAA and PA NTAA is not significant. Moreover, when the mimetic map space of the network topology is compressed to almost zero, the DDoS attack enters an unsupervised blind attack state, that is, an average attack on all nodes in the accessible path detected by the attacker.

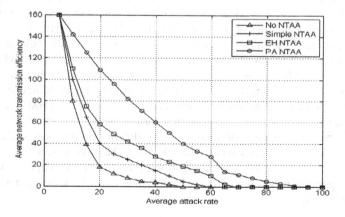

Fig. 6. Results for DDoS attack defense test

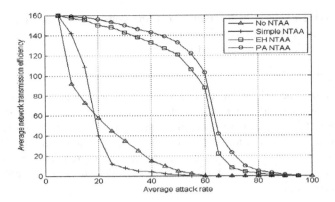

Fig. 7. Results for semi-blind attack defense

5.3   Experiment Against a Semi-blind Attack

Here, it uses a perceptual node edge access system with 20 communication paths for experiments. It can be seen from Fig. 7 that when the edge of the access node is connected to the network, the network transmission delay increases rapidly as the proportion of the received attack path reaches 50%. When the proportion exceeds 60%, the network transmission delay tends to infinity. The average response time of the EH topology association strategy is better than that of the No NTAA but is not as good as that of the Simple NTAA, which is consistent with the analysis presented in [10]. The average response time of the PA NTAA is better than that of the Simple NTAA.

6   Conclusion

Based on a thorough study of the mobile self-organizing characteristics of edge computing networks, this paper combines a moving network transmission with path mimicry adjustment techniques to propose a strict, formal description and definition. An active defense framework for data transmission in an edge computing network based on a link layer and application layer network topology mimetic correlation is designed to ensure scalability of the algorithm. To solve the problem of attacks and to improve defense and transmission quality with a moving periodic adjustment of the network, this research proposes a moving communication path alliance and a mimetic map dislocation transformation method for network topology. Starting from the temporal and spatial dimensions, the model combines moving threshold network anomaly detection and reliability prediction of network security based on the HMM. In this way, the experiment can perform a reasonable transformation of the network, minimize the mimetic adjustment overhead and resolve active defense problems in a DDoS attack and semi-blind attack. Experimental results show that the transmission efficiency of the network topology mimetic association algorithm proposed in this paper is higher than that of other popular methods and the reliability and anti-attack performance are significantly improved.

References

1. Dunlop, M., Groat, S., Urbanski, W., Marchany, R., Tront, J.: MT6D: a moving target IPv6 defense. In: Military Communications Conference, 2011 – Milcom, pp. 1321–1326. IEEE (2012)
2. Bunz, M., Meikle, G.: The internet of things. Sci. Am. **4**(1), 20–25 (2018)
3. Roman, R., Lopez, J., Mambo, M.: Mobile edge computing, Fog et al.: a survey and analysis of security threats and challenges. Future Gener. Comput. Syst. **78**(2), 680–698 (2018). S0167739X16305635
4. Wang, F., Xu, J., Wang, X., Cui, S.G.: Joint offloading and computing optimization in wireless powered mobile-edge computing systems. IEEE Trans. Wirel. Commun. **17**(3), 1784–1797 (2017)
5. Atighetchi, M., Pal, P., Webber, F., Jones, C.: Adaptive use of network-centric mechanisms in cyber-defense. In: IEEE International Symposium on Object-Oriented Real-Time Distributed Computing, pp. 183–192. IEEE (2003)
6. Antonatos, S., Akritidis, P., Markatos, E.P., Anagnostakis, K.G.: Defending against hitlist worms using network address space randomization. In: ACM Workshop on Rapid Malcode, pp. 30–40. ACM (2005)
7. Badishi, G., Herzberg, A., Keidar, I.: Keeping denial-of-service attackers in the dark. IEEE Trans. Dependable Secure Comput. **4**(3), 191–204 (2007)
8. Jafarian, J.H.H., Al-Shaer, E., Duan, Q.: Spatio-temporal address mutation for proactive cyber agility against sophisticated attackers. In: ACM Workshop, pp. 69–78. ACM (2014)
9. Jafarian, J.H., Al-Shaer, E., Duan, Q.: Openflow random host mutation: transparent moving target defense using software defined networking. In: The Workshop on Hot Topics in Software Defined Networks, pp. 127–132. ACM (2012)
10. Zhao, C.: Research on adaptive strategy of end information hopping system. Nankai University (2012)
11. Zhang, X., Niu, W., Yang, G., Zhuo, Z., Lv, F.: APT attack prediction method based on tree structure. J. Univ. Electron. Sci. Technol. China **45**(4), 582–588 (2016)
12. Haggerty, J., Shi, Q., Merabti, M.: Beyond the perimeter: the need for early detection of denial of service attacks. In: Computer Security Applications Conference 2002 Proceedings, pp. 413–422. IEEE (2002)
13. Zhang, J., Gunter, C.A.: Application-aware secure multicast for power grid communications. In: IEEE International Conference on Smart Grid Communications, pp. 339–344. IEEE (2010)
14. Li, H., Ota, K., Dong, M.: Learning IoT in edge: deep learning for the internet of things with edge computing. IEEE Netw. **32**(1), 96–101 (2018)
15. Ai, Y., Peng, M., Zhang, K.: Edge computing technologies for internet of things: a primer. Digital Commun. Netw. **4**(2), 77–86 (2018)
16. Dunlop, M., Groat, S., Urbanski, W., Marchany, R., Tront, J.: MT6D: a moving target IPv6 defense. In: Proceedings of the Military Communications Conference (MILCOM 2011), pp. 1321–1326. IEEE, Baltimore, November 2011
17. Dunlop, M., Groat, S., Urbanski, W., Marchany, R., Tront, J.: The blind Man's bluff approach to security using IPv6. IEEE Secur. Priv. **10**(4), 35–43 (2012)
18. MacFarland, D.C., Shue, C.A.: The SDN shuffle: creating a moving-target defense using host-based software-defined networking. In: Proceedings of the 2nd ACM Workshop on Moving Target Defense, MTD 2015, USA, pp. 37–41 (2015)

19. Skowyra, R., Bauer, K., Dedhia, V., Okhravi, H.: Have No PHEAR: networks without identifiers. In: Proceedings of the 2016 ACM Workshop on Moving Target Defense, MTD 2016, Austria, pp. 3–14 (2016)
20. Sun, J., Sun, K.: DESIR: decoy-enhanced seamless IP randomization. In: Proceedings of the 35th Annual IEEE International Conference on Computer Communications, pp. 1–9. IEEE INFOCOM, April 2016
21. Chen, J., Su, C., Yeh, K.-H., Yung, M.: Special issue on advanced persistent threat. Future Gener. Comput. Syst. 79(Part 1), 243–246 (2018)
22. Yang, L.-X., Li, P., Yang, X., Tang, Y.Y., et al.: A risk management approach to defending against the advanced persistent threat. IEEE Trans. Dependable Secure Comput. 2018, 1 (2018)
23. Wan, J., Chen, B., Imran, M., et al.: Toward dynamic resources management for IoT-based manufacturing. IEEE Commun. Mag. 56(2), 52–59 (2018)
24. Wang, J., Cao, J., Ji, S., et al.: Energy-efficient cluster-based dynamic routes adjustment approach for wireless sensor networks with mobile sinks. J. Supercomput. 73, 3277–3290 (2017)
25. Liang, W., Long, J., Chen, Z., et al.: A security situation prediction algorithm based on HMM in mobile network. Wirel. Commun. Mob. Comput. 2018, 241–257 (2018)
26. Wan, M., Yao, J., Jing, Y., Jin, X.: Event-based anomaly detection for non-public industrial communication protocols in SDN-based control systems. Comput. Mater. Contin. 55(3), 447–463 (2018)
27. Yan, Q., Huang, W., Luo, X., et al.: A multi-level DDoS mitigation framework for the industrial internet of things. IEEE Commun. Mag. 56(2), 30–36 (2018)
28. Vaidya, P., Chandra Mouli, P.V.S.S.R.: A robust semi-blind watermarking for color images based on multiple decompositions. Multimedia Tools Appl. 76, 25623–25656 (2017)

Energy Optimization and Application

Quality-Aware Voice Convergecast in Mobile Low Power Wireless Networks

Mike Adkins[1], Qi Han[1(✉)], and Sudeep Pasricha[2]

[1] Department of Computer Science, Colorado School of Mines,
Golden, CO 80401, USA
michael.h.adkins@gmail.com, qhan@mines.edu
[2] Department of Electrical and Computer Engineering, Colorado State University,
Fort Collins, CO 80523, USA
sudeep@colostate.edu

Abstract. Many disasters have shown the critical need for reliable voice communication for mobile users. Low power ad hoc wireless networks have become a promising solution in emergency scenarios because of their low cost and portability. In order to increase communication amongst moving emergency personnel and disaster victims, we have developed a novel convergecast voice streaming system that guarantees robust voice quality in a low power mobile wireless network. The system integrates routing and mobility-aware admission control along with voice compression adjustment to ensure the quality of voice streams. The system is evaluated using Arduino Due micro-controllers with XBee 802.15.4 radios. Our results show that our system can adequately adapt to changing network and routing conditions to deliver sufficient voice quality by maintaining a certain number of concurrent voice streams. To the best of our knowledge, this work is the first complete system for quality-aware voice streaming in mobile lower power wireless networks.

Keywords: Voice streaming · Low power mobile wireless networks · Admission control

1 Introduction

Today, voice communication is still the primary method for exchanging information in disaster response. Voice communication has obvious benefits: it requires no special training and is hands-free. In the event that users are injured or otherwise incapacitated, available voice communication is critically important for their rescue. We envision that future buildings will be instrumented with a number of low power Zigbee sensor nodes (a.k.a. motes) due to their portability and low cost. These motes will monitor environmental conditions such as toxic gas levels and temperature. During emergency, if cellular service is down, people (including first responders and victims during emergency response) may communicate with

This work is supported in part by NSF grants ECCS-1646576 and ECCS-1646562.

Y. Yin et al. (Eds.): MobiCASE 2019, LNICST 290, pp. 215–229, 2019.
https://doi.org/10.1007/978-3-030-28468-8_16

their low power wireless devices such as smartphones, smart helmets, or other wearables using low-power Bluetooth interfaces. A set of Zigbee/Bluetooth gateway nodes will be deployed to enable communication between people's phones and infrastructure motes. Servers may be deployed near the entrance to enable communication from the low power wireless ad hoc networks to the outside world. This paper focuses on voice convergecast only and leave other communication modes (i.e., boradcast, multicast, unicast) as future work.

Several key issues must be addressed to support voice communication in mobile, low-power, wireless meshed networks (MLWMNs). First, voice streams have relatively high data-rate requirements, but MLWMNs have limited bandwidth (e.g., typical Zigbee nodes only support 250 Kbps). Second, audio streaming over multi-hop LWN often results in unsatisfactory voice quality because of notable loss over low-power wireless links. The problem is exacerbated in scenarios where wireless nodes (i.e., people) are mobile. Third, simultaneously maintaining quality of multiple voice streams over lossy wireless links is difficult.

Our Contributions. We developed a novel quality-aware convergecast mobile audio streaming system (QACM) that maintains the quality of mobile voice streams in an ad-hoc low power wireless network. Specifically,

- We designed an integrated mobility-aware admission control and routing algorithm to ensure the quality of streaming audio in a mobile ad-hoc low power wireless network. Our algorithm guarantees quality of voice streams by choosing routes that maximize the number of audio streams in the network; adjusting routes in reaction to node mobility; minimizing channel contention; and avoiding bottlenecks.
- We implemented our end-to-end system QACM on an Arduino based hardware platform.
- We evaluated the system in both stationary and mobile scenarios.

2   Related Work

We discuss two areas of previous research that are closely related to this work: audio streaming over low power wireless sensor networks and audio streaming in mobile ad-hoc networks (MANETs).

Voice Streaming in Wireless Sensor Networks. Previous work developed audio streaming systems such as QVS [8], ASM [7], FireFly [10], and RT-WMP [15] that are able to provide quality of service in harsh environments, but these systems only worked for stationary nodes. Users must be within the communication range of a radio. This not only limits users mobility, but renders a stationary system useless during an emergency since users are often out of reach of the radio. *As none of these systems are designed to account for node movement, they would perform poorly when nodes move around and network topology dynamically changes. This node movement is exactly the focus of our work.*

Voice Streaming in MANETs. Voice streaming in MANETs has been investigated in several previous studies. These systems [2,3,9,16] monitor the impact of node movement on interference, communication failure, and voice quality in a network. *Although these protocols account for mobility, they are designed for higher bandwidth networks such as 802.11 or require additional information like GPS. Furthermore, most have only been evaluated in a network simulator, and it is unclear of their performance when implemented on actual hardware and evaluated in a more realistic environment.*

3   System Overview and Preliminaries

The architecture of our quality-aware voice convergecast mobile system (QACM) is shown in Fig. 1. QACM is designed to produce satisfying audio in environments where audio streams originate from mobile nodes. In order to handle instability caused by node mobility, QACM makes several audio and routing adjustments. It monitors voice quality in real time and adjusts audio compression and data duplication levels to minimize bandwidth and maintain the guaranteed level of voice quality. It also monitors channel contention among transmitting nodes by controlling the admission or rejection of potential voice streams in order to preserve the necessary throughput at a sink for the already admitted streams. *What distinguishes QACM from existing work is its capability to function in a mobile network as a result of each node continuously adjusting its routing to the sink independently.* The rest of this section presents necessary background for the integrated system and the next section describes our major contribution, i.e., how to manage node mobility with admission control and routing decisions.

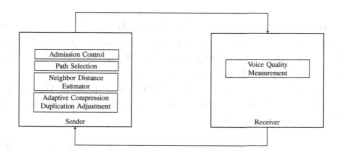

Fig. 1. System Architecture of QACM

In order to calculate voice quality in real time, we adopt the E-model [4] for voice quality measurement, where voice with an R-value above 50 is considered satisfactory. Voice quality is maintained through dynamic audio compression adaptation. We adjust audio compression and packet duplication by following the procedure described in [8]. We use ADPCM [14] to compress 16-bit raw audio into either 5-bit, 4-bit, 3-bit, and 2-bit to reduce bandwidth. We then duplicate a percentage of the packets depending on the amount of packet loss along the path of the audio stream.

Local Capacity Estimation. In order to guarantee high quality while admitting the maximum number of voice streams in the network, nodes must be aware of their saturation rate and contention domain. Contention Domain [8] of Node i refers to the set of nodes whose transmissions directly interfere with Node i's transmissions. Saturation Rate [8] is the maximum throughput observed at a node when all the senders are within the same contention domain. Thus when a node increases its data rate, it must be mindful not to cause the data rate for any contention domains to increase beyond its saturation rate. The local capacity of a node is the minimum local capacity of all nodes in its contention domain.

Although the interference range is larger than a node's communication range, we follow the same simplified assumption as stated in [8]. Only the nodes within a communication range of Node i are members of Node i's contention domain. Although it is well known that interference range exceeds communication range, we calculate saturation rate conservatively to account for the difference between interference and communication ranges.

Traditional Admission Control. For a Node v, we denote $N_p(j)_v$ as the set of nodes that lie from Node v through the first hop neighbor j to the sink. $\mathcal{P}_v$ is the set of all possible routes from Node v to a sink.

$$\mathcal{P}_v = \{N_p(1)_v, \ldots, N_p(j)_v\} \tag{1}$$

We represent all the nodes that are actively sending data in the network that will be affected by a stream s_v along the path $N_p(j)_v$ as $N_a(j)_v$. A route from Node v to a sink must satisfy the following two constraints to become a member of $\mathcal{P}_v$:

1. **Stream Quality Constraints.** Injection rate $\lambda_{in}(s_i)$ for any nodes in the network that forward voice streams $s_1 \ldots s_m$ must be greater than or equal to the threshold rate $\lambda_{th}(s_i)$ to maintain satisfactory voice quality. The threshold rate is derived from the E-model.
2. **Local Capacity Constraints.** For a Node $k \in N_a(j)_v$ the total data rate that flows through itself and the nodes in its contention domain must be no larger than its local capacity B_k.

If a path $N_p(j)_v$ satisfies both constraints, then the path can be added to the set $\mathcal{P}_v$.

4   Integrated Routing and Mobility-Aware Admission Control

In wireless networks comprised of stationary nodes, channel contention, environmental noise, and network congestion are common criteria for admission control. However, mobile nodes complicate admission control decisions. The changing topology of the network makes favorable admission control decisions at time t suddenly detrimental to voice quality at time $t+1$. Several previous works [2,3,9] have adapted traditional admission control to mobility, but often use high bandwidth wireless mediums like 802.11 or have only been evaluated through simulations. We have designed a novel mobility aware algorithm in which routing decisions complement admission control.

Admission control for a quality aware based voice streaming protocol determines if a network can guarantee robust audio throughput for the duration of the audio stream. Although several previous works have created admission control systems that provide good voice quality, mobility is not considered in their design [8].

Previous mobility aware admission control protocols are reactive [3]. These protocols wait until a current path is unusable before searching for an alternative causing unnecessary delay and disruption to an audio stream. Alternatively, our protocol proactively monitors paths to a sink node and automatically switches to superior paths without interruption. Furthermore, the routing decisions strengthen a future voice stream's admission candidacy by seeking paths for current voice streams that have the least impact on the network. Proactive routing algorithms often introduce high levels of overhead. Our system minimizes the maintenance by focusing only on local connections rather than maintaining global knowledge of the network.

4.1   Quality of Path

Path quality is an important metric to be used in our integrated admission control and routing protocol. We define $P_v(j)$ as the set of neighbors affected by a path between Node v via neighbor Node j to a sink. $N(v)$ defines all the neighbors of Node v. We define the cardinality of $P_v(j)$ as **Quality of Path** $(QoP(v))$. A node will use Quality of Path to choose the next hop neighbor on a path to a sink node. Unlike local capacity constraints, $QoP(v)$ accounts for nodes affected by the stream regardless if they themselves are streaming data. The purpose of this metric is to minimize the size of $N_a(j)_v$ and the local capacity constraint for a future stream. To calculate $QoP(v)$, a node takes the number of contention domains affected by its own transmission and unions this set over the set of contention domains along the entire path. The cardinality of the produced set is the $QoP(v)$:

$$P_v(j) = N(v) \cup P_j(i) \tag{2}$$

$$QoP(v) = \min_{j \in N(v)} (\|P_v(j)\|) \tag{3}$$

A path with a larger $P_v(j)$ will lower the local capacity for more neighborhoods and reduce the number of future data streams that can be admitted.

4.2   Integration of Quality of Path with Hop Count and Node-Degree

Selecting the best path between a sender and receiver has significant impact on the data loss and voice quality as discussed in [3,9]. Traditional wireless routing protocols such as Ad hoc On-Demand Distance Vector (AODV) and DSR

[6,11,12] use hop count as a metric to minimize the distance data travels, but these protocols do not account for link quality, utilization, and distance between nodes. Moreover, when two paths are available to a node with identical hop counts, path selection is made arbitrarily. Expected Transmission Count (ETX) [5,8] is an alternative metric that focuses on link quality rather than distance. However, ETX needs to know the number of transmissions and retransmissions along paths before making a routing decision. In mobile networks, historical transmission data is not available since routes change frequently. The delay incurred in collecting this data during a route switch would also reduce the quality of audio communication.

QACM employs a novel route selection protocol that combines the metrics of hop count and the number of neighbors a node has along the path. The goal is to avoid data bottlenecks by minimizing the degree of a node especially if that node is already generating a voice stream. Since QACM is designed for convergecast, it is preferable to avoid converging a large number of streams at a node that is multiple hops from the sink. Any hardware has a maximum data rate it can receive and forward without data loss. Minimizing the number of streams a node has to relay would reduce the likelihood of surpassing this maximum rate and resulting in data loss.

Every time a node moves into the broadcast range of another node and becomes a neighbor, that node must calculate the strengths and weaknesses of this new neighbor becoming its next hop. Contention domain, hop count, quality of path, and the presence of another stream being forwarded by this neighbor are all considered. The order in which these metrics are considered is based on that particular metric's impact on maximizing quality audio and the number of streams in a network. Our decision process is illustrated in Fig. 2.

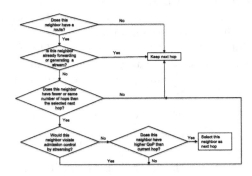

Fig. 2. Process for determining the next hop

4.3   Integrated Path Selection and Admission Control

Our protocol is based on AODV [12]. When a node is activated, it repeatedly broadcasts heartbeat messages to its neighborhood. Neighbors use the information in the heartbeat message to populate its neighborhood table.

When a node has received heartbeat messages from all its neighbors and has populated its neighborhood table, it determines which neighbors have a route to a sink node and marks the chosen neighbor as its next hop to a sink node. This updated information will then be reflected in the node's next heartbeat message.

Once a source node receives and obtains a route through a neighbor, the source node will begin the distributed admission control process. The admission control process regulates the number of voice streams in the network. Its goal is to guarantee that the voice quality of current streams does not fall below the stream quality constraints. Nodes that cannot adhere to the stream quality constraints would send a reject message (REJC) to the sender node. If a sender's injection rate is accepted by the affected nodes along the path, the sender can begin sending data.

The source node adjusts its compression and duplication settings to produce the best quality for the audio stream based on the data loss along the path to the sink. If the source node cannot set the compression and duplication to keep the audio quality above $\lambda_{th}(s_i)$, the audio transmission will be stopped. A full outline of our algorithm is described in Algorithm 1.

Algorithm 1. Integrated Routing and Mobility-aware Admission Control

loop
    broadcast heartbeat message
end loop
Event: Receive heartbeat message
    compute relative distance from RSSI and update neighborhood table
    compute QoP and update neighborhood table
    update next hop from the flowchart and change in relative neighbor distance
    update neighborhood capacity
    update local capacity
Event: Receive INIT
    call Admission Control Algorithm
Event: Receive PATH
    calculate packet loss from upstream neighbor
    update #PathPacketSent and #PathPacketReceived
    forward PATH packet

4.4   Path Adjustment

During audio streaming, intermediate nodes continuously look for lower cost paths to a sink for two reasons. One, a node may determine that a different path to the sink affects fewer contention domains, has fewer hops, or is not sharing a path with another stream. Two, a node may learn that its next hop neighbor is moving outside its contention domain. If either situation arises, a node will switch its next hop neighbor on a different path to a sink node. Although a different path may have fewer hops and be more stable, it must still adhere to both stream-quality and local capacity constraints. To test for local capacity constraints, the intermediate node attempting to switch will begin by broadcasting an initiation (INIT) message as before and continue to follow Algorithm 2.

Algorithm 2. Distributed Implementation of Admission Control

Input: An INIT message generated by source i is received by an intermediate node j

$\lambda_{inc} = 0$;

if It is the first INIT message originated from i **then**

    set a timer T_{ch};

end if

$\lambda_{inc} = \lambda_{inc} + \lambda_{in}(i)$;

if j is on the path from i to the sink **then**

    forward the INIT message;

end if

Event: Timer T_{ch} Fires

if $\lambda_{inc} > B_j$ **then**

    send REJC message to the source node;

end if

The purpose of the path adjustment is to minimize the number of link failures between nodes on a voice stream path and to avoid congested areas in the network. Link failures force sending nodes to pause voice streams and wait until a new path to the sink node is discovered. If a link failure is predicted, this audio stream pause can be avoided. Furthermore, to increase the overall number of voice streams in the network, it is vital to choose paths that interfere with the fewest number of nodes. This path selection process will keep local capacity for nodes high and increase the acceptance rate for future voice streams. If the new path can handle the injection rate, then the intermediate node will switch the route.

4.5 Neighborhood Maintenance

One of the biggest impediments to sustaining a route capable of delivering good audio quality are link breaks. A link break disrupts audio streaming because a new route must be established before streaming can continue. In our work, we use relative distance estimation to predict future link breaks. That is, nodes proactively start a route discovery operation and reroute streams to avoid a future broken link. For a Node i, it tracks the relative distance between itself and its neighbors through RSSI. We use the Path Loss Model [13] to estimate the distance between Node i and its neighbors.

If Node i receives consecutive messages from a downstream neighbor, Node i will search its routing table for neighbors who have paths to the sink with a closer distance. Determining a neighbor's relative distance is important to keep a routing table fresh; it also increases the lifetime of an audio stream despite uncertainty of link stability in the network.

Nodes monitor available paths to the sink. A node may have selected a next hop neighbor, but its next hop neighbor's movement will cause the link to break. If a neighbor moves out of range without a prediction mechanism, the upstream node would have to pause the audio stream and start a route discovery once its neighbor stops receiving voice stream data packets. Predicting link breaks will significantly reduce this delay. Suppose there is a voice stream with the path:

$$N_p(v_1)_{v_0} = \langle (v_0, v_1), \ldots, (v_{k-5}, 2), (8, 7), (9, 10) \rangle$$

Each Node v_i reports its RSSI through its periodic heartbeat messages. The packet loss across the whole path is then reported to the source Node v_0, which will adjust the compression and duplication settings for the stream.

This routing design makes a path completely dynamic. No single node has complete knowledge of its path to the sink. Each node with a route to the sink chooses its next best hop. Nodes try to minimize the number of contention domains affected and initiate a new route discovery before communication with a neighbor is lost.

5   Performance Evaluation

In practice, admission control is designed to reject streams that do not maintain quality audio. However, for our evaluation, in order to test whether our admission control is conservative, we explicitly turned off this feature and only record the admission control decisions while not notifying the sink. In other words, we allow a new stream to join even if it will potentially worsen the voice quality. We can determine the extent that streams would be able to recover. Due to page limitations, more detailed evaluation results can be found in [1].

5.1   Experimental Setup

Our hardware is comprised of a microcontroller, a 802.15.4 radio, and a modular circuit board or Shield to connect the radio to the board. Collision avoidance with CSMA is used as the MAC layer protocol. We chose Arduino Due microcontroller in combination with an XBee 802.15.4 radio to send both network layer and application layer packets.

We performed all evaluations in a nine-square-foot small home office that contained a bookcase, a desk with a computer, and a chair. Although XBee wireless radios are capable of transmitting data up to 100 ft indoor in theory, our preliminary testing showed that distances higher than 3 ft would increase packet loss to 50% when transmitting voice data. Therefore, we configured the

XBee radios to transmit at its lowest radio power of -10 dBm, so that a radio was considered out of range at a distance of 1.5 ft.

QVS [8] is a quality-aware voice convergecast system designed for stationary low power wireless networks and it is the most relevant to our work, so we will compare the performance of QACM with that of QVS. QVS evaluation used custom built hardware called SenEar that has a data rate of 500 kbps; to ensure fair comparison, we implemented QVS using our chosen hardware, the XBee S1 radio, which has only 250 kbps data rate.

5.2   Experimental Results

We begin our evaluation with one mobile stream and then increase the complexity through each additional test by adding more mobile streams, changing straight line movement to random movement, and increasing the number of sinks.

Scenario 1: One mobile node with voice stream. As shown in Figs. 3 and 4, We place the sink node and two relay nodes in a straight line 3 ft apart. We test two scenarios: (1) mobile Node 4 starts about 1.5 ft from Node 3 and moves towards sink; (2) mobile Node 5 is placed about 1.5 ft from the sink node and moves away from the sink. A dashed line indicates the path of the voice streaming data link at time instant t_n. A solid colored line indicates the direction of the moving node. In both scenarios, only the mobile node is sending voice data. The relay nodes only transmit data generated by the mobile nodes.

Fig. 3. Node placement (mobile scenario: one streaming node moves towards sink)   **Fig. 4.** Node placement (mobile scenario: one streaming node moves away from sink)

Figure 5 shows the voice quality of QVS in this scenario. At the start, Node 4 connects to Node 3 which then relays voice data to the sink. Node 4 then starts moving toward the sink. Once mobile Node 4 cannot reach Node 3 anymore, Node 4 ends the voice stream because it does not have a route. Since QVS is designed for stationary nodes, QVS does not adjust its next hop and the connection is lost. Since QVS cannot maintain a voice stream with even one mobile node, we do not further evaluate QVS with more complex scenarios.

Figure 6 shows the results for QACM. Each t_n is the time point when the mobile stream adjusts its next hop. Node 5 starts at a higher R-value and decreases slightly as it moves away from the sink. Moreover, Node 4's R-value marginally increases at it moves closer to the sink. Voice quality is strong throughout both scenarios, which shows QACM can easily support one mobile node sending voice data.

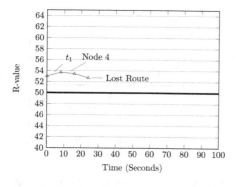

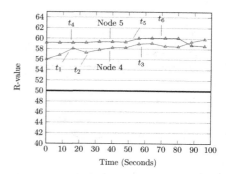

Fig. 5. Voice quality of QVS (one streaming node moves towards the sink)

Fig. 6. Voice quality of QACM in two separate mobile scenarios: streaming node moving towards the sink vs. streaming node moving away from the sink

Scenario 2: One mobile node and one stationary node with voice streams. The only difference in this scenario from the previous one is that we let a stationary node (i.e., Node 3) generate voice streams as well. In this setup, two streams are now competing for both bandwidth and hardware processing at the sink. Also, Node 3 is now both streaming voice data and could potentially be a relay for Node 4. As shown in Fig. 7, Node 4 is unable to establish a connection with Node 3. Until it moves into contact with Relay Node 2, Node 4 cannot start streaming. Node 4's voice quality never reaches an R-value of 50 and Node 3's R-value steadily declines from 51.43 to 44.65. In Fig. 8, Node 4's voice quality starts strong, but as it moves away from the sink, the voice quality decreases because the stream requires more hops to reach the sink. Node 3 starts at an R-value of 49.89, but steadily decreases as Node 4 moves away from the sink. We infer that once Node 4 switches to relay Node 2 at t_5, Node 2 is unable to receive, process, send both Node 3 and Node 4's voice data. From this scenario, it is clear that nodes are not capable of both relaying and streaming with our hardware.

Scenario 3: Two streaming nodes start moving in opposite directions. *Same start time.* We set up two streaming nodes moving in opposite directions. We first evaluate the case when two nodes start moving at the same time (Fig. 9). Figure 10 shows that streaming Node 5 starts near the sink with a voice quality above 50 and Node 4 starts near relay Node 3 with a voice quality slightly below 50. As Node 5 moves away from the sink, its R-value decreases and finishes slightly below 50 at 49.5. Node 4's voice quality initially decreases and then increases as it moves towards the sink and finishes with an R-value of 60.77. This decrease in voice quality for Node 5 and increase for Node 4 shows that an increasing in the number of hops results in lower voice quality.

Random start time. Figure 11 present the results for voice quality when two nodes have a different start time. Node 5 begins moving first, followed by Node 4 30 s

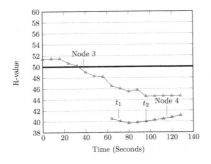

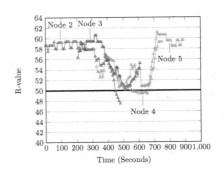

Fig. 7. Voice quality of QACM (mobile scenario: stationary Node 3 streams and also Node 4 streams while moving towards the sink)

Fig. 8. Voice quality of QACM (mobile scenario: stationary Node 3 streams and also Node 4 streams while moving away from the sink)

later. Consistent with previous results, Node 5 begins with strong voice quality since it is only one hop from the sink. Voice quality then decreases as Node 5 moves toward the relay nodes and requires more hops. Node 4 starts with relay Node 3 as its next hop and begins with voice quality below 50. One obvious difference between this and the previous scenario is the number of next hop switches. When moving between Node 3 and Node 2, Node 4 switches back and forth between relay Nodes 2 and 3 14 times. Node 5 also switches more frequently than in previous experiments. Although QACM is designed to mitigate this issue, this ping-pong effect is still possible because of changes in signal strength. QACM prefers a next hop that has the minimum number of next hops to the sink. A node expects a heartbeat message at regular intervals. If a heartbeat message is missed, it is assumed that the sender is now out of range, and the mobile node assumes it must remove this node as a potential next hop resulting in a switch. It is clear that not receiving constant heartbeat messages from both relay Nodes 2 and 3 results in continuous next hop switching.

Random turn. We next evaluate the case when two streaming nodes start moving in opposite directions and then turn 180° at a random time, returning toward their starting location. Figure 12 show the results of this scenario. As described in previous evaluations, streams yield better voice quality when they are streaming directly to the sink or to a relay node that is not forwarding any other streams. Node 4 is streaming directly to the sink. Node 5 is sending its voice data across 3 hops, which results in slightly worse voice quality than Node 4's quality. When the mobile nodes start moving toward each other and must use relay Node 2 simultaneously as their next hop, Node 4's voice quality decreases. After Node 4 turns and begins moving back towards its starting point, its voice quality improves because it is reducing the number of hops to reach the sink. Node 5's voice quality also improves as it moves toward Node 3. Node 5's voice quality improves since it is the only stream using the relay nodes, but its improvement is not as dramatic as Node 4 since its moving away from the sink.

Fig. 9. Node placement: Nodes 4 and 5 start moving in opposite directions at the same time

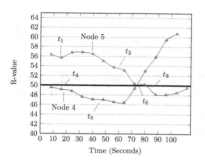

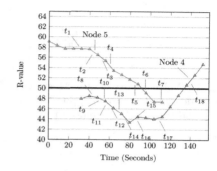

Fig. 10. Voice quality of QACM: Nodes 4 and 5 start moving in opposite directions at the same time

Fig. 11. Voice quality of QACM: nodes 4 and 5 start moving in opposite directions at random times

Scenario 4: Three streaming nodes move randomly with one sink. We next evaluate random movement of streaming nodes at one hop distance. The purpose of this scenario is to evaluate QACM's ability to maintain a quality connection despite continuous movement around the sink node, bandwidth competition, and sink processing power to handle all the streams. Results in Fig. 13 show that all three streams maintain R-value near 50.

Scenario 5: Streaming nodes move randomly with multiple sinks. Lastly, we evaluated one stream with multiple sinks at a one hop distance, since our previous results indicate that voice quality decreases with an increase in the number of hops. Thus, we would like to learn whether having sinks closer to the mobile streaming node can improve the situation; we, therefore, evaluate the case with multiple sinks. The purpose of this experiment was to determine QACM's ability to switch between sinks. Since there was only one stream, interference or bandwidth contention did not affect voice quality.

Figure 14 shows the R-value for one stream switching between multiple sinks. Each numbered node in this figure is a time point when the robot adjusts its direction. The colors of the curves match the colors of the sink nodes, representing the sink where the mobile node is currently sending voice data. The results show that QACM is capable of switching to different sink in order to preserve voice quality.

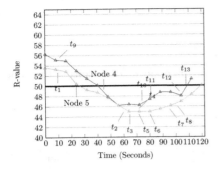

Fig. 12. Voice quality of QACM: streaming Nodes 4 and 5 move in opposite directions and turn back at random times

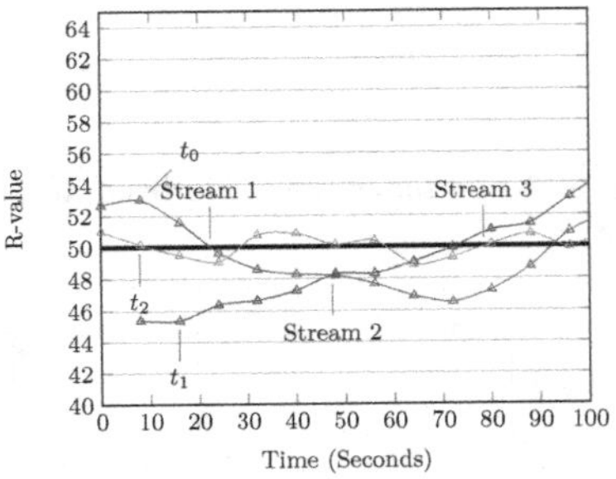

Fig. 13. Voice quality of QACM: three streaming nodes move around the sink

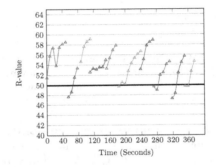

Fig. 14. Voice quality of QACM: one streaming node moves around multiple sinks

6   Concluding Remarks

In this work, we designed and developed a mobile low power voice streaming system (called QACM) that is built on a mobility-aware admission control mechanism integrated with path selection to maximize the total number of concurrent voice streams in the network with satisfactory voice quality. We implemented QACM on Arduino Due microcontrollers and evaluated the system in both stationary and mobile scenarios. Experimental results show that QACM can support up to three concurrent voice streams with quality assurance.

References

1. Adkins, M.: Quality-Aware Voice Convergecast in Mobile Low Power Wireless Networks. Master's thesis, Colorado School of Mines (2017)
2. Calafate, C.T., Malumbres, M.P., Oliver, J., Cano, J.C., Manzoni, P.: QoS support in MANETs: a modular architecture based on the IEEE 802.11 E technology. IEEE Trans. Circ. Syst. Video Technol. **19**(5), 678–692 (2009)

3. Chauhan, G., Nandi, S.: QoS aware stable path routing (QASR) protocol for MANETs. In: Proceedings of First International Conference on Emerging Trends in Engineering and Technology (ICETET 2008), pp. 202–207. IEEE (2008)

4. Cole, R.G., Rosenbluth, J.H.: Voice over IP performance monitoring. ACM SIG-COMM Comput. Commun. Rev. **31**(2), 9–24 (2001)

5. De Couto, D.S., Aguayo, D., Bicket, J., Morris, R.: A high-throughput path metric for multi-hop wireless routing. Wirel. Netw. **11**(4), 419–434 (2005)

6. Johnson, D., Hu, Y.C., Maltz, D.: The dynamic source routing protocol (DSR) for mobile ad hoc networks for IPv4. Technical report (2007)

7. Li, L., Xing, G., Han, Q., Sun, L.: ASM: adaptive voice stream multicast over low-power wireless networks. IEEE Trans. Parallel Distrib. Syst. **23**(4), 626–633 (2012)

8. Li, L., Xing, G., Sun, L., Liu, Y.: A quality-aware voice streaming system for wireless sensor networks. ACM Trans. Sens. Netw. (TOSN) **10**(4), 61 (2014)

9. Lindgren, A., Belding-Royer, E.M.: Multi-path admission control for mobile ad hoc networks. In: Proceedings of the Second Annual International Conference on Mobile and Ubiquitous Systems: Networking and Services, pp. 407–417. IEEE (2005)

10. Mangharam, R., Rowe, A., Rajkumar, R., Suzuki, R.: Voice over sensor networks. In: Proceedings of the 27th IEEE International Conference on Real-Time Systems Symposium (RTSS), pp. 291–302 (2006)

11. Perkins, C.E., Bhagwat, P.: Highly dynamic destination-sequenced distance-vector routing (DSDV) for mobile computers. ACM SIGCOMM Comput. Commun. Rev. **24**, 234–244 (1994)

12. Perkins, C.E., Royer, E.M.: Ad-hoc on-demand distance vector routing. In: Proceedings of Second IEEE Workshop on Mobile Computing Systems and Applications (WMCSA 1999), pp. 90–100. IEEE (1999)

13. Rappaport, T.S., et al.: Wireless Communications: Principles and Practice, vol. 2. Prentice Hall PTR, New Jersey (1996)

14. Rec, I.: G. 726, 40, 32, 24, 16 kbit/s adaptive differential pulse code modulation (ADPCM). International Telecommunication Union, Geneva 18 (1990)

15. Sicignano, D., Tardioli, D., Cabrero, S., Villarroel, J.L.: Real-time wireless multi-hop protocol in underground voice communication. Ad Hoc Netw. **11**(4), 1484–1496 (2013)

16. Zhang, R., Rubin, J.: Robust flow admission control and routing for mobile ad hoc networks. In: Proceedings of IEEE Military Communications Conference (MIL-COM), pp. 1–7. IEEE (2006)

Would I Lie to You - Would You Notice?

Felix Huppert$^{(\boxtimes)}$, Matthias Kranz, and Gerold Hoelzl

University of Passau, Passau, Germany
{felix.huppert,matthias.kranz,gerold.hoelzl}@uni-passau.de

Abstract. The quantified self-paradigm is well established. Its main purpose is to use numbers from sensors to derive self-knowledge. The massive availability of persuasive technology to monitor physiological parameters of humans made the paradigm available to a tremendous number of people. A multitude of different hard- and software platforms are available at the market. They all have different properties at different levels of quality. All in common is their promise to provide accurate and precise data about the humans' physiological condition and performed activities. Basically, they all provide a tool to make people aware of formerly hidden, non-observable, body signals. The gained awareness can then be used by people to e.g. improve their health or fitness level. In this work, we emphasize the perception of the gathered sensory data by the people. We focus on the question of how the trustworthiness of the recorded and presented data is perceived by people. As a fact, non-credible data can be understood by the user as being trustworthy and can have a negative impact on users' behavior. This can be especially critical for human's health in the fitness and medical application domain. It is of high importance to understand how people perceive and correlate their intrinsic body feelings with the data collected and presented by a mobile smart device like a smart watch or a fitness tracker.

Keywords: Fitness tracking · User perceived credibility · Quantified self · Trust in data

1 Introduction

With the rise of consumer-targeted ubiquitous computing technology over the last decade, significant advances in self-tracking and self-monitoring of physical activities and hidden body parameters (e.g. heart-rate and step count) to optimize personal health behaviors have been achieved. Sensing solutions for essential tracking parameters have been implemented into a wide range of affordable everyday pervasive devices such as fitness trackers, smart watches or the omnipresent smart phones. The fundamental concept of any kind of activity tracker device or application can be paraphrased by three essential steps: (I) collect activity related physical sensor measurements, (II) process and analyze gathered measurements to gain semantically abstracted data and (III) provide comprehensible feedback to the user about the tracked activity. In line with the personal informatics and quantified self context, the available feedback from tracking devices and applications

© ICST Institute for Computer Sciences, Social Informatics and Telecommunications Engineering 2019
Published by Springer Nature Switzerland AG 2019. All Rights Reserved
Y. Yin et al. (Eds.): MobiCASE 2019, LNICST 290, pp. 230–243, 2019.
https://doi.org/10.1007/978-3-030-28468-8_17

is intended to be used to reflect on current activity patterns, monitor the progress towards a pursued long-term behavior adaptation or goal and provide motivational support throughout a change process.

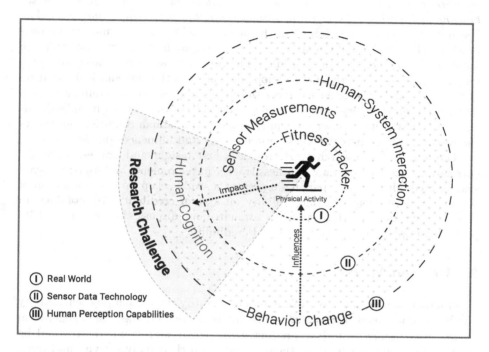

Fig. 1. Layered model, visualizing the abstract activity tracking principle, its dependencies and connectedness between the layers and the related research areas.

To provide a better overview of the essential fitness tracker systems structure, we conceptualized a layered model (cf. Fig. 1). The model visualizes the transitions and relations between the physical activity, sensor data collection and processing, human-computer interaction, psychological influences and impact on the human behavior in the context of activity tracking. Altogether, the model represents a self-regulating circle, where the measured physical activity is followed by an eventual behavior change induced by the feedback from the fitness tracker device, which will have an influence on future activities. The layers and transitions are abstract representations of the related research areas that are omnipresent in the activity tracking context. Research tends to be focused around problems and questions within one of these areas of interest (e.g. data science, psychology or human-computer interaction). Limited multidisciplinary research has been done, where possible transboundary effects - tracker data quality and its impact on human behavior - were evaluated.

As highlighted in the layer model (cf. Fig. 1), we focus on incorporating a wider range of research topics into one combined research effort to investigate the perceived trustworthiness and user expertise in the context of fitness tracking systems and the possible impact of data quality on human behavior. Based on these research intentions, we outlined the research question as follows: *Does a significant variation of pedometer feedback data accuracy from a fitness tracker have an influence on the tracking system credibility perceived by the user?* The research challenge is highlighted in the layer model (cf. Fig. 1) and can be outlined as followed: The physical activity in the research challenge represents the focus on pedometer walking tracking. The sensor measurement and data progressing includes not only the data logging, but also the systematical variation of the data validity in order to assess the research question. The human-system interaction interface presents the system feedback to the user in an understandable way. On the most outer layer of the model, the human cognition represents the research on the perceived system credibility and influences on the users.

The aim of our research is to provide a first insight and impression of the correlation between accuracy of fitness tracker measurements and user-perceived system credibility. In this paper, we present a study setup for the evaluation of the expected influences of data validity on system credibility. We conduct an exploratory, out-of-the-lab study to evaluate and discuss the system and its perceived impact on the user-perceived credibility.

2   Related Work

The fundamental idea to use pedometers to quantify the human physical activity has been established in the 1980s. The intention behind these first generation devices was similar to todays product goals, where step count data would be presented to the users to allow them to reflect on their daily activity and function as a motivational source to be more active [9,17,18]. Due to the primitive implementation and limited range of functions, the general public quickly lost interest and trust in the rudimentary mechanical tracker devices [6,27]. With the rise of smart-devices in the late 2000s, a new era of activity tracking devices was started. The increase in processing power and availability of better sensor technology allowed for complex algorithms and real time evaluation of the movement data, which resulted in more accurate and precise pedometer tracking [27]. These advancements in persuasive technology systems have lead to an increased interest in the related research areas [3,9].

Alongside persuasive fitness tracker devices emerged the personal informatics systems terminology. The description was first brought up by Li et al. in 2010 and was defined as "[Systems that] ... help people collect personally relevant information for the purpose of self-reflection and gaining self-knowledge" [17]. This concept references back to the basics of the quantified self concept. Wolf et al. defined the quantified self movement as the integration and acceptance of continuous data collection technology in the everyday lifestyle [31]. Wrist-worn fitness trackers are a one prime example out of many for a quantified self- and personal informatics systems.

Pedometer measurements represent an integral part of human activity tracking approaches. This common feature integration is justified with the importance of steps in the fundamental human activity [3,29]. The most dominant physical actions typically carried out throughout a day can be associated with taking steps. Steps are objective, intuitive and comprehensible in the context of understanding personal activeness, which makes this measure ideal for humans to reflect on their own physical activity [3]. Most other common fitness tracker measures (e.g. flight of stairs, active minutes, calories burned, etc.) are derived from the pedometer count [8,12,13]. In cross-sectional studies, the negative correlation between steps taken per day and common health issues has been proven. Active individuals, who achieve a higher than average step count per day, were identified to be less likely to have health related issues in the future [3,5,15,30].

Research studies confirm that both accuracy and precision of activity tracking devices have been steadily improved over the last decade [3,8,9,14,16,25,26]. A trustworthy tracking system should offer accurate and precise data transformation under all circumstances to avoid misleading customers [28]. Controlled lab studies where participants walk, jog or run on a treadmill with different testing setups are used by researchers to evaluate the performance of consumer fitness tracker devices [16,25]. The results reveal an optimal accuracy and precision for a typical walking pace of 2.5 mph for most trackers. Faster or slower walking speeds would lead to devices consistently under- or overestimating the step count by 3.5% to 10% [16]. Inaccuracies and precision of the tested devices are consistent and independent of the total steps taken during the study [8]. A high correlation between the results of the examined controlled and field studies was shown, indicating that the findings of lab studies are valid in a real-world setting [9].

Motivation is a key factor especially for physical activity, since unmotivated humans tend to lose interest in their goal [17]. Fitness tracker represent an extrinsic motivation source [1]. Further, motivation is an essential part of the biopsychosocial transtheoretical model [22], which outlines the general process of intentional behavior change. The five stages of change (I Precontemplation, II Contemplation, III Preparation, IV Action and V Maintenance), the influence of decisional balance and the connection to Bandura's self-efficacy theory were first described by Prochaska et al. [23]. The decisional balance describes the user-perceived balance between benefits and drawbacks of the behavior change throughout the stages. Fitness tracker and the common related motivational methods (e.g. gamification, goal setting or social integration) can help shift and maintain a positive decisional balance and support the user to gain higher self-efficacy [10,11,13,23].

The general acceptance and cease of usage motives of the tracker devices has been extensively covered in survey studies [7,19,20,32]. Besides technical difficulties, lack of motivation and support is one of the most common reasons, why users tend to abandon their fitness tracker devices [19]. Furthermore, the perceived trustworthiness of fitness trackers seems to be linked to the long-term user acceptance [24,28]. Presenting the user knowingly false data samples increases the mistrust and decrease the motivation, thus leading users to stop using their fitness tracker. Both motivation and trust in the technology have a significant impact on users pursuing to use fitness tracker devices. The quality of all the gathered activity data has to be interpreted with caution [8, 28]. Long-term adaption of fitness trackers and the related behavior change has been assessed in a wide range of studies [20, 32]. Researcher focused on HCI or human behavior influences, pay little to no tribute to the data quality of the underlying measurement trackers. The impact of false data through inaccuracies on the data reflection process has been untended in this research field.

3   User Study Concept

Our hypotheses for the user study was subject to following wording: *An influence on the pedometer data feedback accuracy has no significant effect on the system credibility perceived by the user when compared to a neutral, unaltered control group.* The chosen study concept was inspired by related work studies and was a combination of survey and long-term field experiments. The controllability and high accuracy means of lab studies were judged to be disadvantageous in the given context, since the unfamiliar surrounding conditions might influence the perception of the study participants (e.g. suspect tracker accuracy is tested). A field study shifts the focus point away from tracker and offers a more realistic application case, which results in higher external validity for gathered data [2].

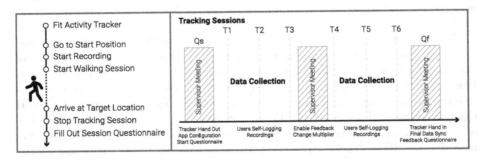

Fig. 2. The left side illustration depicts the study procedure for one data recording session. The right side graph gives an overview of the complete study schedule that spans over a couple of weeks.

For the two-phase, self-guided, longitudinal study design, the participants were instructed to collect regular pedometer data on their walking commute route. An overview of the study schedule is shown in Fig. 2. Initially, a meeting with all willing participants was held to collect pre-study data with a short questionnaire, setup the fitness trackers and provide instructions to the participants. In the first data collection phase, baseline pedometer data sets (3 − 4 per participant) without any provided feedback were recorded. These baseline measurements were recorded to verify the validity and reliably of the used pedometer tracker. After an intermediate meeting with the study supervisor, where additional guidance and an update of the tracking system was provided, another set of commute recordings was collected. In these following sessions, altered feedback values were shown to the participants at the end of each recorded walk. Dependent on the study group, a negative (-15%), neutral (0%) or positive ($+15\%$) alteration multiplier was used. These manipulation values were chosen to provide a significant difference between the baseline and shown measurements without exaggerating the effect, therefore making the changes too obvious. After the second phase had been completed, in a final meeting, the subjective perceived data and tracker credibility was evaluated with a questionnaire.

The procedure for one run of the data collection is illustrated in Fig. 2. After the tracker has been fitted to the wrist of the non-dominant hand, the study participant walks to the starting point on their daily commute route. At this defined location, the recording process is started with our Android control application and the regular commute walk can begin. Once arrived at the target location, the data collection is stopped and the session questionnaire is filled out from inside the app. Both the start and finish locations (e.g. front door, street sign or building) were self-selected by the study participants to provide fixed points of reference for the data collection.

4   Activity Tracking System

Today, the most common consumer-grade fitness tracker are wrist-worn bracelets. Since these rudimentary activity trackers on their own have limited functionality and typically come with a additional smart phone application, we decided to pair the selected tracker with our own Android app. A large variety of purpose-built bracelets are available and most common devices (e.g. Fitbit, Garmin or Polar) have been reviewed or used in some related research [8,16,25,26].

For our study intentions, the Mi Band 2 (cf. Fig. 3) bracelet by Xiaomi was ideal, since it is a relatively popular, low-cost and reliable fitness tracker bracelet. It features an accelerometer based pedometer, photoelectric heart rate sensor, small display and one touch button for user interaction in a small robust wrist-worn package. In a comparative study of 17 different activity trackers in 2015, the first generation Mi Band tracker scored well [8]. The Mi Band achieved an average pedometer accuracy of 96.56% and a variation coefficient of 5.81% across the three study setups (200, 500 and 1000 step trials). It was ranked among the top 5 of the compared devices, which included trackers from many renowned brands. The Mi Band tracker was recommended: "[The] ... Xiaomi Mi Band showed the best package compared to its price." [8].

Access to the pedometer tracker data can be gained with the bluetooth API, which has been reverse engineered by the open source community for Android smart phones. The custom designed application (cf. Fig. 3) was used to (I) start

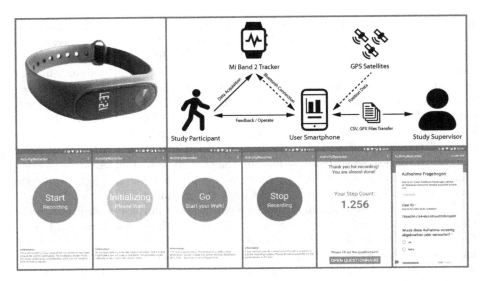

Fig. 3. Illustration of the architecture to record and transfer the collected data from the Mi Band 2 to a central repository of the study supervisor, and to present the user the calculated step count. In addition to the data transfer, a questionnaire to evaluate the run and the perceived step count was implemented.

and stop the recordings sessions, (II) backup the Mi Band data, (III) track GPS location, (IV) show the manipulated feedback score to the user and (V) to fill out the session questionnaires. Both the pedometer and GPS tracking data is stored locally and the latest recordings are transferred over the internet to the study supervisor after a session has been completed. The goal of this implemented system was to have the study participants do the recordings on a self-reliant basis, whilst the remote study supervisor can maintain full control over the study conduction and settings [21].

5   Evaluation

For the user study, eleven student participants from non-technical areas of study were recruited from a selected pool. The mean age was 22.27 years and a median of 23 years with 18.18% being male and 81.81% female. Most participants (90.90%) were right-handed and 81.10% regularly wore a watch-like device (e.g. (smart) watch, fitness tracker). The pre-test questionnaire indicated a predominant interest (81.8%) in technology and 54.5% already use some sort of tracking application or device. In total, six participants completed the all data collection sessions over a duration of four weeks. These six individuals were split evenly into the three test groups (negative, neutral and positive feedback alteration) for the second phase of the user study.

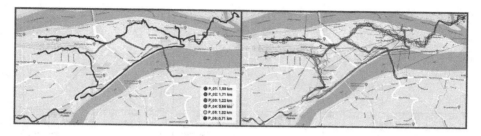

Fig. 4. These maps show the GPS tracks from the pathways the participants recorded during the study. The location data in the left map has been cleaned from outliers and slightly smoothed, while in the maps on the right the raw location data is illustrated.

Due to the self-reliant study design, the GPS position was recorded besides the pedometer data to ensure comparable data sets, free of larger deviations from the typical commute route. All location based data was slight smoothed and larger outliers and measurement glitches removed. The raw and processed GPS data is illustrated in Fig. 4. Over the course of four weeks, a total of 40 usable recordings were collected by the six active participants. No significant deviations were detected in the data set. A descriptive evaluation of the GPS data is listed in Table 1.

Table 1. Descriptive statistics of the recorded GPS data from the commute walks.

Participant	P_01	P_02	P_03	P_04	P_05	P_06
Distance	1.50 km	1.71 km	1.22 km	0.66 km	1.32 km	0.71 km
Time	16:18 min.	19:14 min.	13:11 min.	6:40 min.	14:01 min.	11:23 min.
Speed	5.52 km/h	5.30 km/h	5.55 km/h	5.94 km/h	5.65 km/h	3.74 km/h

The key point of interest is the manipulated pedometer data and the user-perceived system credibility score. The averaged pedometer measures for all six participants are listed in Table 2. The base step count represents the averaged raw step count. The calculated modified data is based on the study group (negative, neutral or positive) for the between subject user study test. The intention of the baseline data collection was to show that the Mi Band 2 has a high measurement reliability. With a repeatability error, which ranges between 2.38% and 3.58% (cf. Fig. 5), the Mi Band 2 produces precise pedometer data comparable with other trackers tested in related work lab studies [8].

The positive and negative 15% step count variation should have presented the study participants with a value that is significantly lower or higher than the baseline step count, but not too large of a deviation to give away the research intention. A paired sample t-test was conducted on the pedometer data measurements to confirm the statistical significant difference. The results of the t-test

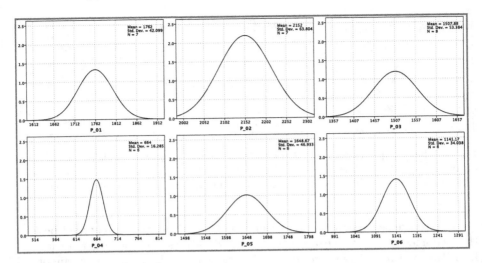

Fig. 5. Deviation of steps counts per study participant during the baseline data collection. Knowing the deviation from the users path, it was possible to deduce the +/− 15% manipulation threshold for the real value that was presented to the user.

(cf. Table 2) indicated a significant difference between the baseline and manipulated pedometer feedback for the positive and negative study groups. For the neutral control group no significant distinction was identified, which was to be expected since the data was not altered.

Table 2. The significance of the difference between the averaged baseline and manipulated pedometer data is evaluated in a t-test and the precision of the baseline data set is shown in this table.

Participant	P_01	P_02	P_03	P_04	P_05	P_06
Manipulation	Positive	Negative	Neutral	Neutral	Negative	Positive
Base step count	1.762	2.152	1.507	664	1.648	1.141
Mod. step count	1.992	1.846	-	-	1.427	1.317
Base Precision	2.38%	2.96%	3.54%	2.84%	2.45%	2.98%
Sig. test	1.9%	1.8%	80.5%	92.5%	1.2%	4.1%

A post-study questionnaire and short interview session was carried out to evaluate the credibility and perceived accuracy of the used fitness tracker. The likert scale questions were derived from related survey research work. We used a one to five scale, where a one indicates a negative denotation and a rating of five presents a positive statement towards the asked question. This answer scale is reflected in the result representation in Fig. 6. Negative answers are color coded with red color nuances and positive statements are denoted with green nuances. The amount of fill of each circle represents the percentage split of people that gave that respective answer. Figure 6 clearly presents the overall consenting appraisal of the survey questions.

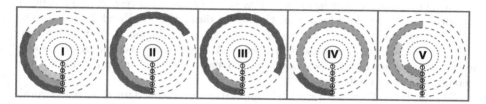

Fig. 6. Visualization of the results from the post-study likert scale questionnaire, where the participants had to evaluate (I) relevance of the feedback, (II) expected value match, (III) trust in the fitness tracker, (IV) perceived accuracy of the measurements and (V) possibility of influence. (Color figure online)

The overall personal relevance (I) of the step feedback was rated above average (median 4), which is an indication that the participants interpret the shown feedback as valid. The impact (V) of the pedometer feedback on behavior change was judged as possible. Furthermore, some participants mentioned in the interview that a lower feedback value would increase their personal interest to be more active. These statements indicate that the fitness tracker would be used as intended to monitor the daily activity and provide progress feedback towards being more active.In regard to the expected step count value (II), 83% mentioned an exact match between the presented feedback value and their expectations. One participant pointed out slightly higher pedometer feedback values, even though the individual was in the negatively influenced study group.

Five out of the six participants evaluated the presented pedometer score as accurate (IV) and one rated it to be very accurate. One participant mentioned in the interview that the used wrist-worn tracker provided "better" accuracy than other prior tested methods. This positive statement was also emphasized in two other interviews, where the shown feedback of the Mi Band 2 was judged to be more accurate than tracking methods already used by some participants.

The credibility (III) of the fitness tracker used during the user study was assessed as very credible by all six participants, indicating a high trust in the Mi Band and its measurement capabilities.

Overall, the trust and credibility evaluation provides coherent results that indicate a high trust in the data validity regardless of the manipulated feedback.

6   Result Discussion

Relating back the Fogg et al. definition of credibility in the context of computer systems [10], where credibility was defined as trustworthiness and expertise of a system. The user study participants indicated an overall knowledgeable system, since their confidence in the data measurements and validity of the presented feedback values was high. Trustworthiness was defined by Fogg et al. as the perceived goodness of system. Regarding the trust for our given tracking system, the participants judged the used fitness tracker as very reliable and trustworthy in the questionnaire and interview. Based on the general computer credibility definition and the clear trends in the study data, the Mi Band 2, despite the added inaccuracies, was rated as credible. As a conclusion to the user study, the outlined research question is answered: A significant variation of pedometer feedback data accuracy does not seem to have a significant influence on the perceived system credibility.

The Mi Band 2 tracker provided repeatable step count figures with an overall precision of 2.85%. The intentional manipulated pedometer feedback values were significantly higher or lower by 15%, depended on the study group. From the evaluation of the post-study questionnaire and the interview session, it is clear that the participants had little to no awareness of the intentional induced data inaccuracies. This was further underlined by the statements that the provided wrist-worn fitness tracker was more accurate and trustworthy than other already used smartphone applications, since the Mi Band 2 is a "purpose-build" device. The difference between the independent user measurements with a smartphone and the shown feedback from our Mi Band setup were not further questioned and seemingly had no influence on the credibility rating. The statistical assessment indicated no significant difference in the perceived system trust and accuracy between the neutral and groups with manipulated feedback.

In related work, authors [8,9,28] expect users to think critical about tracking technology and the data quality. One of the key factors for long-term behavior change through the usage of fitness tracker systems is the data reflection process [17]. Users reflect on their hourly, daily or weekly achievements and try to adapt their behavior. Our presented study shows that especially inexperienced fitness tracker users can not associate well between their real-life activity and the presented feedback values, even for short-term tracking. They did not reminisce precisely about details of the logged activity. The verification of the data validity and reliability was assumingly based more on the overall user experience with the tracker rather than the perceived walking activity during the recorded sessions. The users seem to lack a understanding of the correlation between these data values. Inexperienced, first time tracker users seem to take the system credibility for granted, until some major inaccuracies raises concerns [4,9,11]. This almost careless attitude about fitness tracker technology and the accompanying possibility of false feedback might have a significant impact on the intended long-term behavior change.

7   Conclusion

Would I Lie to You - Would you Notice? - A question we can definitely answer with No, you wouldn't notice.

Based on the fact that activity trackers only provide very abstract data (e.g. step count or minutes active) it is nearly impossible, even for the informed users to judge if the values presented by the fitness trackers are trustworthy or not. End users have next to no possibilities to verify the validity of their recorded fitness- or health data. The tracker always has more information and dependent on the quality of the algorithms, or the intent of the App developers, can present even statistically significantly changed values, without the user being able to identify them as being not trustworthy. This problem domain can be seen as closely related to the market of lemons paradigm. Users have to see their smart devices as a black box, thus have no control over the data processing and feedback generation.

In a first explorative study, we introduced a 15% offset in step count value for daily commute walks over the span of four weeks. Three study groups received either negative, neutral or positively influenced feedback values. The participants had to reflect on the shown pedometer feedback and rate the credibility of the shown values. The results indicated that the variation of the step count value had no significant impact on the user-perceived credibility and awareness, thus the users didn't notice the change. This is especially interesting as the overall walking distance was short and recallable by the users. We argue that although the walking distance was short, users were not able to judge the values correctly. This means in fact, the less recallable the activities they perform are, the more variation can be in the abstract data without them being able to judge if the the data is trustworthy or not.

Participants blindly trusted the wrist-worn fitness tracker devices and did not question the presented mismatched information at all, which was also con- firmed in the post-study interview when the research intention was revealed. With this paper, we provide a first thought-provoking impulse to question the impact of fitness feedback data quality on the user-perceived trustworthiness. It is of highly importance to understand that people have a high trust in technol- ogy and no way to proof if the data is correct or not. Especially in the fitness and health domain, it can expose risks and health issues to the users or influ- ence them to change their behaviour based on wrong assumptions. Up until now, researchers, manufacturers and users assumed the abstract feedback data to be valid and easily usable for studies without prior detailed verification. Even users were adjudged the capability to spot inaccuracies and compensate for mislead- ing information. In the conduced user study, we have demonstratively shown major flaws in the widespread fundamental belief that user can judge general data quality and fitness tracker credibility.

References

1. Asimakopoulos, S., Asimakopoulos, G., Spillers, F.: Motivation and user engage- ment in fitness tracking: heuristics for mobile healthcare wearables. In: Informatics, vol. 4, p. 5. Multidisciplinary Digital Publishing Institute (2017)
2. Attig, C., Franke, T.: I track, therefore i walk-exploring the motivational costs of wearing activity trackers in actual users. Int. J. Hum. Comput. Stud. **127**, 211–224 (2018)

3. Bassett, D.R., Toth, L.P., LaMunion, S.R., Crouter, S.E.: Step counting: a review of measurement considerations and health-related applications. Sports Med. **47**(7), 1303–1315 (2017)
4. Benedetto, S., Caldato, C., Bazzan, E., Greenwood, D.C., Pensabene, V., Actis, P.: Assessment of the Fitbit charge 2 for monitoring heart rate. PloS one **13**, e0192691 (2018)
5. Bravata, D.M., et al.: Using pedometers to increase physical activity and improve health: a systematic review. Jama **298**(19), 2296–2304 (2007)
6. Crouter, S.E., Schneider, P.L., Bassett, J.D.: Spring-levered versus piezo-electric pedometer accuracy in overweight and obese adults. Med. Sci. Sports Exerc. **37**(10), 1673–1679 (2005)
7. Day, S.: Self-tracking over time: the fitbit® phenomenon. In: The 7th Annual Conference of Computing and Information Technology Research and Education New Zealand (CITRENZ2016) and the 29th Annual Conference of the National Advisory Committee on Computing Qualifications, Wellington, New Zealand, pp. 1–6 (2016)
8. El-Amrawy, F., Nounou, M.I.: Are currently available wearable devices for activity tracking and heart rate monitoring accurate, precise, and medically beneficial? Healthc. Inform. Res. **21**(4), 315–320 (2015)
9. Evenson, K.R., Goto, M.M., Furberg, R.D.: Systematic review of the validity and reliability of consumer-wearable activity trackers. Int. J. Behav. Nutr. Phys. Act. **12**(1), 159 (2015)
10. Fogg, B.J.: Persuasive technology: using computers to change what we think and do. Ubiquity **2002**, 5 (2002)
11. Fritz, T., Huang, E.M., Murphy, G.C., Zimmermann, T.: Persuasive technology in the real world: a study of long-term use of activity sensing devices for fitness. In: Proceedings of the SIGCHI Conference on Human Factors in Computing Systems, pp. 487–496. ACM (2014)
12. Gouveia, R., Pereira, F., Karapanos, E., Munson, S.A., Hassenzahl, M.: Exploring the design space of glanceable feedback for physical activity trackers. In: Proceedings of the 2016 ACM International Joint Conference on Pervasive and Ubiquitous Computing, pp. 144–155. ACM (2016)
13. Harjumaa, M., Segerståhl, K., Oinas-Kukkonen, H.: Understanding persuasive software functionality in practice: a field trial of polar FT60. In: proceedings of the 4th International Conference on Persuasive Technology, p. 2. ACM (2009)
14. Hoelzl, G., Kranz, M., Schmid, A., Halbmayer, P., Ferscha, A.: Size does matter - positioning on the wrist a comparative study: smartwatch vs. smartphone. In: IEEE International Conference on Pervasive Computing and Communications Workshops (PerCom Workshops), pp. 703–708, March 2017
15. Katzmarzyk, P.T., et al.: The international study of childhood obesity, lifestyle and the environment (ISCOLE): design and methods. BMC Public Health **13**(1), 900 (2013)
16. Leth, S., Hansen, J., Nielsen, O.W., Dinesen, B.: Evaluation of commercial self-monitoring devices for clinical purposes: results from the future patient trial, phase I. Sensors **17**(1), 211 (2017)
17. Li, I., Dey, A., Forlizzi, J.: A stage-based model of personal informatics systems. In: Proceedings of the SIGCHI Conference on Human Factors in Computing Systems, pp. 557–566. ACM (2010)
18. Liu, X., et al.: Characterizing smartwatch usage in the wild. In: Proceedings of the 15th Annual International Conference on Mobile Systems, Applications, and Services, pp. 385–398. ACM (2017)

19. Maher, C., Ryan, J., Ambrosi, C., Edney, S.: Users' experiences of wearable activity trackers: a cross-sectional study. BMC Public Health **17**(1), 880 (2017)
20. Mercer, K., Li, M., Giangregorio, L., Burns, C., Grindrod, K.: Behavior change techniques present in wearable activity trackers: a critical analysis. JMIR mHealth and uHealth **4**(2), e40 (2016)
21. Pilgram, N., Mohamed, A., Kranz, M., Hoelzl, G.: Biofeedback in the wild - a smartwatch approach. In: IEEE International Conference on Pervasive Computing and Communications Workshops (PerCom Workshops), pp. 312–317, March 2018
22. Prochaska, J.O., DiClemente, C.C.: Transtheoretical therapy: toward a more integrative model of change. Psychother. Theor. Res. Pract. **19**(3), 276 (1982)
23. Prochaska, J.O., DiClemente, C.C.: Toward a comprehensive model of change. In: Miller, W.R., Heather, N. (eds.) Treating addictive behaviors. ABBI, vol. 13, pp. 3–27. Springer, Boston (1986). https://doi.org/10.1007/978-1-4613-2191-0_1
24. Rupp, M.A., Michaelis, J.R., McConnell, D.S., Smither, J.A.: The impact of technological trust and self-determined motivation on intentions to use wearable fitness technology. In: Proceedings of the Human Factors and Ergonomics Society Annual Meeting, vol. 60, pp. 1434–1438. SAGE Publications, Los Angeles (2016)
25. Sears, T., Alvalos, E., Lawson, S., McAlister, I., Eschbach, L.C., Bunn, J.: Wrist-worn physical activity trackers tend to underestimate steps during walking. Int. J. Exerc. Sci. **10**(5), 764–773 (2017)
26. Shcherbina, A., et al.: Accuracy in wrist-worn, sensor-based measurements of heart rate and energy expenditure in a diverse cohort. J. Pers. Med. **7**(2), 3 (2017)
27. Troiano, R.P., McClain, J.J., Brychta, R.J., Chen, K.Y.: Evolution of accelerometer methods for physical activity research. Br. J. Sports Med. **48**(13), 1019–1023 (2014)
28. Trommler, D., Attig, C., Franke, T.: Trust in activity tracker measurement and its link to user acceptance. Mensch und Computer 2018-Tagungsband (2018)
29. Tryon, W.W.: Activity Measurement in Psychology and Medicine. Springer Science & Business Media, Boston (2013)
30. Wattanapisit, A., Thanamee, S.: Evidence behind 10,000 steps walking. J. Health Res. **31**(3), 241–248 (2017)
31. Wolf, G.: Know thyself: Tracking every facet of life, from sleep to mood to pain (2009). https://www.wired.com/2009/06/lbnp-knowthyself/
32. Yang, R., Shin, E., Newman, M.W., Ackerman, M.S.: When fitness trackers don't'fit': end-user difficulties in the assessment of personal tracking device accuracy. In: Proceedings of the 2015 ACM International Joint Conference on Pervasive and Ubiquitous Computing, pp. 623–634. ACM (2015)

Author Index

Printed in the United States
By Bookmasters